# PUNISHING HATE

Frederick M. Lawrence

# Punishing Hate

Bias Crimes under American Law

**HARVARD UNIVERSITY PRESS**

Cambridge, Massachusetts, and London, England   1999

Library of Congress Cataloging-in-Publication Data

Lawrence, Frederick M.
    Punishing hate : bias crimes under American law / Frederick M. Lawrence.
       p.   cm.
    Includes bibliographical references and index.
    ISBN 0-674-73845-4 (alk. paper)
    1. Hate crimes—United States.   I. Title.
KF9345.L39   1999
345.73'025—dc21                                                    98-49780

*For*

*Joseph F. Lawrence*
*Beatrice D. Lawrence*
*the late Ben Kurtzman*
*Sally Kurtzman Gold*
*the late Jack Gold*

*who taught me that the end of bigotry begins not with the*
*punishment of hate, but with the practice of love.*

# Contents

# Preface

My interest in understanding and combating racism and other forms of bigotry goes back before my career at Boston University, to my stint as an Assistant United States Attorney in New York, and indeed before that as well. I share with many a deeply felt intuition that bias crimes are in some sense worse than otherwise similar crimes that lack bias motivation. The very depth of this widely shared intuition, however, raises an ironic question about the nature of this book: some have suggested to me that the book's dimensions are necessarily limited, because for work about bias crimes to be truly path-breaking it must disprove, rather than embrace, the shared intuition.

There is another new path for scholarly work, one that seeks to establish a firm theoretical, philosophical, and legal grounding for the shared intuition. I fear that much contemporary scholarship celebrates the counterintuitive. My work, or at least this book, does not. I hope that *Punishing Hate* does indeed break new ground, offering a theoretical argument about a vital contemporary topic that has not been offered before. I have been told that people interested in this topic will be sympathetic to my conclusions, and thus attracted to this book. The attraction, however, should begin but not end with this sympathy. It is the persuasiveness of the argument and the comprehensiveness of the discussion by which this, or any, book should be judged.

A story is told of a man who was to introduce the late Jonas Salk at a banquet. He was quite at a loss for a proper introduction for such an extraordinary figure. As he was getting dressed in his tuxedo, his child came into the room, and the following discussion took place:

*Child:* Why are you getting dressed up?
*Father:* I have to go to a dinner tonight.
*Child:* Why are you getting dressed so fancy?
*Father:* I have to give a speech. I have to introduce a very famous person.
*Child:* Who are you going to introduce?
*Father:* Dr. Jonas Salk.
*Child:* Who is Dr. Jonas Salk?
*Father:* He discovered the cure for polio.
*Child:* Daddy, what's polio?

And with that, he knew that he had his introduction for Jonas Salk.

In giving this book to my children, it is my fondest hope that, when they give it to their children, the latter will be puzzled as to why their grandfather should have spent so much time on something as inconceivable as racial violence.

.

## PUNISHING HATE

# Introduction:
# The Challenges
# of Punishing Hate

What we need in the United States is not division; what we need in
the United States is not hatred; what we need in the United States is
not violence or lawlessness, but love and wisdom, compassion toward one another, and a feeling of justice toward those who still suffer within our country, whether they be white or they be black.

—Robert F. Kennedy, on the death of Dr. Martin Luther King, Jr.,
Indianapolis, April 4, 1968

Crimes that are motivated by racial hatred have a special and
compelling call on our conscience. When predominantly black churches
were in flames across the South during the summer of 1996, it took only a
matter of weeks for Congress to enact and President Clinton to sign the
Church Arson Prevention Act of 1996.[1] Consider the public attention given
to the following three cases because of their close connection to issues of
race.

- On October 23, 1989, Carol DiMaiti Stuart, a pregnant white woman,
  was shot to death after a birthing class at a hospital in Boston. Ms. Stuart's husband told police that the killer was a black man. For weeks
  thereafter, the investigation of this killing—including the wrongful targeting of a black man as a suspect in the crime—was one of the major
  news stories in Boston. Public preoccupation did not fully cease until
  Charles Stuart died in an apparent suicidal leap off the Tobin Bridge after he was implicated in his wife's death.[2]
- On March 3, 1991, Rodney King was kicked and beaten by three
  officers of the Los Angeles Police Department while more than a dozen
  others looked on. Not since the police attacks on civil rights workers in
  the South during the 1960s had the nation's attention been so focused
  on an assault of this nature, a focus that largely lasted from the time of
  the beating through the acquittal of the officers on state criminal

1

charges in 1992 and their subsequent conviction on federal charges in 1993. At the time of the state verdict, an astonishing 99 percent of respondents in one poll had heard or read about the verdict.[3]

- In the early morning hours of Sunday, June 7, 1998, in Jasper, Texas, James Byrd, a forty-nine-year-old black man, was beaten and tied to the back up a pickup truck and dragged nearly three miles to his death. The accused perpetrators of the crime were members of a white supremacist group. The murder of Byrd immediately became a matter of national concern, prompting public condolences by the President and widespread calls for a new federal hate crime law.[4]

Contrast the public attention that these cases received with the concern shown over the myriad violent crimes that occur in Boston, New York, or Los Angeles on a regular basis. Numerous assaults occur in this country every day, yet these assaults receive relatively little, and then only local, attention. Similarly, the general public ordinarily cares little whether any particular assault leads to a prosecution of the perpetrators and, if it does, whether any particular prosecution results in a conviction. This pattern of public indifference contrasts sharply with the reaction to crimes that implicate race relations.

This book looks at the nature of racially motivated violence and provides a foundation for understanding bias crimes in America. The study of bias crimes occurs at the intersection of three fundamental values of the American polity: equality, free expression, and federalism. These values frame the three fundamental questions upon which this book focuses:

- Must a society that is dedicated to equality treat bias crimes differently from other crimes, and must it enhance the punishment of these crimes?
- May a society that is also dedicated to freedom of expression and belief enhance the punishment of bias crimes?
- Is a prominent federal role in the prosecution and punishment of bias crimes consistent with the proper division of authority between state (and local) government and the federal government in our political system?

I answer each of these fundamental questions in the affirmative. The enhanced punishment of bias crimes, with a substantial federal-enforcement role, is not only permitted by doctrines of criminal law and constitutional law but also mandated by our societal commitment to the equality ideal.

The balance of this Introduction presents the arguments of the book in brief, summarizing the way in which each of these fundamental questions is addressed. The questions are deceptively complex at points: the closer the consideration, the more difficult it is to assert simple answers with confidence. This Introduction, therefore, is designed to provide a road map, a concise chapter-by-chapter summary of the entire argument. As with any road map, the reader may find that it is helpful to consult this one not only at the beginning of the journey, but at various points along the way as well. It is my intention that background knowledge of criminal and constitutional law, though obviously helpful, is by no means necessary in order to follow the flow of the discussion.

## Setting the Context: The Introductory Questions

The first chapter takes up essential definitional issues. The exploration of American bias crime law begins with three key introductory questions.

What precisely is a bias crime? The ultimate answer will look both to the motivation of the criminal and to the results of his conduct. (I opt for the male pronoun because the overwhelming majority of bias criminals are men or boys.) But the key factor in identifying an actor as a bias criminal is the *motivation* for his conduct, what is known as *mens rea* in criminal law doctrine. Consideration of specific cases, real and hypothetical, helps to concretize this analysis of motivation. For example, Colin Ferguson's December 1993 shooting spree on the Long Island Rail Road—carefully directed only at white and Asian-American passengers—is a bias crime; an interracial fight between a landlord and a tenant that erupts following an argument over the level of heat provided is not a bias crime; and the unconscious racism driving the murder of Yusef Hawkins in Bensonhurst, New York, in November 1988 is a bias crime but for reasons that are far more subtle and complex than in the Ferguson case.

Which biases count for "bias motivation"? Who is a bias crime victim? The answers have their roots in society's very self-definition. As a normative matter, "bias" should include bigotry on the basis of race, ethnicity, religion, national origin, sexual orientation, and, in certain instances, gender. As a descriptive matter, the scope of "bias" adopted by a polity is a significant statement of its values and its sense of equality. In this book I use "race" in "racial animus," or in such terms as "racially" motivated violence or "racial" intolerance, inclusively, not exclusively, encompassing motivation based not only on the race, but also on the color, ethnicity, religion, or national origin of the victim. In many states, gender and sexual orientation are covered by bias crime laws as well.

Is the problem of bias crimes actually becoming worse, or is it only our perception that it is worsening? Here, as elsewhere in criminal law (such as the incidence levels of rape or domestic violence), perception and problem are related. As we broaden our understanding of what constitutes a bias crime, the desecration of a graveyard that may have been dismissed as a "prank" in an earlier time is revealed for what it is: bias-motivated vandalism. On the other hand, the growth of violence associated with so-called militias strongly suggests an increase in hate crimes that is far more than a matter of perception.

## Understanding Bias Criminals, Bias Crime Victims, and Bias Crime Laws

Chapter 2 turns to the legal and factual foundations of our study of bias crimes. First, I discuss the development of American bias crime laws themselves. Two models of bias crime statutes have evolved over the past two decades or so. One model, the "racial animus" model, requires that the defendant has acted out of hatred for the victim's racial group or the victim for being a member of that group. The other model, the "discriminatory selection" model, requires that the defendant has selected his victim because of the victim's membership in a particular group. What these models have in common is that each is primarily concerned with the state of mind of the bias criminal and the manner in which this differs from that of other criminals. Where these models differ is in the definition of the requisite mental state. Most state and federal statutes that deal with bias crimes can be understood in terms of these two models of bias crimes, although precise categorization is often difficult.

I then demonstrate that the resulting harm of a bias crime exceeds that of a similar crime lacking bias motivation (what I call a "parallel crime") on each of three levels: the nature of the injury sustained by the immediate victim of a bias crime; the palpable harm inflicted on the broader target community of the crime; and the harm to society at large. Consider, for example, a cross-burning on the lawn of a black family who has just moved into a largely white neighborhood. Such are the facts of the infamous cross-burning in St. Paul, Minnesota, that gave rise to the Supreme Court decision in *R.A.V. v. City of St. Paul* (1992), which we will discuss further, especially in Chapter 5. This crime causes a greater injury to the immediate victims than would a non–racially motivated act of vandalism. Moreover, it causes a direct and identifiable harm to the local black community and to the community generally that would not have resulted from a non–racially motivated crime.

## Punishing Hate

Chapters 3–6 examine the major issues that emerge from the three fundamental questions outlined above. These are the issues that must be confronted when analyzing bias crime laws in America:

- Should we enhance the punishment of bias crimes? (Chapter 3); and how do we determine who is guilty of committing a bias crime? (Chapter 4)
- Are bias crime laws constitutional, given our commitment to free expression? (Chapter 5)
- What ought to be the role of the federal government in the prosecution of bias crimes? (Chapter 6)

Chapter 3 explains why bias crimes ought to receive enhanced punishment. I begin with an overview of the purpose of criminal punishment and proceed with an examination of the role of proportionality in punishment. The need for "the punishment to fit the crime" is a critical aspect of all punishment theories and, in order to determine the relative punishments for various crimes, there must be a means by which to measure the relative seriousness of those crimes. When the level of intentionality for two crimes is roughly the same—as is the case with an intentional assault and an intentional bias-motivated assault—the relative seriousness of the crimes is best measured by the harm caused. Although we cannot measure relative harm with arithmetic precision, much can be said to guide our understanding of harm. I then apply this analysis of relative harm to bias crimes, concluding that bias crimes warrant harsher punishment than parallel crimes.

Chapter 4 considers the aspects of bias crimes that are relevant to the punishment of an individual offender. Whereas the harm caused by bias crimes *generally* justifies the enhanced punishment of these crimes, the resulting harm to a *particular* victim does not, in and of itself, warrant the enhanced punishment of the perpetrator. Bias motivation of the perpetrator, and not necessarily the resulting harm to the victim, is the critical factor in determining whether someone has committed a bias crime. The arguments presented in Chapter 4 form the basis for conclusions that are set out in Chapter 7 concerning a model bias crime statute.

## The Conflict between the Punishment of Hate and Freedom of Expression

Thus far, the book has argued that bias criminals deserve enhanced punishment and has offered a theory as to the best means of defining who is a bias criminal. In Chapter 5, I move on to the subject in this field that has generated the greatest attention, not only from legal scholars, but also from journalists and other commentators: does the enhanced punishment of bias criminals comport with our commitment to freedom of expression and belief? I refer to this as the "bias crimes–hate speech paradox." Is it possible to punish racially motivated violence when the right to free expression of ideas, no matter how distasteful or hateful, is a fundamental constitutional principle? How much intolerance a liberal democracy should tolerate is a question that has fueled debate for years.

I argue that the apparent paradox of seeking to punish the perpetrators of bias-motivated violence while being committed to protecting the bigot's rights to express his prejudice is a false paradox. Put simply, we are making this problem harder than it needs to be. We must focus on the basic distinction between "bias crimes," criminal conduct that is motivated by the race or similar characteristic of the victim and deserves enhanced punishment, and "racist speech," articulation of racist views, which, no matter how unpleasant, is protected. This distinction has been blurred (or denied) by commentators and courts alike, including, for example, the United States Supreme Court in *R.A.V. v. City of St. Paul,* in which the St. Paul, Minnesota, cross-burning ordinance was struck down, and again in *Wisconsin v. Mitchell* (1993), in which the Wisconsin bias crime law was upheld. Others have suggested either that both bias crimes and racist speech are protected, or that both may be punished. I reject these extremes and present a middle position.

The basic distinction between a bias crime and racist speech lies in the underlying motivation of the actor, which we can ascertain by looking at the nonbias element of the behavior involved. The nonbias element of racist speech is expression, a form of behavior that, however offensive, is protected and cannot be made criminal in our legal system. Speech advocating racial superiority is, bias aside, the expression of an opinion. The nonbias element of a bias crime, however, is an actual parallel crime that is punishable. Burning a cross on the lawn of a black family, bias aside, is still at least trespass and probably is some form of endangerment, assault, or arson.

Free expression protects the right to express offensive views but not the right to behave criminally. This is true even when the parallel crime consists solely of speech. Speech that is intended to frighten someone seriously is a verbal assault that may be punished. Bias-targeted behavior that is intended to create fear in its targeted victim is a bias crime, whether the behavior is primarily verbal or physical. Behavior that vents the actor's bigotry, and perhaps upsets the addressee greatly, is racist speech that is protected by the First Amendment. The enhanced punishment of bias crimes, therefore, is fully consonant with our constitutional guarantees of free expression.

## The Federal and State Roles in the Punishment of Bias Crimes

Chapter 6 takes up the third of the three fundamental questions addressed at the outset: the proper division of authority between state (and local) government and the federal government. This issue figured prominently in the federal government's decision to retry, in federal court, the police officers involved in the beating of Rodney King who were initially acquitted on California state charges. Ordinarily, crimes of violence are left to state and local authorities for criminal prosecution.

I trace the evolution of federal law enforcement's developing role in the punishment of racially motivated violence from the Reconstruction Era through the early part of this century, the New Deal Period, the Second Reconstruction during the 1960s, and up to the present. I argue that a prominent federal role in the prosecution of bias crimes is both constitutionally permissible and socially vital.

## The Broader Framework

Chapter 7 pulls together the conclusions developed throughout the book and proposes a broader framework from which to view bias crimes. I propose a model for bias crime statutes that focuses on the racial motivation of the actor. Moreover, I return to the general justifications for criminal punishment and augment that discussion of the expressive value of punishment. Punishment represents societal condemnation of certain behavior and thus expresses deep social values. The expressive value serves less as a justification of punishment than as a critical illustration of the impact of punishment. It cannot help us answer the initial question of whether or not society may punish its members, but once we answer that question affirmatively, societal denunciation must inform our decisions about the nature of that punishment.

Because racial harmony and equality are among the highest values held in our society, crimes that violate these values should be punished more harshly than crimes that, although otherwise similar, do not violate these values. If bias crimes are not punished more harshly than parallel crimes, the message expressed by the criminal justice system is that racial harmony and equality are not among the highest values held by our society. Put differently, it is impossible for the punishment choices made by the society *not* to express societal values. The only question is the content of that expression and the resulting statement of those values. The punishment of bias crimes as argued for in this book, therefore, is necessary for the full expression of commitment to American values.

## CHAPTER 1

# What Is a Bias Crime?

A bias crime is a crime committed as an act of prejudice. Bias crimes thus differ from the two broad categories that largely compose the universe of violent crimes. The first of these broad categories contains all crimes committed without regard to any personal characteristics of the victim. This category includes a wide array of crimes such as random muggings, drive-by shootings, and most robberies and burglaries. It also includes crimes in which the choice of victim is dictated solely by the requirements of the crime. The bank teller is assaulted as a means of robbing a bank, not because of any individual characteristic of the teller.

The second broad category contains all crimes committed precisely because the victim is who he or she is. This category includes revenge crimes and most so-called crimes of passion. In these crimes, the victim could not be interchanged with someone else.

Bias crimes differ from both broad categories. Unlike the first category, bias crimes are crimes in which distinct identifying characteristics of the victim are critical to the perpetrator's choice of victim. Unlike the second category, bias crimes are crimes in which the individual identity of the victim is irrelevant. A bias crime occurs not because the victim is *who* he is, but rather because the victim is *what* he is.

We will explore the precise nature of bias motivation below. Here, however, it is important to address a key misconception about the nature of bias motivation. The source of this misconception may be the popular term "hate crime" that is often used in connection with bias crimes. Not every crime that is motivated by hatred for the victim is a bias crime. Hate-based violence is a bias crime only when this hatred is connected with antipathy for a racial or ethnic group or for an individual because of his membership in that group. The use of "hate" in the title of this book is meant in this sense. I use the term "bias crime" rather than "hate crime" to emphasize that the key factor in a bias crime is not the perpetrator's hatred of the victim per se, but rather his bias or prejudice toward that victim.

What of the case of a "mixed motive," that is, when the perpetrator of a violent crime is motivated by a number of different factors in the commission of the crime? Although ultimately the search for bright lines is elusive, we can say that to constitute a bias crime, the bias motivation must be a substantial motivation for the perpetrator's criminal conduct. We might assess the role of bias motivation in a crime by asking the "but for" question: but for the ethnicity of the victim, would this crime have been committed?

These initial considerations about defining bias crimes may be brought to bear on two of the three cases mentioned in the Introduction: Colin Ferguson's shooting spree on the Long Island Rail Road, and an interracial fight between a landlord and a tenant that erupts following an argument over the level of heat provided. (I will leave the third case, the murder of Yusef Hawkins in Bensonhurst, New York, for Chapter 4 because—as a case raising issues of unconscious racism—it is more complex than the other two cases.)

- On December 7, 1993, Colin Ferguson, a black man originally from Jamaica, walked through a crowded commuter train, shooting only at white and Asian-American passengers, killing six and injuring nineteen. There is little difficulty classifying this as a bias crime because, although Ferguson may have had other reasons for his shootings besides his victims' ethnicity, it is clear that ethnicity was a substantial part of his motivation. But for their ethnicity, the victims would have been left unharmed.[1]

- Suppose that an argument between a landlord and a tenant of different races erupts because of the tenant's claim that the apartment is inadequately heated. As the argument becomes more intense, angry words are exchanged, including racial epithets. Ultimately, the argument boils over into an altercation in which one of the parties assaults the other. Should we consider this assault to be a bias crime? The answer will turn on the role that prejudice played. If we conclude that the argument itself was the primary reason for the eruption of the fight and that the assault would have occurred regardless of the racial difference between the two, then this is not a bias crime. If, by contrast, we conclude that the victim's race played a substantial role in the assault, that is, that the assault would not have occurred had the victim not been of his race, then this is a bias crime.

## Who Is a Bias Crime Victim?

There are two ways of asking the question posed here:

(1) To which victim categories *do* bias crime laws apply in America?
(2) To which victim categories *should* bias crime laws apply in America?

The first question is strictly descriptive and is thus straightforward. If we review all the state and federal bias crime statutes in the United States, we find that all encompass race, color, ethnicity, national origin, and religion—what I call the classic bias crime categories. Many reach sexual orientation or gender as well, and some include other categories such as age or disability. (A chart of all state bias crime laws is provided in Appendix A.)

The second question is normative. It is less straightforward, but it is also far more interesting because it requires us to look more deeply at the nature of bias crimes. To consider this question, we play less the role of researcher, culling the law of the various jurisdictions that punish bias crimes, than the role of advisor to a hypothetical state legislature considering the scope of its bias crime law. What should we advise them?

We must return to first principles. I said at the outset that a bias crime is a crime committed as an act of prejudice. Prejudice, in this context, is not strictly a personal predilection of the perpetrator. A prejudiced person usually exhibits antipathy toward members a group based on false stereotypical views of that group. But in order for this to be the kind of prejudice of which we speak here, this antipathy must exist in a social context, that is, it must be an animus that is shared by others in the culture and that is a recognizable social pathology within the culture.

Two simple examples help make the point. Suppose that A decides in advance of meeting B that he does not like B because B is Jewish and A believes that Jews cannot be trusted. A is acting out of prejudice. A's dislike for B is based on false stereotypical views of B's religious group. Anti-Semitism in America is a group antipathy that has a social context. If, on the other hand, C decides in advance of meeting B that he does not like B because B has blue eyes and C believes that blue-eyed people cannot be trusted, we consider C to have a rather odd peccadillo where eye color is concerned—like the narrator in Poe's *The Tell-Tale Heart,* who obsesses over his victim's "pale blue eye, with a film over it"—but we would be hard pressed to call his behavior prejudiced in a deep sense.[2] C's dislike for B, like that of A, is based on false stereotypical views of B because of B's membership in a group, that is, people with blue eyes. Here the similarity ends. "Eye colorism" is not a group antipathy that has a social context. There may be more people than just C who think that blue-eyed people cannot be trusted, but there is no history of discrimination against people with blue eyes in our culture, nor is there any ideology or world view that connects those who do not trust them.

Having seen that some characteristics, like religion, fall within the scope of bias crimes, and that others, like eye color, fall outside of consideration, we must try to sharpen the distinction between the two categories. We proceed in two stages. First, we determine which characteristics are appropriate for consideration. Second, we consider how a legislature chooses among these groups.

The first stage looks initially at a case of discrimination based on any particular characteristic. Do the discriminators and those discriminated against understand themselves to be members of a group? Is there some self-consciousness of these collections of individuals as groups?[3] This methodology sharpens the focus and gives some structure to our intuition concerning religious bigotry on the one hand and "eye colorism" on the other. In our society, adherents to a religion self-consciously perceive this to be a group to which they belong. The same, of course, cannot be said for people who all happen to have blue eyes. But now we can also say that, in American society, race, ethnicity, national origin, gender, and sexual orientation, like religion, are characteristics that yield groups and not random collections of people. A case could well be made that there are other such characteristics, for example, those criteria that define disabled people, veterans, or the elderly. Indeed, the potential list is extensive. With respect to identifying bias crime categories, the list will be overly inclusive, that is to say, it will include groups that no legislature would include in a bias crime law. But at this first stage of the process, where we seek characteristics that yield self-regarding groups, we should be expansive. Selectivity will enter our process at the second stage.

At the second stage, a legislature determines which of the characteristics that yield self-regarding groups ought to be included in its bias crime law. These are the characteristics that implicate societal fissure lines, divisions that run deep in the social history of a culture. Here the strongest case is for race. Racial discrimination, the greatest American dilemma, has its roots in slavery, the greatest American tragedy. The depth of the racial divide in this country has been extensively documented.[4] Strong cases can also be made for the other classic bias crime categories—color, ethnicity, religion, and national origin—on the basis of our complex history of commitment to equality and inclusiveness, mixed with a painful reality of exclusions over time of such groups as Latinos, Jews, Catholics, Mexicans, Irish, Eastern Europeans, and, at some times, immigrants generally.

Race, color, ethnicity, religion, and national origin are all examples of national social fissure lines. But bias crime laws need not be limited to national issues. A state legislature, or for that matter a city council, engaged in drafting a bias crime law or ordinance might well look beyond national fissure lines and include characteristics that, as a statewide or local matter, implicate deep social divides. Consider, for example, the characteristic of union membership in a strongly pro-union town. Such a context gave rise to a noncriminal, civil rights claim that reached the Supreme Court in the case of *United Brotherhood of Carpenters and Joiners of America v. Scott*.[5] Paul Scott and James Matthews were employees of A. A. Cross Construction Company. Cross had a contract with the Department of the Army for a construction project near Port Arthur, Texas, well known as a "union town." Cross, however, had a practice of using non-union labor on its projects, and the Port Arthur project was no exception. In Port Arthur, in 1975, bringing non-union labor to a construction project was a dangerous thing to do. This led not only to violence, in which both Scott and Matthews were beaten, but to the kind of violence against which the local authorities of Port Arthur had little interest in interfering, investigating, or prosecuting.[6] Under these circumstances, the drafters of a bias crime statute for a jurisdiction such as Port Arthur might well conclude that union membership, or the absence thereof, is an appropriate characteristic for inclusion.

In this book, I do not propose to identify a definitive list of characteristics that yield groups that might properly be included in a bias crime statute; nor will I identify an exhaustive list of societal fissure lines. Rather, I seek to describe the proper methodology for going about the business of constructing such a list. Once a state legislature has left the relatively safe port of national fissure lines such as race, color, ethnicity, religion, and national origin, and considered any particularly divisive local issues, how is it to proceed?

Consider briefly the arguments for and against inclusion of two particular characteristics in bias crime laws—gender and sexual orientation. Not only are these characteristics the most hotly debated in bias crime legislation today, but analyzing them yields significant insights into an appropriate methodology to determine which victim categories give rise to bias crimes and which do not.[7] Both categories clearly satisfy the first stage of our methodology. In American society, gender and sexual orientation are characteristics that yield self-regarding groups and not random collections of people. Both gender and sexual orientation thus tell us something very important about how states go about determining where societal fissure lines exist.

Legislators and commentators have taken two approaches in deciding where societal fissure lines fall. One approach is to begin with the classic societal fissure lines and to look for common elements in other groups to determine if they should be included in bias crime laws.[8] This approach has been applied most frequently to gender. Opponents generally do not argue that women as a class are unsuitable for bias crime protection. Sex is generally an immutable characteristic, and no one seriously argues that women are not victimized as a result of their gender. Instead, opponents argue that crimes against women are not *real* bias crimes, that is, that they do not fit the bias crime model.

The other approach looks to the qualities of the characteristic itself, an approach taken most frequently with respect to sexual orientation. Many legislators, either because they view sexual orientation as a choice and not as an immutable characteristic, or because they are wary of giving special rights to gays and lesbians, argue that homosexuals do not deserve inclusion in bias crime statutes.[9] These two examples are thus highly illuminating for our purposes.

### Should Gender Be Included in Bias Crime Laws?

Those who argue that gender should not be a bias crime category assert that gender-related crimes do not fit the standard bias crime model. For our immediate purposes, it is sufficient to know that the chief factor in classic bias crimes is that the victim is attacked because he possesses the group characteristic. From this chief factor, two things follow:

(1) victims are interchangeable, so long as they share the characteristic; and
(2) victims generally have little or no pre-existing relationship with the perpetrator that might give rise to some motive for the crime other than bias toward the group.

Those who oppose the inclusion of gender in bias crime laws argue, among other things, that victims of many gender-related crimes are not interchangeable,[10] and that victims often have a prior relationship with their attackers.[11] Because assailants are acquainted with their victims in many gender-related cases, the argument goes, the victims are not interchangeable and the crime does not fit into the bias crime category. Particularly in cases of acquaintance rape and domestic violence, the prior personal relationship between victim and assailant makes it difficult to prove that gender animus, and not some other component of the relationship, is the motivation for the crime.

Some commentators and legislators have added a pragmatic argument against including gender: it is not necessary to include gender in bias crime statutes because violence against women is already covered well under existing criminal laws, although these laws may be under-enforced. Rape, for example, is not punished merely as assault; rape is punished as a separate crime that, in most states, is second only to murder in terms of severity of punishment. Similarly, in the context of domestic violence, many states have become increasingly active in trying to develop specialized responses by law enforcement. As Texas State Representative Scott Hochberg stated as he opposed the inclusion of gender in the Texas bias crime law, "we have very specific rape statutes, and we have sexual abuse statutes, and we have family violence statutes . . . Crimes against women that are gender-specific crimes, we have other mechanisms to take care of."[12]

Those who believe that gender should be included in bias crime statutes argue that gender belongs with the classic societal fissure lines. This is most obviously true in cases of stranger rape or random violence against women. The case of Marc Lepine makes the point powerfully. Lepine was a twenty-five-year-old unemployed Canadian man who killed fourteen women with a semiautomatic hunting rifle at the engineering school of the University of Montreal on December 7, 1989. After the shootings, Lepine took his own life. The killings were clearly gender-motivated. Lepine killed six women in a crowded classroom after separating the men and sending them out into the corridor. Before shooting, he told the women students, "You're all a bunch of feminists." He left behind a three-page statement in which he blamed feminists for spoiling his life. He listed the names of fifteen publicly known women as the apparent objects of his anger.[13]

Lepine's crime plainly fits the model of classic bias crimes: his victims were shot solely because they were women and, from his point of view, could well have been a different group of individuals, so long as they were women. It has been argued that even victims of domestic violence and acquaintance rape ultimately are interchangeable in the minds of their assailants. The perpetrator, according to this argument, would have assaulted any woman with whom he was involved, and would have done so because she was a woman.[14] The violence involved in these crimes is not directed at the victim as an individual. Rather, these crimes attack women as a means of enforcing a particular social hierarchy.[15] The existence of a prior relationship between victim and perpetrator, moreover, is not incompatible with the existence of a bias crime. The lack of a prior relationship may be a description of most bias crimes, but it is not a *sine qua non* for all bias crimes.

An attacker's acquaintance with his victim would not make a race- or religion-based crime any less a bias crime. Recall the hypothetical case of the interracial fight between the landlord and the tenant. We concluded that this *might* not constitute a bias crime but also that it very well might: the identification of the crime turned on the relative role played by the victim's race. If it were a substantial motivating factor in the crime, that is, if the assault occurred only because the victim was of his particular race, then this is a bias crime.[16] Conceding that motive can be difficult to prove in a gender-related crime, advocates of including gender in bias crime laws still contend that proof of discriminatory motive is difficult for any bias crime, and yet this has not and should not preclude the enactment of bias crime laws.[17]

Finally, those who believe that gender should be included in bias crime laws reject the pragmatic argument that such inclusion is unnecessary because crimes against women are already criminalized. This argument, if applied generally, would lead to unacceptable conclusions concerning bias crimes. Consider the argument made by Colorado State Representative Jim Congrove in opposition to bias crime legislation in the state: "It's illegal now to beat someone up. Assault is illegal. Shooting people is illegal. Hurting them, beating them or harming them in any way is illegal."[18] Congrove, generalizing from the pragmatic argument against the need for including gender in bias crime laws, mounted an argument against bias crime laws altogether. The same point may be illustrated with reference to homicide. Murder may be the most serious criminal offense in every jurisdiction in the nation, but it is virtually impossible to argue that lynching—that is, racially motivated murder—need not be considered a bias crime.

The arguments for including gender in bias crime laws illustrate the complexity involved in determining the scope of bias crimes. At this stage of our discussion that is reason alone to review these arguments. Even here, however, something more should be said. We can make two observations about the ultimate issue of whether gender ought to be in a bias crime statute.

First, the arguments against including gender in bias crimes share a common proposition: that bias crimes should include only gender-*motivated* violence and not all crimes that happen to have female victims. The argument, indeed, is precisely over which crimes are gender-*motivated*. This observation permits us to see that some crimes against women are bias crimes and some are not. A prime example of the subset that are bias crimes is random violence clearly motivated by hatred of women, such as the Lepine shootings in Montreal. None of the arguments against including gender as a protected category applies to this sort of crime. There was no previous relationship between Lepine and his victims, and there is no question that the victims were interchangeable in the eyes of the perpetrator. Even motive, had Lepine survived, would have been relatively simple to prove. Crimes such as this clearly share all the characteristics of bias crimes, and should be punished as such.

A prime example of those crimes against women that are not bias crimes are those in which the gender of the victim is utterly irrelevant to the perpetrator, such as a mugging of the "next person" who happens to go to the automatic cash machine. In evaluating other categories of cases, reasonable people may differ, but they will be considering the same issue: whether the crime is primarily one with gender-based motivation. In confronting the question of whether stranger rape, acquaintance rape, or domestic violence is a bias crime, this is the issue that legislatures should be addressing.[19]

The second observation about the ultimate issue of including gender in bias crime statutes has to do with the statement made when a state decides the issue. Failure to include gender in bias crime statutes in some manner, at least to cover cases such as the Lepine shootings, implies that women are not as deserving of protection as racial, religious, or ethnic minorities. Simply put, the state makes a normative statement when it frames its bias crime statute—there is no such thing as a "neutral" bias crime law. We will return to this subject in the final chapter.

*Sexual Orientation*

It is difficult to make a strong argument that crime motivated by bias based on sexual orientation—"gay bashing"—does not fit the bias crime model. The factors that make some gender-related crimes so problematic—existence of a personal relationship or the lack of victim interchangeability—are not present in most crimes against homosexuals that are motivated by their sexual orientation. Many such crimes share all the characteristics of bias crimes.[20] If one of the purposes of bias crime statutes is to protect frequently victimized groups, sexual orientation is particularly worthy of inclusion. Some surveys indicate that more than 50 percent of homosexuals in the United States have been the victims of attacks motivated by sexual orientation.[21] A Department of Justice report noted that "homosexuals are probably the most frequent victims of hate crimes."[22] Several legislators who have supported the addition of sexual orientation to state and local bias crime laws did so at least partly in response to an increase, or at least an increase in reported, bias-motivated crimes against homosexuals.[23]

The debate over the inclusion of sexual orientation in bias crime laws has turned primarily on a different factor: whether homosexuality as a category deserves bias crime protection. At times, this argument has been couched in terms of whether homosexuality is an immutable characteristic the way race, color, ethnicity, or national origin are. Texas State Representative Warren Chisum, fighting to exclude sexual orientation from a state bias crime bill, argued that including sexual orientation "would give minority status to a human act, as opposed to being born black or brown or a woman, which are unavoidable indoctrinations into a minority group. [The bill says] now you can opt to be minority by making a human thought."[24] Similarly, Louisiana State Representative Tony Perkins unsuccessfully tried to eliminate sexual orientation from a state bias crime bill, arguing that sexual orientation is a choice and that therefore gays and lesbians do not merit added protection.[25]

The argument for exclusion of sexual orientation from bias crime laws because of the nonimmutability of homosexuality is weak for two sets of reasons. First, immutability of homosexuality is far from clear. There is much evidence that sexual orientation is indeed immutable, whether for genetic reasons alone, or for some combination of genetic and environmental reasons.[26] Even if this evidence is not conclusive, there is certainly no scientific basis to conclude that sexual orientation is a matter of personal choice. The assertions of Representatives Chisum and Perkins are not a solid basis upon which to make public policy.

Second, immutability turns out to be a multilayered concept. Part of Representatives Chisum and Perkins's argument is the notion that homosexuality is chosen behavior: one can "choose" not to be gay, whereas one cannot choose not to be black. Even if we were to assume that homosexuality is chosen behavior, there is a serious problem with this argument. The problem is that this same argument could be made with respect to religion, one of the classic bias crime characteristics. The choice not to remain Jewish or Catholic is certainly more real than the choice not to remain black. The reason that religion, along with race, color, ethnicity, and national origin, is protected by virtually all bias crime statutes is that we deem it unreasonable to suggest that a Jew or Catholic might just choose to avoid discrimination by giving up her religion. Indeed, we deem it outrageous. Understood in this light, the question of immutability collapses into a basic value-driven question: are homosexuals somehow less deserving of protection than other groups?

Many legislators who oppose the inclusion of homosexuality have explicitly made their arguments on such value-based grounds. Maryland Representative Ellen Sauerbrey, the minority leader of the Maryland House of Delegates, for example, summarized this view about a bias crime reporting law when she said, "I just don't think we should be always separating out gays and lesbians . . . I don't think we should be creating special categories for homosexuals for everything that comes along."[27] In the debate over including sexual orientation in the Indiana bias crime law, Representative Woody Burton, offering an amendment to remove sexual orientation as a protected category, argued that including homosexuals in hate crime statutes would be "opening the door toward . . . teaching that kind of lifestyle to our children."[28]

In determining whether or not sexual orientation should be included in a state's bias crime law, the legislature is inescapably faced with a value-driven question. It is not, however, the stark question that Representative Burton poses as to whether we should be "teaching that kind of lifestyle to our children." Rather, it is the value-driven question of whether the state should protect homosexuals from discrimination.

The recent decision of the Supreme Court in *Romer v. Evans* is instructive on this point.[29] In *Romer*, the Court struck down Colorado's "Amendment 2," a state constitutional amendment that prohibited any governmental action designed to protect the civil rights of homosexuals. An explicit denial of rights to gays and lesbians is irrational and thus unconstitutional. Only ten years after upholding the Georgia sodomy statute in *Bowers v. Hardwick*,[30] the Supreme Court concluded that Amendment 2 was "inexplicable by anything but animus toward the class that it affects."[31] We need not conclude that omission of sexual orientation from a bias crime law is unconstitutional in the same sense as the expressed denial of protection at issue in *Romer*. We may conclude, however, that states which exclude sexual orientation from bias crime statutes are making a normative statement about the nature of homosexuality and the treatment of gays and lesbians.

Just as we saw concerning gender in bias crime statutes, the state makes a normative statement about the treatment of gays and lesbians when it frames its bias crime law. Failure to include sexual orientation implies that gays and lesbians are not as deserving of protection as racial, religious, or ethnic minorities, and that sexual orientation is not as serious a social fissure line as race, religion, and ethnicity. We see once again that there is no "neutral" bias crime law.

## Is the Bias Crime Problem Getting Worse?

During the 1980s, public concern over the level of racially motivated violence in the United States rose dramatically. This decade saw the most significant legislative response to the problem of bias crimes since Reconstruction. Prior to 1980, only five states had any type of bias crime statute. Most of the pre-1980 bias crime statutes were enacted to combat the activities of the Ku Klux Klan. As a result, most of the laws addressed cross-burning and the wearing of hoods or masks in public.[32] Only one state, Connecticut, had a statute prior to 1980 that addressed the problem of racially motivated assaults outside the traditional forum of Ku Klux Klan assaults.[33] Today, nearly every state has a bias crime law, and federal law enhances punishment for federal crimes committed with bias motivation.[34]

Such public concern and the consequent enactment of bias crime statutes across the United States probably stemmed, at least in part, from an apparent worsening of the bias crime problem during this period. It remains difficult, however, to gauge whether the bias crime problem has actually worsened or merely appears to have done so. Though statistics gathered by both independent and governmental organizations support the conclusion that the bias crime problem has worsened, these statistics remain inconsistent and incomplete. Moreover, the statistics gathered toward the end of the 1980s and throughout the early to mid-1990s reflect not only a growth in the bias crime problem, but also an obscuring growth in legislative and administrative response to this problem. Likewise, socioeconomic trends, though they also point to a worsening of the problem, remain laden with guesswork and ambiguity. In effect, determining the true magnitude and morphology of the bias crime problem presents myriad problems.

In general, experts and commentators agree that bias crimes had, from the mid-1980s through the early 1990s, increased annually.[35] For example, the Anti-Defamation League (ADL), the Southern Poverty Law Center (SPLC), and the National Gay and Lesbian Task Force (NGLTF), organizations that collect data on the subject, all reported such persistent growth. The NGLTF reported that antigay and lesbian incidents increased from 2,042 in 1985 to 7,031 in 1989.[36] Similarly, the ADL, in its Audit of Anti-Semitic Incidents for 1994, reported an all-time high of 2,066 religious bias incidents for that year, coming at the end of a series of significant increases during the early 1990s. Recently, however, some of these groups have reported decreases in bias crimes. For instance, in their 1997 audit, the ADL reported a 24 percent decrease in the number of anti-Semitic incidents since 1994,[37] and the National Coalition of Anti-Violence Programs, a nationwide alliance of gay and lesbian advocacy groups, reported a similar decline in antigay incidents in 1996.[38]

These trends are difficult to interpret. There is evidence that bias crimes, even if less numerous, have become more violent. Monitoring groups have observed a shift from racially motivated property crimes such as spray painting, defacement, and graffiti, to personal crimes such as assault, threat, and harassment.[39] In 1990 the SPLC's data-gathering arm, Klanwatch, reported that homicides linked to white supremacists or bias motivation had more than tripled since 1989, reaching a total of twenty.[40] By 1993, Klanwatch noted a "shocking reversal" in the racial profile of the perpetrators and victims of these deadly crimes. Though law enforcement officials had charged whites with all of 1989's and all but one of 1990's racially motivated slayings, of the fifty-eight such slayings reported nationwide from 1991 to 1993, law enforcement officials charged African-Americans with twenty-seven—a full 46 percent.[41] This shift in the bias crime role of African-Americans—from victims only to perpetrators as well—marked a significant departure from the traditional perception of the bias crime problem. Minorities were no longer only victims, and whites, no longer only victimizers.

This surprising shift in the bias crime problem, however, elicited charges of inaccurate reporting from numerous bias crime experts and commentators. For instance, Reverend Joseph A. Lowery, the president of the Southern Christian Leadership Conference, questioned the Klanwatch figures, citing the inclusion of a resistant robbery victim as an example of erroneous recording.[42] In this case, Lowery explained, the African-American robbers probably killed their victim not because he was white but because he had attempted to intercede during the commission of the robbery. Hence, the SPLC incorrectly labeled this homicide bias-motivated.

In a more dramatic denunciation of bias crime reporting, Lawrence E. Lockman, the vice-chairman of Concerned Maine Families, flatly asserted that the state attorney general's office "inflates statistics on hate crimes against gays, [thereby] 'creat[ing] the false impression that Maine is a hot-bed of anti-gay bigotry.'"[43] Though this denunciation, unlike the former, indicates personal bias and lacks convincing proof, it carries with it the same message of distrust for current methods of bias crime data-gathering. Ultimately, such observers argue, data centers fail to gauge accurately, or attempt to manufacture actively, the worsening of the bias crime problem in the United States.[44]

In an effort to provide trustworthy statistics for bias crime observers and simultaneously to address heightened concern over the bias crime problem, Congress in 1990 passed the Hate Crime Statistics Act (HCSA).[45] Under this act, the Department of Justice must collect statistics on the incidence of bias crimes in the United States as part of its regular information-gathering.[46] The Attorney General delegated the development and implementation of the HCSA to the Federal Bureau of Investigation's (FBI) Uniform Crime Reporting Program for incorporation among its 16,000 voluntary law enforcement agency participants.[47] Accordingly, the FBI initiated intensive education and training of state and local law enforcement personnel in the investigation, identification, reporting, and appropriate handling of bias crimes.[48]

Since the HCSA's implementation in 1991, the FBI has documented a general rise in bias crimes. The data collected under the HCSA reveal the following number of bias crimes:[49]

1991—4,558
1992—7,442
1993—7,684
1994—7,498
1995—7,947
1996—8,759

However, these figures, like those reported by other data-gathering organizations, remain vulnerable to charges of inaccuracy. Because the FBI's numbers simply mirror the numbers reported by state and local law enforcement agencies, and because agency participation under the HCSA is voluntary, the completed data more aptly reflect popular perception of the bias crime problem than they do the problem itself.[50] For example, the near 70 percent increase in bias crimes reported between 1991 and 1993 evidences a simultaneous increase in the reporting of such crimes. Specifically, only 2,771 police departments in 32 states participated in data collection and reporting in 1991 while, in 1993, 6,840 police departments in 46 states and the District of Columbia did so.[51] In addition to such inconsistent reporting, the FBI's data also suffer from consistent under-reporting: even with nearly 7,000 agencies participating under the HCSA in 1993 and 1994, more than 9,000 agencies throughout the country failed to report altogether, many of them located in major urban centers.[52] As a result, it is, as Michael A. Sandberg of the ADL's Chicago office admitted, difficult to draw reliable nationwide conclusions on the basis of HCSA data because law enforcement participation has not yet reached an optimum, nor even a representative, level.[53]

There is a mutual-feedback relationship between the bias crime problem and both the popular perception and the official response to the problem. A perceived increase in bias crime as fostered by independent data-gathering and reporting leads to increased public concern regarding such crimes. Such concern leads, in succession, to legislative and administrative response, to increased official reporting, and, in effect, to an even greater perceived increase in bias crime, and so on. Thus problem and perception conflate, and the apparent growth in bias crime becomes not simply a reflection of increased hatred and apathy (as the statistics alone would suggest), but also an indication of increased understanding and action (as the increased response to the problem suggests).

On the other hand, some organizations, including the National Institute Against Prejudice and Violence, report that, despite increased bias crime reporting by police agencies, a majority of bias crime victims do not report incidents at all.[54] In fact, "[d]ue to factors such as [the victim's entrenched] distrust of the police, language barriers, the fear of retaliation by the offender, and the fear of courting exposure," even organized attempts to collect bias crime data, such as the HCSA, probably fail to provide an accurate count of hate crimes and their changing face in America.[55] Some bias crime victims view an incident as simply too minor to report, thus skewing the statistics even further. Given that intimidation constitutes the most frequently perpetrated bias behavior, and given that intimidation sometimes appears "minor," the problem of under-reporting takes on even greater urgency.[56] Under-reporting by law enforcement agencies, when coupled with under-reporting by victims, points to drastic under-reporting of bias crimes in general.

In addition to all the problems with measuring the current level of hate crimes, we also face a significant problem with establishing a base-line for a meaningful comparison. The abysmal data available on the hate crime problem prior to the mid-1980s exacerbate the difficulties of gauging whether this problem has actually worsened or only appears to have done so. For instance, it was not until 1978 that the Boston City Police Department became the first law enforcement agency to track racially motivated crimes;[57] it was not until 1981 that Maryland became the first state to pass a reporting statute;[58] and it was not until the mid- to late 1980s that several other states implemented similar recording statutes.[59] Furthermore, the SPLC's Klanwatch Project only began gathering statistics on bias crime across the nation in 1979. Likewise, the ADL began gathering and publishing statistics on bias crimes in 1979, but these statistics covered only anti-Semitic incidents, thus leaving a wide gamut of other bias crimes untouched and unreported.

In light of these incomplete data, we must also look to social trends to determine whether bias crime incidence has actually risen or just appears to have done so. SPLC attributes the continued increase in the number of hate groups to such social trends as communication among racist groups through the Internet, broader dissemination of hate-oriented music with lyrics advocating violence against members of minority groups, and the approach of the millennium's inspiring hate groups with a perverse image of an impending racial Armageddon.[60] Perhaps indicative of the authenticity of this rise is the criminological observation that white, teenage males are, both historically and currently, the "most common [perpetrators] of hate crime," in tandem with the propensity among some groups of teenagers toward racial hostility and the acceptance of violence as a means of dispute resolution.[61] Though these observations create something of a tautology (white teenage males commit more bias crimes because they are racist and violent; because they commit more bias crimes, white teenage males appear racist and violent), they nonetheless point to a disturbing trend: individuals more willing and, therefore, more apt to commit bias crimes than those of the previous generation now occupy the age cohort most likely to commit such crimes.

This trend, however, evidences an internal irony. Although white teenage males commit most bias crimes generally and most violent bias crimes specifically, they often cite reasons other than actual bias as their true motivation for committing these crimes. For example, students at both Norman Thomas High School in New York City and Greenwich High School in Greenwich, Connecticut, where incidents manifesting bias occurred in the spring of 1995, said that the invocation of racial or religious slurs often reflects the perpetrators' "larger insecurities, frustrations, petty rivalries, hostilities and other emotions that are a part of coming of age."[62] Thus, rather than accurately depicting bigoted beliefs, bias behavior actually masks deeper and largely dissimilar feelings of personal inadequacy.[63] In effect, the increase in teenage-perpetrated crimes that appear to be bias-motivated may stem from overestimating cases of actual bias motivation and may, therefore, fail to evidence a worsening of the bias crime problem.

By contrast, widely recognized parallels between economic trends and bias crime incidence more soundly support the conclusion that the bias crime problem has actually worsened in recent years. In general, bias incidents spike during periods of economic unrest. We may understand this in two different but related ways. First, economic difficulties lead to displaced aggression and scapegoating of disadvantaged groups, which in turn leads to increased racism. Second, economic difficulties may lead to increased criminal behavior such that racism, previously exhibited privately, takes the form of racially motivated violence. Whatever the explanation, there is compelling empirical evidence of the connection between racial violence and economic hardship.[64] For example, during the 1830s and 1840s, fueled by the economic Panic of 1837 and the subsequent economic depression, many Americans blamed their difficulties on German and Irish immigrants, thus popularizing anti–Roman Catholicism.[65] Likewise, after the Civil War, the Ku Klux Klan gained prevalence throughout the South and, during the economic difficulties of the early 1920s, gained similar prevalence in the North.[66] Although lynching by citizens' mobs declined during the Great Depression, those involved in lynchings and other forms of racial violence came from the poorest parts of the white community.[67] Moreover, as lynchings waned, a new means of accomplishing the same end while maintaining a semblance of due process emerged: during the 1930s, use of the perfunctory death penalty trial increased greatly throughout the South.[68] Finally, bias crime incidence also increased during the late 1970s.[69]

Today, the shrinking of the middle class, along with the rise of a tenuous, service-oriented economy, has likely led to a similar increase in intolerance and a consequent growth in bias crime.[70] For the first time in a century, many Americans believe that their children will not inherit a better standard of living than they currently enjoy; they further believe that they cannot ameliorate this situation. Because personal effort thus appears ineffectual in combating the adverse economy, displaced aggression, stereotyping, scapegoating, and, inevitably, bias crime have once again grown pervasive.[71] When individuals laden with economic woes combine this hatred with action, bias crime—as history shows—becomes not only possible but inevitable.

Moreover, political leaders of the 1980s and early 1990s, rather than pacifying or constructively channeling the economic frustrations of Americans, utilized negative racial rhetoric and demagogic messages, thereby heightening intergroup antagonisms and likely (though perhaps unwittingly) fueling an actual increase in bias crime.[72] For instance, in 1993 American politicians increasingly blamed immigrants for the country's economic problems, and in that same year, anti-immigrant sentiments appeared in more than half the crimes reported against Asians and Latinos.[73] A more concrete example of these damaging political tactics was George Bush's infamous use of Willie Horton—a convicted African-American rapist—as a political symbol during the 1988 Presidential campaign. By aligning blacks and crime, Bush successfully played upon racial stereotypes to advance his conservative agenda and may, thereby, have exacerbated interracial tensions.[74] Another seemingly harmless example of this damaging rhetoric was the "buy American" crusade initiated by American business people and public officials during the late 1980s.[75] This slogan's latent anti-Japanese message gripped the nation, and its widespread acceptance may have helped legitimize the kind of beliefs that lead to increased acceptance of racial violence and, by extension, increased incidence of bias crime. Similarly, the controversy surrounding California's Proposition 187 in 1996, denying benefits such as medical care and education to illegal immigrants, may have contributed to the increase in anti-Asian violence in that state.[76]

In addition, the growth of organized "hate groups" throughout the United States may further evidence, or perhaps foreshadow, a worsening of the bias crime problem. While it appears that "most hate crimes are committed by individuals who are not associated with any organized group," the greater militancy and violence, as well as the increased membership, of these groups has many observers worried.[77] And rightly so.

Klanwatch has reported that, though membership in the traditional Ku Klux Klan has decreased, increased membership in other white supremacist groups has offset this older group's decline.[78] For example, the Skinhead movement has expanded its ranks from between 1,000 and 1,500 throughout twelve states in 1988 to between 3,300 and 3,500 throughout forty states in 1993.[79] Even more frightening than these membership numbers alone, however, is this group's "extraordinary [and increasing] record of violence."[80] Between 1991 and 1993, the Skinhead movement claimed responsibility for twenty-two murders, some perpetrated against minorities, some against fellow Skins.[81] In the preceding three years, the group had claimed responsibility for only six such murders.[82]

Still, one "hate group" has dominated public attention since the bombing of the Oklahoma City Federal Building on April 19, 1995: the militia movement. On the surface, the hatred espoused by this group differs from that of other hate groups. While "traditional" hate groups place racial or religious bigotry at the center of their agendas, the militia movement focuses its hatred on the federal government.[83] This hatred (or perhaps fear) manifests in the militia groups' belief that an impending armed conflict with the federal government necessitates paramilitary training and weapons stockpiling.[84]

But the militia movement has deep connections with white supremacist and neo-Nazi organizations. More than 137 such militia groups and "patriot organizations" possess ties to racist groups. Moreover, people with histories of racial and religious bigotry often occupy positions of leadership in the militia movement.[85]

Although antigovernment sentiment may form the bond between these volatile white supremacist groups and the militias, the confluence of developed and organized racial and religious hate groups with armed and ready citizens' militias has produced an increased threat on the personal, rather than on the political, level.[86] In addition, because some leaders of organized hate groups have sought to discard "gutter racism" and "reinvent themselves as respectable American Patriots" in order to secure a larger following, they have easily melded with the militia movement.[87] Thus, by "exploiting the broader issues of immigration, gun control, states' rights, abortion and homosexuality," Klanwatch Director Danny Welch explained, "these racists and anti-Semites are tapping into a larger audience than they've been able to reach in years."[88]

Nonetheless, although the militias' political agenda resembles a mere guise for racial and religious bias, members of the movement have not claimed, nor have law enforcement officials charged them with, any bias crimes. For example, Charles Trocci, the press secretary for the Pennsylvania state police, noted that, despite close monitoring of militia activity, the police have not discovered any illegal activity.[89] "In all fairness to [the militias]," stated Trocci, "there's been an absence of criminal activity [on the part of militia members]."[90] Even so, the infiltration of these groups by violence-prone hatemongers remains cause for alarm. After all, as Floyd Cochran, a former member of the Aryan Nations, stated in an interview with CNN, "[It is] fairly easy [to] . . . get people to hate . . . People [are] receptive to the message of hate."[91] Perhaps they are even more so when they hate already—even if they only hate an entity (the federal government) rather than a person or group of persons.

Although it is not possible to say with confidence the extent to which bias crimes are increasing and the extent to which the increase is in our perception, there are several things that we may say with confidence, and it is important that we do so. First, the obvious relationship between perception and problem in no way undercuts the severity of the problem. Our ability to measure the trajectory with precision may be limited, but we are able to confirm the existence today of a serious level of bias-motivated crime. Second, the mutual-feedback relationship between the level of bias crime and the popular perception of this level does not necessarily undermine our determination of the severity of the problem. As we broaden our understanding of what constitutes a bias crime, that which may have been dismissed as a "prank" in an earlier time is now properly revealed as bias-motivated criminal conduct. This does not mean that we are "over-counting" bias crimes today. On the contrary, it means only that previously we were "under-counting" these crimes. In sum, we should be wary of the risk of overkill but not freed from the obligation of vigilance.

## CHAPTER 2

# How Are Bias Crimes Different?

It is no overstatement to say that the past twenty years have seen a revolution in the legal response to racially motivated violence. Prior to 1980, Connecticut alone criminalized bias crimes. Bias crime laws have become pervasive in the American legal culture. With the enactment in 1997 of bias crime statutes in Arizona, Nebraska, and Louisiana, virtually every state now expressly criminalizes bias crimes.

Two subjects require initial attention in the study of these laws: the typology of bias crime laws and the harm that results from bias crimes. The landscape of the various laws proscribing racially motivated violence is best understood through focusing on the state of mind of the bias criminal. A close analysis of the many bias crime statutes that have been enacted within the last two decades allows us to observe certain legal trends, and to categorize these laws into the "racial animus" model—requiring that the defendant has acted out of hatred for the victim's racial group or the victim for being a member of that group—and the "discriminatory selection" model, requiring only that the defendant has selected his victim because of the victim's membership in a particular group. The mental state of the perpetrator is critical in distinguishing these statutes.

At the other end of the spectrum from the inward focus on the mind of the bias criminal is the outward focus on the harm caused to bias crime victims. The resulting harm of a bias crime is best thought of in comparative terms, relative to the harm caused by a parallel crime. Harm may be examined on each of three levels: the immediate victim of a bias crime, the broader target community of the crime, and society at large. On each level, bias crimes cause a harm that is greater than that caused by parallel crimes.

## The "Discriminatory Selection Model" and the "Racial Animus Model" of Bias Crimes

We often speak about "bias crime laws" as if these laws took a single form. Quite the contrary. There are two analytically distinct, albeit somewhat overlapping, models of bias crimes. I refer to these models as the "discriminatory selection model" and the "racial animus model."

The discriminatory selection model of bias crimes defines these crimes in terms of the perpetrator's discriminatory selection of his victim. Under this model, it is irrelevant *why* an offender selected his victim on the basis of race or group; it is sufficient that the offender did so. Alternatively, the racial animus model of bias crimes defines crimes on the basis of the perpetrator's animus for the racial or ethnic group of the victim and the centrality of this animus in the perpetrator's motivation for committing the crime. (Sample discriminatory selection statutes are provided in Appendix B and sample racial animus statutes in Appendix C.)

Many cases of discriminatory victim selection are in fact also cases of racial animus—perhaps most, but not all. The distinction between the racial animus model and the discriminatory selection model of bias crimes will be discussed in depth below. It may prove helpful even at this introductory stage, however, to provide several hypotheticals to help focus the nature of this distinction.

Consider a purse snatcher who preys exclusively upon women because he believes that he will better achieve his criminal goals by grabbing purses from women rather than by trying to pick wallets out of men's pockets. The purse snatcher has discriminatorily selected his victims on the basis of gender, but he has not acted with animus toward women as a group. Similarly, consider the mugger who preys solely upon white victims because he believes that white people, on average, carry more money than nonwhites. He, too, has selected his victim on the basis of race but has done so without bias motivation.

The discriminatory selection model of bias crimes received much attention because it was a statute of this model that was upheld by the Supreme Court in 1993 in *Wisconsin v. Mitchell*.[1] *Mitchell* was the first case in which the Supreme Court expressly sustained a modern bias crime law.[2] Because *Mitchell* represents the constitutional authority for the enactment of bias crime laws, the Wisconsin statute warrants close examination. It is to this statute and the litigation that led to its consideration by the Supreme Court that we now turn.

### The Supreme Court's Affirmation of the Discriminatory Selection Model

On October 7, 1989, in Kenosha, Wisconsin, Todd Mitchell, a nineteen-year-old black man, directed and encouraged a number of young black men and boys to attack a fourteen-year-old white boy, Gregory Riddick. Mitchell selected Riddick solely on the basis of his race. Mitchell was convicted of aggravated battery for his role in the severe beating—a crime that carries a maximum sentence of two years under Wisconsin law.[3] His crime also implicated the Wisconsin bias crime statute, which provides for the enhanced penalty of racially motivated crimes.[4] Under this statute, the potential penalty for an aggravated battery is increased by five years if the perpetrator of the assault selected his victim on the basis of the victim's race. In addition to Mitchell's conviction for battery, he was also found to have acted out of racial bias in the selection of the victim. Mitchell, whose maximum possible sentence for this offense was seven years, received a prison sentence of four years.[5]

The Wisconsin bias crime statute provides that the maximum sentence and/or fine for certain crimes of violence shall be increased if the offender "[i]ntentionally selects" his victim "because of the [victim's] race, religion, color, disability, sexual orientation, national origin or ancestry."[6] Mitchell challenged his conviction under this statute, claiming that the enhancement of his prison term was a violation of his right to freedom of expression under the First Amendment. The Wisconsin appellate court upheld his conviction, but that state's Supreme Court reversed.[7] Ultimately, the United States Supreme Court upheld Mitchell's sentence, including the enhanced portion.

The penalty-enhancement statute upheld in *Mitchell* was a discriminatory selection model law. The nature of this model was crucial to the manner in which the state of Wisconsin portrayed its statute before the Supreme Court. Wisconsin was intent upon distinguishing its statute from the cross-burning ordinance that had been struck down by the Supreme Court just one year earlier in *R.A.V. v. City of St. Paul*. As discussed below, the distinction between the discriminatory selection model and the racial animus model, so significant in the argument advanced by Wisconsin, was largely lost in the Court's decision in *Mitchell*. Nonetheless, *Mitchell* must be seen both as a challenge to the Wisconsin statute itself and as part of an ongoing judicial consideration of the constitutionality of bias crime laws.

At the time that the *Mitchell* case was working its way through the Wisconsin state courts and up to the United States Supreme Court, the conflict between bias crimes and freedom of expression was the central legal issue of concern for those who study and those who enforce these laws. Although this conflict will be examined in detail in Chapter 5, we must examine it briefly here in order to understand the significance of the choice of bias crime model in *Mitchell*. The Supreme Court's 1992 decision in *R.A.V. v. City of*

*St. Paul* dominated the bias crime debate at the time.[8] The *R.A.V.* decision raised serious doubts as to the constitutionality of bias crime legislation generally. The doubts were so pervasive that the FBI sent out a letter to more than 16,000 local law enforcement agencies to inform them that the decisions in *R.A.V.* did not affect their obligations to collect data under the Federal Hate Crimes Statistics Act of 1990.[9]

In *R.A.V.*, the Supreme Court unanimously struck down a municipal ordinance prohibiting cross-burning and other actions "which one knows or has reasonable grounds to know" will cause "anger, alarm or resentment in others on the basis of race, color, creed, religion or gender."[10] The majority of the Court found that the St. Paul ordinance was an unconstitutional content-based regulation of speech.[11]

The reasoning of the Court in *R.A.V.* receives close scrutiny in Chapter 5, where we focus on issues of expression and the potential conflict between the punishment of bias crimes and First Amendment jurisprudence. For now, it is sufficient to note the Court's general problem with the St. Paul ordinance. While the Court acknowledged that the ordinance was aimed only at "fighting words," a category entitled to less protection than general expression, it found that the statute punished not fighting words generally but only a certain kind of fighting words.[12] The Court concluded that St. Paul had established a regulation aimed directly at racist speech and biased beliefs rather than at all fighting words or even a subgroup of fighting words selected for reasons other than the content of those words. In so doing, the ordinance impermissibly chose sides in the debate over racial or religious prejudice.

The reasoning in *R.A.V.* became the paradigm for other courts reviewing bias crime statutes. For example, this view was adopted, with some modification, by the Ohio Supreme Court[13] and by the Wisconsin Supreme Court in its decision reversing the enhancement of Todd Mitchell's sentence for aggravated battery.[14] Following the decision in *R.A.V.*, the focus of attention among those who sought to enforce bias crime laws turned to limiting the reach of that case or distinguishing its holding so as not to apply to other bias crime statutes. In Massachusetts, for example, the state attorney general convened a special task force to reexamine the constitutionality of the Massachusetts Civil Rights Crimes statute in light of *R.A.V.*[15] When the Supreme Court decided to hear *Mitchell*, the critical issue to the parties was the applicability of *R.A.V.* to the Wisconsin penalty-enhancement statute.

In defending its bias crime statute from constitutional attack, Wisconsin seized upon the precise form and content of that statute and the fact that it was a statute of the discriminatory selection model of bias crimes. The Wisconsin penalty-enhancement law is the only explicit discriminatory selection model statute in the country. As noted, it expressly states that penalty enhancement is applicable if the offender "[i]ntentionally selects the person against whom the crime . . . is committed . . . because of the race, religion, color, disability, sexual orientation, national origin or ancestry of that person."[16] The first clause of the relevant section of the provision, unique among American bias crime laws, requires "intentional selection" of the victim on the basis of race. This provided a key element in Wisconsin's argument that its statute withstood the holding in *R.A.V.* Wisconsin contended that *R.A.V.* was concerned with the regulation of expression. The Wisconsin bias crime statute proscribed not expression but conduct—the conduct of intentional discriminatory selection of a victim. The speech-conduct distinction, though of dubious validity, plays a key role in judicial First Amendment analysis.[17]

The focus on the discriminatory selection aspect of the Wisconsin statute was an attempt not only to frame the statute on the permissible side of the line between the regulation of speech and that of conduct, but also to defend the bias crime statute from the claim that it punished "motivation." The Wisconsin Supreme Court in *Mitchell* had held that the Wisconsin bias crime law impermissibly strayed beyond the punishment of act and purposeful intent and went on to punish motivation. The Court held that "[b]ecause all of the [parallel] crimes are already punishable, all that remains is an additional punishment for the defendant's motive in selecting the victim. The punishment of the defendant's bigoted motive by the hate crimes statute directly implicates and encroaches upon First Amendment rights."[18]

In order to portray the statute as punishing something other than motivation, Wisconsin argued that Mitchell's discriminatory selection of Riddick because of Riddick's race was wholly distinct from whatever Mitchell's actual motivation for doing so may have been.[19] Mitchell may have been motivated by Riddick's race or merely by the desire to show off in front of his friends.[20] But so long as Mitchell chose Riddick on the basis of his race, his conduct would trigger the Wisconsin penalty-enhancement statute.

Ironically, although Wisconsin was successful in defending the constitutionality of its bias crime statute, it was unsuccessful in explaining the nature of the discriminatory selection model to the Court. For that matter, the state failed to persuade the Court that the distinction between discriminatory selection and other models of bias crimes was relevant to the Court's consideration of the issue. On the one hand, the Court understood Mitchell's sentence to have been enhanced because he "intentionally selected his victim on account of the victim's race."[21] This appears to be consistent with the state's construction of its statute. But elsewhere, the Court described the Wisconsin bias crime penalty-enhancement law as one that "punishes criminal conduct [but also] enhances the maximum penalty for conduct *motivated by a discriminatory point of view* more severely than the same conduct engaged in for some other reason or for no reason at all."[22] Here, the understanding of the elements of the bias crime seems to turn less on the strict discriminatory selection of a victim than on the "point of view" that underpins that selection.

The Court's lack of focus on the specific nature of the bias crime statute under review in *Mitchell* perhaps stemmed from the fact that it was not persuaded by the argument that the statute impermissibly punished motive rather than conduct or intent.[23] The exact nature of the motivation punished by Wisconsin was therefore not deemed to be of great relevance. Had the Court focused on the statute itself, it would have seen that the bias crime law it was upholding was directed solely at the discriminatory selection of the victim.

### The Racial Animus Model of Bias Crimes

The Wisconsin statute may be contrasted with state statutes that target the racist motivation of the bias crime offender. These are statutes of the racial animus model. New Jersey, for example, enhances the criminal penalty for a crime that is motivated, at least in part, by "ill will, hatred, or bias due to race, color, religion, sexual orientation or ethnicity."[24] The elements of a bias crime in Connecticut, Maryland, Pennsylvania, Florida, and New Hampshire also include hatred toward the victim's race and not mere discriminatory selection of that victim. Other states have statutes that, although less explicit as to the role of animus in a bias crime, implicitly require the existence of racial animus for criminal conduct to be a bias crime. The racial animus model of bias crimes is the one that bias crime scholars[25] and law enforcement agencies most typically adopt.[26] This model is consonant with the classical understanding of prejudice as involving more than differential treatment on the basis of the victim's race. This understanding of prejudice, as reflected in the racial animus model of bias crimes, requires that the offender have committed the crime with some measure of hostility toward the victim's racial group and/or toward the victim because he is part of that group.[27]

The racial animus model of bias crimes is well illustrated by the regulations promulgated by the FBI to implement the Hate Crime Statistics Act of 1990.[28] These regulations define a bias crime as criminal conduct motivated, in whole or in part, by a "preformed negative opinion or attitude toward a group of persons based on their race, religion, ethnicity/national origin, or sexual orientation."[29] The regulations provide for a set of "bias indicators" to guide the classification of a particular crime as a bias crime. These indicators primarily involve direct evidence of racial animus on the part of the offender.[30] Some of the indicators are consistent with a discriminatory selection model of bias crimes,[31] and others are equally consistent with either model.[32] What distinguishes the FBI definition from a discriminatory selection model such as that utilized in Wisconsin, however, is the use to which discriminatory selection indicators are put under the FBI regulations. A discriminatory selection criterion is relevant to the FBI only insofar as it allows for the inference of animus. In this manner, the FBI regulations are distinct from the Wisconsin model. For purposes of the FBI regulations, discriminatory selection of a victim, in and of itself, is irrelevant to the identification of conduct as a bias crime. Discriminatory selection of a victim becomes relevant only if that selection is probative of an underlying racial animus. As observed earlier, whereas all cases of racial animus are cases of discriminatory selection, the converse is not true.

### Where Do Most State Statutes Fit?

The discriminatory selection model law represented by the Wisconsin penalty-enhancement statute and the racial animus model adopted by the FBI and enacted by such states as Florida, New Hampshire, Pennsylvania, New Jersey, Connecticut, and Maryland are two distinct models of bias crime laws. But the majority of bias crime statutes cannot be unambiguously placed in one category or the other. Of those states whose punishment for bias crimes is distinct from the general punishment of the relevant parallel crime, the majority have employed neither Wisconsin's "intentionally selects" language nor New Jersey's "ill will, hatred, or bias due to race" language. California, for example, provides for the enhancement of criminal penalties for certain crimes if committed "*because of* the [victim's] race, color, religion, ancestry, national origin, or sexual orientation."[33]

The *because of* or *by reason of* formulation has been adopted in some form by most states with bias crime laws. Many of these states have enacted simple *because of* bias crime statutes. Such statutes require only that the defendant has committed the parallel crime and that the crime be committed *because of* the victim's race. This is also the formulation utilized in federal civil rights crimes statutes. (See Appendix D.) Other states augment this "because of the victim's race" element of the bias crime with an additional element of "maliciousness."(See Appendix E.)

*Because of* bias crime statutes—either in the simple form or with the additional element of maliciousness—evade easy classification as either racial animus or discriminatory selection laws. These statutes lack explicit reference either to animus as found in New Jersey's law or to discriminatory selection as found in Wisconsin's statute. Several observations may be made, however, as to the classification of these laws. First, the simple *because of* model is most consistent with a discriminatory selection model. One state court construed the phrase "intentionally injures [a victim] . . . because of [the victim's] race" as a proscription against targeting a victim on the basis of the victim's race, concluding that "one need not hate at all to commit this crime."[34]

*Because of* is more typically found in civil statutes than in criminal proscriptions and, in the civil rights context, looks to an actor's actual discriminatory choice rather than to his reasons for making that choice. In the employment discrimination context, the federal antidiscrimination law Title VII utilizes a *because of* formulation that in no manner requires racial animus on the part of the employer. Title VII mandates that "[i]t shall be an unlawful employment practice for an employer . . . to fail or refuse to hire or to discharge any individual . . . *because of* such individual's race." *Because of* under Title VII is understood to be sufficiently removed from animus to include acts that, although neutral on their face, have a discriminatory impact on a protected class.[35] Similarly, the understanding of discriminatory intent for purposes of the equal protection clause of the Fourteenth Amendment of the Constitution requires neither animus nor conscious awareness of discrimination.[36]

The *because of* formulation that requires maliciousness does suggest a greater concern with the motivation of the offender. The very term "maliciousness" lends itself to a requirement that the perpetrator demonstrate a hatred for his victim.[37] Even this formulation, however, is consistent with the discriminatory selection model and has been interpreted in this manner. The Washington Supreme Court recently construed a *because of* statute that required maliciousness as a discriminatory selection statute in the case of

*Washington v. Talley.* The Washington bias crime statute under review in *Talley* provided that a person was guilty of malicious harassment if he caused personal injury or damage to another's property "maliciously and with the intent to intimidate or harass another person because of, or in a way that is reasonably related to, associated with, or directed toward, that person's race, color, religion, ancestry, national origin, or mental, physical, or sensory handicap." The Washington Supreme Court understood the statute to deal strictly with the offender's discriminatory selection of a victim. It stated that "the statute punishes the selection of the victim, not the reason for the selection . . . The statute is triggered by victim selection regardless of the actor's motives or beliefs."[38]

*Because of* statutes that require maliciousness are, however, certainly consistent with a racial animus model, and it is fair to say that even those *because of* statutes that do not require maliciousness are at least not inconsistent with the racial animus model. These laws, after all, do not explicitly refer to the "discriminatory selection" of a victim and thus permit a court to interpret the mental-state requirement that an offender has acted *because of* the race of the victim as a requirement of racial animus.[39] Certainly this is true where prosecutors must show the added element of maliciousness.

Classification of *because of* bias crime statutes is thus made difficult by the fact that these laws are consistent with either the discriminatory selection model or the racial animus model. Moreover, few of these laws have received definitive judicial construction.[40] Thus these statutes, as yet, may not be classified as examples of either the discriminatory selection model or the racial animus model.

To a certain extent, it is not so surprising that classification of bias crime laws poses such thorny problems. Proponents of bias crime laws themselves, apparently unaware of the potential ambiguity of the language used in bias crime statutes, have shown little interest in resolving the ambiguity. The 1994 federal legislation that enhances criminal penalties for bias crimes provides a good example. The legislation, as eventually enacted, uses *because of* language and the discriminatory selection model. A "hate crime" is defined as "a crime in which the defendant intentionally selects a victim, or in the case of a property crime, the property that is the object of the crime because of the actual or perceived race, color, religion, national origin, ethnicity, gender or sexual orientation of any person." By contrast, Senator Diane Feinstein, the chief sponsor of the bill, argued for its passage using language that clearly reflects the racial animus model. She said that "[s]omeone who selects a victim of a crime based on bigotry and hatred should be subject to the stiffest penalties."[41]

One additional category of bias crime laws requires some mention as to the mental state of the bias crime offender: the treatment of institutional vandalism. Many states have statutes that specifically punish defacement and destruction of such institutions as houses of worship, cemeteries, or religious schools. (See Appendix F.)

Institutional vandalism statutes do not require animus on the part of the offender; they require only knowledge that the institution attacked or defaced was, in fact, one protected by the law. With one exception, these statutes are discriminatory selection model statutes. I classify institutional vandalism statutes as discriminatory selection laws because, ordinarily, these cases involve actors who selected their target because of the racial or religious nature of the institution. If strictly read, however, these laws allow for a finding of guilt based on a much lower showing of culpability by the actor. So long as the actor *knows* that the institution he defaces is a church or a synagogue, it matters neither whether he was motivated by religious animus nor whether he selected the institution for that reason. This standard goes beyond not only the racial animus model, but also the discriminatory selection model. As a practical matter, however, knowledge of the religious nature of the institution that is vandalized is deemed to be a surrogate for discriminatory selection of that institution because of its religious identification. So understood, these are discriminatory selection statutes.[42]

The landscape of state bias crime law thus consists of a few statutes falling clearly within the discriminatory selection model or the racial animus model and a substantial number of bias crime laws that are ambiguous as to what they punish. (See Appendix A.) Several states, including Wisconsin, have adopted an explicit discriminatory selection statute governing bias crimes against a person, although virtually all state institutional vandalism laws are of this model. Several states have explicitly adopted the racial animus model. But the majority of states with bias crime laws are not clear as to which models they employ.

In Chapter 4, I return to the ambiguity created by the two models of bias crimes and the resulting lack of clarity in state bias crime statutes. I argue that the racial animus model is preferable; states should either abandon discriminatory selection as a model for bias crimes or recognize that cases of discriminatory selection in the absence of racial animus present defendants who are less blameworthy for the commission of a bias crime than the bias criminal who acts out of racial animus. The argument for the virtues of the racial animus model, however, must await Chapter 4. In order to reach the conclusions of Chapter 4, two other pieces of the puzzle must be set in place, one sociological and factual in the balance of this chapter, the other philosophical and legal in the chapter that follows.

## The Outward Manifestations of Bias Crimes

### The General Nature of the Bias Crime and Its Impact on the Victim

The picture that most of us carry in our heads of the prototypical bias crime is of a group of assailants terrorizing an individual victim whom they have never met before, solely because of that victim's race, and ultimately causing their victim great physical harm. This picture is in fact quite accurate. Recent sociological and criminological research allows us to begin to paint a picture of bias crimes collectively and to distinguish these crimes from parallel crimes collectively. For the moment, it is helpful to understand these empirical findings, not in terms of any legal or philosophical conclusions that might be drawn, but in a purely descriptive sense. The normative implications of these descriptive findings will be addressed in the next chapter.

Bias crimes are far more likely to be violent than are other crimes. This is true on two levels. In the first place, crimes committed with bias motivation are dramatically more likely to involve physical assaults than do crimes generally. One study conducted in Boston found that approximately half of all bias crimes reported to the police involved assaults. This is far above the average for crimes generally, where we find that only about 7 percent of all crimes reported to the police involve assaults.[43] Secondly, bias-motivated assaults are far more likely than other assaults to involve serious physical injury to the victim. The Boston study, for example, found that nearly 75 percent of the victims of bias-motivated assaults suffered physical injury, whereas the national average for assaults generally is closer to 30 percent.[44] As opposed to the perpetrators of other crimes, perpetrators of bias crimes are more likely to be strangers to their victims, having focused *exclusively* on race in selecting the victim.[45] This fungibility of victims to the bias-motivated criminal is so integral to the bias-motivated crime that courts have looked to it as a critical element for identifying bias crimes.[46] Bias crimes are also distinguishable as a group from parallel crimes on the basis of the number of perpetrators; bias crimes are significantly more likely to be committed by groups than by individuals.[47]

Bias crimes may also be distinguished from parallel crimes on the basis of their particular emotional and psychological impact on the victim. The victim of a bias crime is not attacked for a random reason—as is the person injured during a shooting spree in a public place—nor is he attacked for an impersonal reason, as is the victim of a mugging for money. He is attacked for a specific, personal reason: his race. Moreover, the bias crime victim cannot reasonably minimize the risks of future attacks because he is unable to change the characteristic that made him a victim.

A bias crime thus attacks the victim not only physically but at the very core of his identity. It is an attack from which there is no escape. It is one thing to avoid the park at night because it is not safe. It is quite another to avoid certain neighborhoods because of one's race. This heightened sense of vulnerability caused by bias crimes is beyond that normally found in crime victims. Bias crime victims have been compared to rape victims in that the physical harm associated with the crime, however great, is less significant than the powerful accompanying sense of violation.[48] The victims of bias crimes thus tend to experience psychological symptoms such as depression or withdrawal, as well as anxiety, feelings of helplessness, and a profound sense of isolation.[49] One study of violence in the workplace found that victims of bias-motivated violence reported a significantly greater level of negative psychophysiological symptoms than did victims of nonbias–motivated violence.[50]

The marked increase in symptomatology among bias crime victims is true regardless of the race of the victim. The psychological trauma of being singled out because of one's race exists for white victims as well as for members of minority groups.[51] This is not to suggest, however, that there is no difference between bias crimes committed by white perpetrators against people of color and those bias crimes in which the victim is white, as in *Wisconsin v. Mitchell*. A difference exists between black and Hispanic victims and white victims concerning a second set of factors—that is, defensive behavioral changes. Although bias crimes directed at minority victims do not produce a greater level of psychological damage than those aimed at white victims, they do cause minority bias crime victims to adopt a relatively more defensive behavioral posture than white bias crime victims typically adopt.[52]

The additional impact of a bias-motivated attack on a minority victim is not attributable solely to the fact that the victim was selected because of an immutable characteristic. This much is true for all victims of bias crimes. Rather, the very nature of the bias motivation, when directed against minority victims, triggers the history and social context of prejudice and prejudicial violence against the victim and his group. The bias component of crimes committed against minority group members is not merely prejudice per se but prejudice against a member of a historically oppressed group. In a similar vein, Charles Lawrence, in distinguishing racist speech from otherwise offensive words, described racist speech as words that "evoke in you all of the millions of cultural lessons regarding your inferiority that you have so painstakingly repressed, and imprint upon you a badge of servitude and subservience for all the world to see."[53] Minority victims of bias crimes therefore experience the attack as a form of violence that manifests racial stigmatization and its resulting harms.

Stigmatization has been shown to bring about humiliation, isolation, and self-hatred.[54] An individual who has been racially stigmatized will often be hypersensitive in anticipation of contact with other members of society whom he sees as "normal" and will even suffer a kind of self-doubt that negatively affects his relationships with members of his own group.[55] The stigmatized individual may experience clinical symptoms such as high blood pressure[56] or increased use of narcotics and alcohol.[57] In addition, stigmatization may present itself in such social symptoms as an approach to parenting that undercuts the child's self-esteem and perpetuates an expectation of social failure.[58] All of these symptoms may stem from the stigmatization that results from nonviolent prejudice. Nonviolent prejudice carries with it the clear message that the target and his group are of marginal value and could be subjected to even greater indignities, such as violence that is motivated by the prejudice. An even more serious presentation of these harms results when the potential for physical harm is realized in the form of the violent prejudice represented by bias crimes.[59]

### The Impact of Bias Crimes on the Target Community

The impact of bias crimes reaches beyond the harm done to the immediate victim or victims. There is a more widespread impact on the "target community"—that is, the community that shares the race, religion, or ethnicity of the victim—and an even broader based harm to the general society. Members of the target community of a bias crime experience that crime in a manner that has no equivalent in the public response to a parallel crime. The reaction of the target community not only goes beyond mere sympathy with the immediate bias crime victim, but exceeds empathy as well.[60] Members of the target community of a bias crime perceive that crime as an attack on themselves directly and individually. Consider the burning of a cross on the lawn of an African-American family or the spray-painting of swastikas and hateful graffiti on the home of a Jewish family. Others might associate themselves with the injuries done to these families, having feelings of anger or hurt, and thus sympathize with the victims. Still others might find that these crimes triggered within them feelings similar to the sense of victimization and attack felt by these families, and thus empathize with the victims. The reactions of members of the target community, however, will transcend both empathy and sympathy. The cross-burning and the swastika-scrawling will not just call up similar feelings on the part of other blacks and Jews, respectively. Rather, members of these target communities may experience reactions of actual threat and attack from this very event. Bias crimes may spread fear and intimidation beyond the immediate victims and their friends and families to those who share only racial characteristics with the victims.[61] This additional harm of a personalized threat felt by persons other than the immediate victims of the bias crime differentiates a bias crime from a parallel crime and makes the former more harmful to society.

This sense of victimization on the part of the target community leads to yet another social harm uniquely caused by bias crimes. Not only may the target community respond to the bias crime with fear, apprehension, and anger, but this response may be directed at the group with which the immediate offenders are either rightfully or, even more troubling, wrongfully, identified. Collective guilt always raises complicated questions of blaming the group for the acts of certain individuals. But it is one thing when groups are rightfully identified with the immediate offenders, for example, the association of a bias crime offender who is a member of a Skinhead organization with other members of that organization. It is quite another when groups are wrongfully identified with the immediate offenders. Consider, for example, the association of those individuals who killed Yankel Rosenbaum with the Crown Heights black community generally, or of those who killed Yusef Hawkins with the Bensonhurst white community generally. In addition to generating concern and anger over lawlessness and the perceived ineffectuality of law enforcement that often follow a parallel crime, therefore, a single bias crime may ignite intense and long-standing inter-community tensions.[62]

### The Impact of Bias Crimes on Society as a Whole

Finally, the impact of bias crimes may spread well beyond the immediate victims and the target community to the general society. This effect includes a wide array of harms, from the very concrete to the most abstract. On the most mundane level—but by no means least damaging—the isolation effects discussed above have a cumulative effect throughout a community. Consider a family, victimized by an act of bias-motivated vandalism, that begins to withdraw from society generally; the family members seek safety from an unknown assailant who, having sought them out for identifiable reasons, might well do so again. Members of the community, even those who are sympathetic to the plight of the victim family and who have been supportive of them, may be reluctant to place themselves in harm's way and will shy away from socializing with these victims or having their children do so. The isolation of this family will not be solely their act of withdrawal; indeed, a societal act of isolation as well injures both the family that is cut off and the community at large.

Bias crimes cause an even broader injury to the general community. Such crimes violate not only society's general concern for the security of its members and their property but also the shared value of equality among its citizens and racial and religious harmony in a heterogeneous society. A bias crime is therefore a profound violation of the egalitarian ideal and the anti-discrimination principle that have become fundamental not only to the American legal system but to American culture as well.[63]

This harm is, of course, highly contextual. We could imagine a society in which racial motivation for a crime would implicate no greater value in that society than the values violated by a criminal act motivated solely by the perpetrator's dislike of the victim. It is not easy to imagine such a society, but it is possible. It is indicative of racism's pervasiveness that real-world examples are hard to come by and require us to look to another time and a distant place. In the 1930s, the anthropologist Ethel John Lindgren reported findings about the Tungus and the Cossacks, who, although racially and culturally distinct, lived in close proximity without conflict. Although the Tungus were Mongolian nomads and the Cossacks were Caucasoid Christian village-dwellers, neither group believed itself to be racially superior, and they maintained supplementary and complementary relations.[64]

We may thus hypothesize that an assault committed by a Cossack against a Tungus out of bias against the Tungus race would cause no greater injury to the victim, the Tungus community generally, or the entire society, than would a simple assault. The animus against the Tungus held by this individual Cossack would represent only an individual abnormal psychological profile. It would not implicate the broad and deep fabric of racial and ethnic prejudice that such acts implicate in our society. It would be roughly akin to an assault in our culture committed against a victim with blue eyes because the perpetrator held a deep antagonism for all blue-eyed people.

Whatever may be said of the Tungus' and Cossacks' society, it is very clear that its level of racial harmony and the absence of racial tension are not present in our society. Bias crimes implicate a social history of prejudice, discrimination, and even oppression. As such, they cause a greater harm than parallel crimes to the immediate victim of the crime, the target community of the crime, and the general society.

## CHAPTER 3

# Why Are Bias Crimes Worse?

Any question of criminal law enforcement ultimately turns on a justification for the imposition of criminal punishment. Any proposed justification for punishment must in turn confront and satisfy two critical requirements of just punishment: (1) only the guilty should be punished; and (2) the punishment of the guilty should be proportionate to the crime committed. The next two chapters take up these requirements for the punishment of bias crimes in reverse order.

This chapter argues that bias crimes ought to receive punishment that is more severe than that imposed for parallel crimes. First I explore the proportionality requirement in depth, demonstrating that some level of fit between the seriousness of a crime and the harshness of the criminal penalty is essential to modern theories of punishment. Next, I turn to the means by which the seriousness of a crime may be measured. This entails an analysis of the manner by which harm may be assessed. Finally, I will apply the theories of proportionality and harm that have been developed to the context of bias crimes, concluding that the harmful consequences particular to bias crimes warrant their enhanced punishment.

## Why the Punishment Must Fit the Crime

The relevance of the harms caused by bias crimes to the punishment of those crimes springs from the requirement of proportionality between crime and punishment. Most punishment theorists accept and indeed defend this doctrine. Although a full analysis of alternative theories of punishment is beyond the scope of this discussion, an overview of why we punish is in order.

There are two general schools of punishment theory. The first, retribution, justifies punishment by the wrongdoer's desert. This is a deontological approach to punishment, unconcerned with the consequences of punishing the criminal and focused upon giving the criminal his "just desert." The other school of punishment theory draws its justification from a utilitarian rationale and thus focuses precisely on the consequences of punishment. To the utilitarian, or "consequentialist," punishment is justified to the extent that it improves the overall welfare of society. H. L. A. Hart thus described the purpose of punishment as that of achieving crime reduction.[1] Four justifications are subsumed under the consequentialist rubric: general and specific deterrence and rehabilitation and incapacitation. General deterrence justifies punishment of the convicted individual by its tendency to discourage others from committing similar (or perhaps any) crimes. The other three consequentialist justifications focus on the criminal himself. Specific deterrence grounds punishment in its tendency to discourage the punished individual from committing future offenses. Rehabilitation seeks to use punishment as a means of reforming the criminal such that he will emerge from his sentence unlikely, or at least less likely, to commit future crimes. Finally, incapacitation, doubting the possibility of affecting the convict's character or moral calculus, seeks to reduce crime by taking the convict off the streets.

With this background of why we punish in mind, we may return to the issue of proportionality. Our discussion here begins with an analysis of the traditional defense of proportionality associated with retributivists and then proceeds to show that consequentialists, as well as modern eclectic punishment theorists, embrace the proportionality requirement. We may then apply these views of proportionality to the context of bias crimes.

### Proportionality of Punishment under Retributive Punishment Theory

Retribution theory offers a justification of proportionality that is inherent in the very nature of punishment. For the retributivist, the offender deserves punishment because he has violated the norms of society imbedded in the criminal law. The sheer fact that the defendant deserves to be punished—not social utility—justifies the punishment.[2] Retributivists do not agree on a single basis for this "desert," and it is from the various answers to this inquiry that different strands of retributive thought emerge.

The simplest form of retribution theory is one of vengeance: the criminal has harmed society, and therefore he deserves to be harmed *by* society. This brittle form of retributive theory need not detain us long. As George Fletcher put it, retribution "is obviously not to be identified with vengeance or revenge, any more than love is to be identified with lust."[3]

More sophisticated theories of retributive punishment look in two directions for a foundational concept of "desert." One theory, following Hegel, grounds the punishment of the offender in his "right to be punished." Through punishment for a crime, society demonstrates its respect for the criminal; a criminal's fundamental right to be treated as an autonomous human being requires punishment for his choice to violate the law.[4] The other strand of retributive thought is based upon the offender's obligation to pay the proverbial "debt" that he owes to society as a result of his criminal activity. The classic statement of the debt metaphor as a justification for punishment is that of Kant. A civilized society requires a legal system that confers substantial benefits on its citizens in return for their adherence to the rules of the system. When a member of that society breaks the law, he incurs a debt to society because, having enjoyed the benefits of the legal system, he has not accepted its burdens. The extent to which he has rejected the burdens of abiding by the law, that is, the extent to which he has broken the law, establishes a debt that he now owes. This "debt" is "paid" through punishment.[5]

A common ground shared by all forms of retributive thought—simple vengeance, personhood-based or debt-based retribution—concerns the level of appropriate punishment.[6] Punishment, to be morally justifiable, must be proportional to the crimes for which it is imposed.[7] This concept of proportionality need not mean a mechanical application of *jus talionis* requiring that the punishment of the offender be identical to the crime he committed, that is, "eye for an eye, tooth for a tooth." Indeed, *jus talionis* will often lead to an immoral result. Although reasonable people will disagree as to the morality of executing the murderer, it would be immoral to suggest raping the rapist. In other instances, it is impossible to attain identity of crime and punishment. An adult, for example, may not be subjected to identical punishment for child abuse. Finally, literal *jus talionis* will often be highly speculative at best. How do we know all the damage suffered by a crime victim, physical and psychological, and how would we create an identical harm to the offender? [8]

The retributive concept of proportionality need not look to simplistic notions of an "eye for an eye." The minimum requirement for proportionality of punishment under a retributive theory is that the punishment for a particular crime, when placed along the spectrum of all criminal punishments, stands at the same point as that occupied by the crime in the spectrum of all crimes.[9] This requirement is essential under both debt-based and personhood-based retribution. Proportional punishment satisfies the offender's debt under a debt-based notion of retribution because the offender is re-quired to "pay" the relative amount of punishment that corresponds to the relative amount of harm that he caused society. Under personhood-based retribution, proportional punishment recognizes the legitimate rights of both wrongdoer and offended party because it is geared to the relative harm done to the victim and caused by the offender.

### Proportionality of Punishment under Consequentialist Punishment Theory

Proportionality of crime and punishment is not the unique province of re-tributive punishment theorists. Most consequentialists also embrace some concept of proportionality in their justification for criminal punishment. In the simplest consequentialist model, punishment for a category of crimes must be set at a level that is sufficient to deter the commission of those crimes.[10] However, because consequentialist punishment turns on the temptation of future criminal activity, this is a concept of proportionality that is wholly extrinsic to the nature of the crime committed.

The problems presented by such a wooden consequentialist theory are ap-parent. A framework for punishment concerned only with the likelihood of the offender to commit future crimes looks only to the minimum amount of punishment necessary to attain rehabilitation or specific deterrence of the offender. In certain instances, this will yield highly problematic results that most theorists would be unwilling to embrace. Because the goal is solely the deterrence of future criminal behavior, the level of punishment will be keyed only to the strength of the offender's attraction to commit crimes and not to the nature of the crimes. Fixing punishment at the minimum level necessary to deter the offender from further criminal behavior could lead to shockingly disproportionate penalties. Herbert Packer warned of a theory of punishment under which "the violent psychopath and the incorrig-ible writer of bad checks might find themselves side by side in lifelong de-tention."[11]

This concern led to efforts among consequentialist punishment theorists to find a means of importing a concept of proportionality. Like retributivists, they sought to ground proportionality in the gravity of the crime, but they sought to do so without reliance upon retributive argument. Alfred Ewing, for example, argued that ideas of "proportion between guilt and penalty are too deeply rooted in our ethical thought to be dismissed lightly, however hard they may be to rationalise."[12] He located proportionality in the educative aspect of criminal punishment. This educative role of punishment was an extension of traditional deterrence theory. The total utilitarian benefit achieved through punishment was not restricted to the specific deterrence of the offender himself, or even to the general deterrence of potential wrongdoers, but also embraced the general moral education of society.[13]

In his explanation of the educative effect of punishment, Ewing sought to find a utilitarian grounding of both the general concepts of desert and proportionality. He sought to reach these results "without the *prima facie* irrationality" of retributive theory.[14] As to desert, the moral education of society could be accomplished only if those who were guilty of wrongdoing were punished:

> The moral object of a punishment as such is to make people think of a certain kind of act as very bad, but, if it were inflicted otherwise than for a bad act, it would either produce no effect of this sort at all or cause people to think an act bad which was not really bad, and this is why we must first of all ask—is a punishment just?[15]

Ewing also grounds the requirement of proportionality between crime and punishment in the educative role of punishment. For Ewing, punishment must do more than provide a crude moral education that bifurcates all conduct into the good and the bad. Punishment must also teach the relative seriousness of various forms of impermissible conduct. The criminal law should "compare the degrees of badness presupposed on the average by different offenses, and, having done that . . . lay down the principle that a lesser offense should not be punished so severely as a greater one."[16]

Ewing's goal—to establish both desert and proportionality without reference to retributive argument—was not fully achieved. His argument remained susceptible to critique from the standard, and most telling, argument against pure consequentialist theories of punishment. Theoretically, moral education could be achieved through the punishment of the wholly innocent. As long as the authorities concealed the fact of the defendant's innocence, the punishment of the innocent might have a strong educative effect.[17] The utilitarian rejoinder to this critique is that the educative effect of punishment is, by definition, served only by the punishment of the guilty; punishment of the innocent fails to impart the proper moral education.[18] The flaw in this rejoinder is that it confuses punishment and publicity. Punishment itself neither deters nor educates beyond the defendant himself. As J. D. Mabbot wrote: "A judge sentences a man to three years' imprisonment not to three years *plus* three columns in the press."[19] General moral education, like general deterrence, turns on publication of the punishment and, so long as the publication excludes reference to the innocence of the defendant, the punishment will achieve Ewing's educative purpose.

Ewing's theories, however, set the stage for much of the debate over the justification for punishment.[20] What Ewing sought to do solely within a utilitarian framework has been better accomplished by those who have developed "mixed theories" of punishment, drawing on aspects of both utilitarian and retributivist thought. These eclectic approaches embrace proportionality of punishment and guilt, not as a theory that serves to justify punishment in its own right, but as a limiting principle of a justification for the imposition of criminal punishment. Two prominent illustrative examples will suffice.[21]

H. L. A. Hart's distinction between the "general justifying aim" for punishment and the limiting principles governing the "distribution" of punishment allow a significant role for proportionality.[22] Lengthy sentences for minor crimes might be effective in deterring the commission of such crimes, and might even produce a total benefit outweighing the total cost of this punishment, but, to Hart, it is "wrong to employ them." Such sentences are wrong neither for the retributive reason that there is a "penalty 'naturally' fitted to [the crime's] degree of iniquity," nor for the traditional utilitarian reason that the imposition of such a sentence would impose a greater cost to the offender than benefit to the society.[23] Rather, "[t]he guiding principle is that of a proportion within a system of penalties between those imposed for different offenses where these [penalties] have a distinct place in a commonsense scale of gravity."[24] This "commonsense scale" is a central aspect of Hart's synthesis of consequentialist and retributive theories. Hart relies on "very broad judgments both of relative moral iniquity and harmfulness of different types of offense." Without the conformity of punishment to such a scale, common morality may be confused or the law may be held in contempt.[25]

Herbert Packer also embraces a critical role for proportionality between crime and punishment. Packer's "integrated theory of punishment" places proportionality as one of the issues of the minimal doctrinal content of criminal law.[26] "It is inescapable," Packer wrote, "that some offenses are to be taken more seriously than others and that the severity of the available punishment should be proportioned to the seriousness with which the offense is viewed."[27]

Proportionality is a key element of the justifications for punishment. Whether through the retributive argument in its Kantian and Hegelian roots and its modern interpretations, through the position advanced by such utilitarian theorists as Ewing, or through the contemporary eclectic theorists, it is, as Packer said, "inescapable" that some crimes are worse than others and must be punished more severely as a result. Before this understanding of proportionality may be brought to bear on our ultimate question—the punishment of bias crimes—the question of what it means for one crime to be "worse" than another deserves further attention.

## Evaluating the Severity of Crimes

### The Role of Culpability and Harm in Criminal Law Doctrine

Murder, the intentional and unjustified taking of a human life, is worse than an equally intentional and unjustified crime in which the victim is not killed. Murder is also worse than an accidental killing. These two assertions are incontrovertible. They are also the point of departure for a fuller understanding of what it is that makes some crimes worse than others. Our two basic assertions about murder demonstrate that there are two elements of a crime that describe its seriousness: culpability of the offender and harm caused to the society.[28] Before going any further, we must clarify some necessary terminology. Terms such as "culpability," "mental state," and *mens rea* are often used interchangeably. I believe that this is a mistake. I use here the terms "culpability" and *mens rea* and understand them to have distinct meanings. I use "culpability" as a descriptive term, meaning state of mind. This is the way in which this term is used, for example, in the influential Model Penal Code that defines culpability categories of "purposely," "knowingly," "recklessly," and "negligently."[29] I use the term *mens rea*, by contrast, as a normative term, arising out of assessment of blame or wrongdoing.[30]

Let us now return to the two assertions with respect to the relative severity of the crime of murder. Murder is a more serious crime than intentional assault because of the harm caused. Although the offender acts willfully in both instances, the murder victim is dead, whereas the assault victim is only injured. Murder is also a more serious crime than an accidental killing owing to the actor's culpability. Although a death results in each case, the murderer acts willfully whereas the accidental killer acts without intent.

Much has been said about the role of culpability in the assessment of the seriousness of a crime. It is not an overstatement to say that the entire thrust of the study and articulation of modern criminal law has been toward a focus on the state of mind or culpability of the accused. This focus does not mean that the results of the conduct are unimportant. Rather, punishment under the criminal law, whether based on a retributive or a consequentialist argument, has been critically linked to the actor's mental state.

Nowhere is the centrality of the accused's mental state to consequentialist theory more clearly visible than in the Model Penal Code. The code's organizing principle is culpability, and the grading of offenses is based upon the defendant's culpability in each element of the crime.[31] Moreover, the code prescribes the same punishment for the crimes of attempt, solicitation, and conspiracy as for the crime that is attempted or solicited, or that is the object of the conspiracy. This is a marked departure from the common law, under which inchoate crimes are punished less severely than the target offense.[32]

Retribution theory also centers on the culpability of the individual. This is most readily apparent in the form of retributive theory that justifies punishment strictly based on the incorrect moral choice made by the individual to do wrong.[33] Culpability is of equal import to those retributivists who are primarily concerned with consequences. Herbert Morris, for example, has argued that the accused's duty to suffer punishment flows both from his moral choice and from the consequences of his conduct.[34] That results are relevant to some retributivists does not negate the critical role of individual choice that underpins any deontological theory of punishment. Choice can be understood only in the context of culpability.

Culpability and its role in understanding the seriousness of a particular crime may be drawn directly from substantive criminal law. In extreme terms, culpability is necessary at some level for the existence of guilt. The utter absence of culpability negates the possibility of guilt.[35] We can also draw much finer distinctions about culpability from existing criminal law doctrine. Culpability provides the general organizing mechanism within which the Model Penal Code assigns levels of punishment. For most crimes under the code, purposeful or knowing conduct warrants a more severe penalty than does reckless conduct, which itself gives rise to harsher punishment than negligent criminal behavior.[36] Moreover, the doctrines relating to excuse generally, and to provocation or diminished capacity in particular, are premised upon the relationship between the offender's culpability and the seriousness of his crime.[37]

In contrast to this doctrinally and theoretically well developed understanding of the relationship between culpability and the level of punishment, the role of harm in assessing this relationship has been largely unexplored. This is surprising because the intuitive case for harm as a key component in assessing a crime's seriousness is at least as strong as it is for culpability.

We may demonstrate the intuitive claim easily by holding the culpability of the criminal actor constant and varying the harm caused by him. Society punishes an intentional murderer with greater severity than it does an equally intentional nonlethal assaulter. From a culpability standpoint, the murderer and the assaulter are the same, yet their punishments differ. The same point may be illustrated at the lower end of the homicide scale. Reckless conduct—that is, reckless risk creation—resulting in death constitutes the felony of manslaughter.[38] If the identical conduct with the identical culpability does not result in death, however, the actor is guilty of a far lesser crime, often only a misdemeanor such as the Model Penal Code's "reckless endangerment."[39]

Although resulting harm clearly matters in assessing crime severity, criminal law doctrine tells us surprisingly little about the role of harm. For a richer theory of harm that is useful across a broad range of crime, one must reason from first principles.

## A Theory of Measuring Harm

Two initial propositions inform the evaluation of relative harms. First, the kind of harms that we wish to measure cannot be restricted to the individual reactions of particular victims. Because the purpose in gauging harms is to inform the criminal law, the weighing process must entail a large aspect of aggregation. Second, the relative harms caused by various crimes need not be universal and will often be contextual to a particular society. Although most societies will consider murder worse than assault, the relative harms caused by trespass, theft, and simple assault may vary with a culture's valuation of private property and physical integrity. The calculus of harms may be helpfully visualized either ex ante or ex post.

EX ANTE MEASURING OF HARMS: THE RELATIVE RANKING OF RISK  The ex ante analysis ranks the harms that result from various crimes in terms of the relative risk preferences of a rational person.[40] The least harmful crime of all is the one that a rational person would risk facing, given a choice between risking this crime and any other crime. Ex ante analysis thus imagines a person faced with the unfortunate choice between risking two different crimes. Consider a person, "Driver," who is driving along the dock area of a city's waterfront late at night when his or her car breaks down. Driver has called the authorities and been informed of the following: help will arrive in one hour; in the meantime, the police will pick up Driver so that he or she may spend that hour in a safer location. Driver supposes two things to be true: waiting with the car reduces the chances of the car's being stolen, but increases the chances of Driver's being mugged; conversely, accepting the ride and leaving the car reduces the chances of Driver's being mugged, but increases the chances of the car's being stolen. Driver is asked to make an ex ante analysis of the harms associated with mugging and car theft. I suspect that most people faced with Driver's choice would accept the ride. If that is the case, then the ex ante analysis would conclude that mugging causes a more serious harm to its victim than does car theft.

The same thought experiment could be brought to bear on all crimes. Once every crime has been considered, a rough ranking of crimes will exist, from the least to the most harmful.[41] This process produces only a rough ranking because there are several necessary qualifications. The first qualification stems from the first general proposition discussed above—that is, that the measurement of harm calls for an aggregation of individual harms. Although each crime causes a unique harm to its victim, our purpose is not to measure these individual subjective assessments of harm but rather to probe for an aggregated, societal assessment of the harm associated with the commission of a crime. The aggregation of harm assessments of all rational actors in a society renders it impossible to create a strict ranking of all harms in a numerical order. The first qualification, therefore, is that the ranking of crimes by harm caused produces not a strict numerical ranking but a series of groupings of harm, and these groupings may be small in number. This small number of groupings does not, however, raise serious problems for our effort to measure harm. The purpose of assessing relative harms is to give content to the goal of assigned punishment based on the seriousness of the crime. A small number of "harm levels" correlates with the similarly small number of discrete crime levels that most jurisdictions maintain. The Model Penal Code, for example, provides for only six levels of crimes: felonies of the first, second, and third degree, misdemeanors, petty misdemeanors, and violations. Most states have roughly similar regimes.[42]

This difficulty in comparing unlike harms requires a second qualification to the ex ante ranking of crimes by harm. It is one thing to say with some confidence that the rational person would risk suffering a petty larceny before risking grand larceny and, therefore, the harm of the former is less than that of the latter. It is quite another thing to ascertain the rational person's choice between the theft of a substantial sum of money and a fraud causing an approximately equivalent loss. This qualification also finds its solution in the small number of harm groupings. For example, in ranking fraud, theft, assault, and petty theft, most of us would probably think the following:

(1) The fraud and the theft represent roughly the same risk level and therefore ought to be grouped together for purposes of assessing the resulting harm of these crimes;

(2) I would risk either fraud or theft of a substantial sum of money before risking assault with a deadly weapon;

(3) I would risk neither fraud nor theft of a substantial sum of money before risking a petty theft.

We can thus rank the harms caused by the crimes of fraud, theft, assault, and petty theft in this manner.

EX POST MEASURING OF HARMS: RANKING WHAT THE VICTIM LOST    Relative harms may also be assessed through an ex post analysis that focuses on the nature of the resulting harm. This analysis seeks to rank crimes according to what the victim has lost as a result of the crime. Andrew von Hirsch and Nils Jareborg have articulated a powerful analytic tool in their proposal for measuring harm in this manner through reference to a "living standard analysis."[43]

To understand "living standard analysis," it is first helpful to understand what the "living standard" is not. First, it is not limited to issues of relative economic affluence, as in the traditional meaning of "standard of living" in economic literature.[44] Von Hirsch and Jareborg adopt a broader meaning, developed by Amartya Sen, which encompasses not only economic abilities but also economic and noneconomic factors, all of which bear on a person's sense of well-being.[45] Second, the living standard is not limited to those issues that affect an individual's ability to make choices about his life.[46] A broad conception of living standard captures the nature of certain harms— for example, serious bodily injury—through which the victim loses more than the ability to make life choices.

Harm, as measured by loss or negative impact upon living standard, becomes a far-reaching concept that draws upon our assessment of what it means to live a good life—a key question raised both in everyday life and in complex social inquiry.[47] This measuring device allows for a meaningful comparison of harms based on the interests that are implicated by a particular crime. Reckless driving and aggravated assault might produce the same physical injury to a victim, but the assault will likely offend the victim psychologically whereas the car accident will not. The aggravated assault is thus the more serious crime of the two.[48] A satisfactory measurement of harms for the purpose of understanding the relative seriousness of crimes must have a means by which to capture the distinction between these two crimes.

The living standard measure of harm is necessarily contextual. Properly understood, this contextuality is a virtue and not a shortcoming. Sensitivity to cultural variation is an essential element of any attempt to measure harm. Living standard analysis is contingent upon the values that society holds. The identical conduct may cause far greater harm in one culture than in another as a function of the values held by those cultures.[49] Although intercultural comparisons of harm may therefore be difficult to achieve, comparisons of harm within a culture will be possible.

The living standard analysis admittedly is vague: what does it mean to compare various injuries that could be caused to the respective victims' sense of well being? But although the analysis cannot produce a precise formula for measuring harm, neither is it a mere foil for unguided discretion and unprincipled intuition. Living standard analysis does not provide a precise formula for assessing harm and assigning levels of criminal punishment, nor is it intended to do so. For several reasons, no such precise formula is possible. First, those who actually employ this analysis or any analysis in the creation of a listing of comparative harms will necessarily have to use their judgment in doing so. Second, no workable theory can produce more than a reasonably small number of discrete harm categories. Final assignment of crimes within these categories will also require judgment on the part both of criminal law drafters and of sentencing judges. The purpose of the living standard analysis is not to determine harm levels but to provide a consistent vocabulary for the discussion of harm and a set of principled limitations on that discussion. It thus enables us to address questions that are essential to understanding whether the enhanced punishment of bias crimes may be justified.

Living standard analysis seeks to take account of those harms that, by their very nature, are difficult, and perhaps even impossible, to quantify. My contention is that, with all the difficulties in describing injuries such as those to dignity and autonomy, no analysis of harms is complete or even minimally useful without factoring in these types of injury. As Geoffrey Hawthorn wrote about Sen's conception of the living standard, "we have to reject being precisely wrong in favor of being vaguely right."[50]

Measuring harms with the living standard analysis requires a focus on two key variables. The first variable is the severity of a particular crime's invasion upon a victim's overall "personal interest." Consider the personal interest represented by the traditional economic term *standard of living*. At one end of this spectrum are the most primal and basic issues of standard of living—survival with the barest of human functional capacity. Crimes that cause injury on this level are the most serious of all. At the other end of the spectrum is deprivation of a relatively high level of comfort. This injury, although real, is not great. Between these end points, a potentially infinite number of gradations of well-being exist. In order to provide a scale that will be consistent in application and suggest no greater accuracy than it may fairly claim, a relatively small number of interim points is appropriate.[51]

The second variable for living standard analysis is the various kinds of interests that may be violated by a crime. These interests begin, but do not end, with physical safety and the protection of material possessions. At a minimum, a full understanding of living standard must also include a recognition of personal dignity interests as well as those of individual autonomy.[52]

We may then discuss the harm caused by various crimes in terms of how deep an injury is sustained and what kinds of interests are affected. Murder affects physical safety at the most profound level and is thus a crime of the gravest harm evaluation. Burglary may have a minimal effect on physical safety, particularly if it occurs at a time when the dwelling would likely be unoccupied. Burglary will, however, have some greater impact on living standard with respect to material possessions. This might interfere only with a level of relative comfort (the taking of a VCR) or with the level of primal basic needs (the taking of a car from a house in the desert with no other means of transportation and no means of communication). But neither of these interests captures the full harm caused by a burglary. The deepest harm caused by a burglary may well stem from the violation of the victim's sense of autonomy. Victims of burglaries often describe the ongoing injury they feel as they continue to live in houses that perpetrators unlawfully entered.[53]

The final stage of living standard analysis calls for a combination of the injuries to various interests caused by a single crime. Such injuries may vary in severity. In the case of burglary, for example, the injury to physical safety might be minimal, the injury to material possession variable, and the injury to autonomy significant. In order to determine the relative harm caused by the crime of burglary we must aggregate these various injuries in some manner.

We might assess the relative harm caused by crimes by beginning with the deepest injury inflicted upon any interest by a crime and setting harm, at minimum, at this level. If we decide that burglary causes a very serious—but not the most profound—injury to autonomy interests, we would set its harm level at a "very serious" level. This "level" would be one of a small number of discrete levels of harm. As we noted earlier, this small number of harm levels corresponds to the small number of levels of crimes. But what of the other interests affected by burglary? Depending upon the severity of the intrusion, these interests may be used to increase the measure of harm caused by burglary within the "very serious" harm level.[54] Living standard analysis permits not only an assignment of crimes to a small number of harm levels, but also a rough set of rankings within these broad ranges.

Both the ex ante ranking of harms in terms of the relative risk preferences of a rational person and the ex post ranking of harms through use of a living standard analysis help clarify the harms caused by crimes. Harm, along with culpability, lies at the heart of measuring the seriousness of a crime. Armed with the above discussion, I now return to the context of bias-motivated violence.

## The Relative Seriousness of Bias Crimes

### Reconsideration of the Unique Harm Caused by Bias Crimes

The seriousness of a crime, as noted above, is a function of the offender's culpability and the harm caused. It follows, therefore, that the relative seriousness of bias crimes and parallel crimes will also turn on the culpability and harm associated with each.

In order to compare the culpability attached to parallel crimes and bias crimes we must return to the central relationship between the two. Every bias crime contains within it a parallel crime against person or property. In the case of a bias-motivated assault, for example, the parallel crime of assault exists alongside the bias crime. In a sense, the parallel crime exists "within" the civil rights crime. Thus, bias crimes are two-tiered crimes, composed of a parallel crime with the addition of bias motivation.[55] The comparison of culpability for parallel crimes and bias crimes will thus weigh the single-tiered *mens rea* of the parallel crime against the two-tiered *mens rea* of the bias crime. The requisite *mens rea* for the parallel crime will generally be recklessness, knowledge, or purpose. This is both the requisite culpability for the parallel crime and the requisite culpability for the first tier of the bias crime.

The parallel crimes of most bias crimes are offenses against the person or property, such as vandalism or assault. To be guilty of these parallel crimes, the accused must have possessed a specific intent with respect to the elements of the crime. The Model Penal Code has broadened the traditional concept of specific intent to include not only purposefulness—that is, conduct that is driven by the conscious desire to achieve the criminal end—but also "knowledge." Under the code:

A person acts knowingly with respect to a material element of an offense when:

(i) if the element involves the nature of his conduct or the attendant circumstances, he is aware that his conduct is of that nature or that such circumstances exist; and

(ii) if the element involves a result of his conduct he is aware that it is practically certain that his conduct will cause such results.[56]

It is possible, however, that there will be instances in which the culpability for the parallel crime will be less than specific intent and in which recklessness will suffice for criminal liability. The Model Penal Code defines recklessness as follows:

A person acts recklessly with respect to a material element of an offense when he consciously disregards a substantial and unjustifiable risk that the material element exists or will result from his conduct. The risk must be of such a nature and degree that, considering the nature and purpose of the actor's conduct and the circumstances known to him, its disregard involves a gross deviation from the standard of conduct that a law-abiding person would observe in the actor's situation.[57]

Consider, for example, an offender who throws rocks at a place of worship. Although specifically motivated by the religious affiliation of the institution, it is not his purpose to cause any actual property damage. Culpability with respect to bias is certainly purposeful, but culpability with respect to the parallel crime of vandalism is only recklessness. In several states he would be guilty of the bias crime of religiously motivated vandalism.[58]

Whatever culpability distinction does exist between parallel crimes and bias crimes resides at the second-tier *mens rea* of the latter. To establish a bias crime, the prosecution must prove, along with the first-tier *mens rea* that is applicable to the parallel crime, that the accused was motivated by bias in the commission of the parallel crime. Under both federal and state law, the burden is on the prosecution to show motivation.[59] This proof would be necessary whether we are applying the racial animus model or the discriminatory selection model of bias crimes. Under the racial animus model, the offender must have purposefully acted in furtherance of his hostility toward the target group. Under the discriminatory selection model, the offender must have purposefully selected the victim on the basis of his perceived membership in the target group. Under either model, nothing short of this *mens rea* of *purpose* will constitute the requisite culpability for the second tier of a bias crime. Unless the perpetrator was motivated to cause harm to another because of the victim's race, the crime is clearly not a bias crime.[60]

The culpability associated with the commission of parallel crimes and bias crimes is thus identical in terms of *what* the offender did and differs only in respect to *why* the offender did so. The relevance of this difference to the calculation of crime seriousness depends upon the reason that the culpability itself is relevant to crime seriousness.

Why is it that the intentional murderer ought to be punished more severely than the negligent killer? The result of the conduct of each is the death of the victim; they differ only as to their culpability. To the consequentialist, the murderer is punished more because he was more likely to cause death than was the negligent killer, or because the social value of his activity resulting in death was less relative to the chance of death.[61] If this is the role of culpability in the calculation of crime seriousness, then the culpability associated with bias crimes makes these crimes more severe than parallel crimes. Bias crime offenders are more likely to cause harm than are those who commit the same crimes without bias motivation. As discussed above, bias crimes generally are more likely to be assaults than are parallel crimes, and bias-motivated assaults are far more likely to be brutal. Moreover, the social value of activity resulting in bias crimes is far less than even the antisocial behavior that results in the parallel crime.

An alternative explanation for punishing the murderer more severely than the negligent killer is that his act of intentionally killing is more blameworthy.[62] If culpability is relevant to crime seriousness because it bears on blameworthiness, then the argument that the culpability associated with bias crimes makes these crimes more serious than parallel crimes is as compelling as it was for the consequentialist. The motivation of the bias crime offender violates the equality principle, one of the most deeply held tenets in our legal system and our culture. To the extent that crime seriousness is designed to capture a deontological concept of blameworthiness, bias crimes are more serious than other crimes. The rhetoric surrounding the enactment of bias crime laws suggests that most supporters of such legislation espouse a thoroughly deontological justification for the punishment of racially motivated violence.[63]

This trend is well illustrated by an unusual punishment for bias crimes proposed in Marlborough, Massachusetts. The Marlborough city council unanimously approved an ordinance that would deny public services, such as local licenses, library cards, or even trash removal, to those convicted of bias crimes. Supporters of the ordinance drew upon the community's disdain for the racial prejudice demonstrated by the bias criminal rather than the harm caused by the criminal's conduct.[64]

Culpability analysis, therefore, advances the argument for the relatively greater seriousness of bias crimes. The argument is equally supported by culpability theory based upon consequentialist and nonconsequentialist justifications for punishment.

A harms-based analysis also demonstrates that bias crimes are more serious than parallel crimes, regardless of the theory of punishment we assume. Under an ex ante analysis, the question is whether the rational person would risk a parallel crime before he would risk a bias crime. For several reasons, the answer is almost certainly yes. Consider first the context of vandalism. The parallel crime arising out of the defacement of a building or home is primarily a nuisance to the victim. The loss is insurable and, if not insured, is suffered in terms of time or money or both. However, if that vandalism is bias motivated, the defacement might take the form of swastikas on the home of a Jewish family or racist graffiti on the home of an African-American family. The harm here is not a mere nuisance. The potential for deep psychological harm, and the feelings of threat discussed earlier, exceed the harm ordinarily experienced by vandalism victims. No one can buy insurance to cover these additional harms.

The case of an electrical fire that destroyed a Boston-area synagogue provides the framework for a useful hypothetical example of the rational person's relative willingness to bear the risk of parallel vandalism versus bias-motivated vandalism.[65] In the short period immediately after the fire, prior to the determination of the cause, there was widespread concern that the fire was the result of bias-motivated arson. The news that it was not was met with great relief. Part of this relief may be attributed to the fact that the fire had occurred accidentally and was not the result of arson, bias motivated or otherwise. But this explanation does not capture the entire reaction, part of which is attributable to the fact that anti-Semitism was ruled out as a cause. Had the fire been caused by foul play without bias motivation—for example, by pecuniarily motivated arson without any trace of anti-semitism—surely the reaction of both victims and the general community would have exceeded the reaction that would have followed an accidental fire, but would not have been as great as if the cause were determined to have been religiously motivated. Faced with the choice between racist and nonracist vandalism, the rational person would risk the parallel crime before risking the more personally threatening bias crime with its longer-lasting effects.

This analysis applies to attacks against persons just as it does to those against property. In the parallel crime of assault, the perpetrator generally selects the victim (1) randomly or for no particular conscious reason, (2) for a reason that has nothing to do with the victim's personal identity, such as the perpetrator's perceiving that the victim is carrying money, or (3) for a reason relating to personal animosity between the perpetrator and the victim. A random assault or mugging leaves a victim with, at least, a sense of being unfortunate and, at most, a sense of heightened vulnerability. An assault as a result of personal animosity causes, at most, a focused fear or anger directed at the perpetrator. Unlike a parallel assault, a bias-motivated assault is neither random nor directed at the victim as an individual, and this selection and the message it carries cause all the harms discussed earlier. The perpetrator selects the victim because of some immutable characteristic, actual or perceived. As unpleasant as a parallel assault is, the rational person would still risk being victimized in that manner before he would risk the unique humiliation of a bias-motivated assault.

An ex post analysis provides further clarity and support for this conclusion. A living standard analysis focuses on depth of injury caused by a crime to interests of physical safety, material possessions, personal dignity, and autonomy. Recall that when we compare a parallel crime with a bias crime, we are comparing the same crime with the addition of the perpetrator's bias motivation. The parallel assault crime and the bias assault crime will cause roughly similar injuries to the physical safety and material possessions of the victim. But the bias crime victim's injury to autonomy—in terms of his sense of control over his life—and to his personal dignity will exceed that inflicted upon the parallel assault victim. This is clear from the far greater occurrence of depression, withdrawal, anxiety, and feelings of helplessness and isolation among bias crime victims than is ordinarily experienced by assault victims.[66]

Moreover, in order to assess completely the impact of bias crimes on living standards, we must look beyond the individual victims of these crimes. Here, too, we see a far greater societal injury caused by bias crimes than by parallel crimes. A parallel crime may cause concern or even sorrow among certain members of the victim's community, but it would be unusual for that impact to reach a level at which it would negatively affect their living standard. By contrast, bias crimes spread fear and intimidation beyond the immediate victims to those who share only racial characteristics with the victims. Members of the target group suffer injuries similar to those felt by the direct victim of the actual crime.[67] Unlike the sympathetic nonvictims of a parallel crime, members of the target community will suffer a living standard loss in terms of a threat to dignity and autonomy and a perceived threat to physical safety. Bias crimes, therefore, cause a greater harm to a society's collective living standard than do parallel crimes.

A bias crime, as a matter of culpability or harm—and whether analyzed under retributive or consequentialist justifications for punishment—is more serious than the relevant parallel crime. Bias crimes thus warrant enhanced criminal punishment.

## CHAPTER 4

# Who Is Guilty of a Bias Crime?

Having argued that bias crimes ought to receive more severe punishment than parallel crimes, I now turn to the legal definition and critical elements of a bias crime. I begin by returning to the relationship between culpability and harm discussed in the previous chapter but now do so in the context of understanding individual guilt. Whereas the seriousness of bias crimes *generally* justifies the enhanced punishment of these crimes *collectively,* the resulting harm to a particular victim does not, in and of itself, warrant the conclusion that a particular perpetrator is guilty of a bias crime. Bias motivation of the perpetrator, and not the resulting harm to the victim, is the critical factor in determining an individual's guilt for a bias crime. For these purposes, "bias motivation" may entail either racial animus or discriminatory selection.

## The Crucial Role of the Offender's Mental State

The result of the criminal conduct alone does not ultimately tell us much concerning the guilt or innocence of an actor accused of a bias crime. The most compelling basis for deciding whether an individual has committed a bias crime lies in the mental state of the actor. The modern trend in the study of criminal law, as noted above, has been toward a focus on the state of mind, that is, the "culpability," of the accused. Punishment theorists—retributivists and consequentialists alike—have generally considered the degree of guilt to be linked critically to the actor's culpability. If the focus of punishment is shifted from the accused's culpability to the results of his conduct, then guilt may be triggered by events and circumstances that are beyond his control. The occurrence of harmful results is often fortuitous and therefore outside the realm of that which provides a justifiable indication of the actor's blameworthiness.[1]

A result-oriented focus is particularly inappropriate for determining guilt in the context of bias crimes. In many cases, the harms associated with a bias crime depend entirely on whether the victim, the target group, and the society perceive the perpetrator's bias motivation. But a perpetrator may often have little control over the perception of others; the victim, the target group, and the community may mistakenly perceive a bias motive when none is present, and they might fail to perceive a bias motive that is in fact really there. A harms-based guilt standard might have some legitimacy in the civil context, which permits a focus on the harm caused and the consequent need to compensate the victim.[2] If this view were applied to the criminal context, however, it would allow for the punishment of bias crimes solely for the harm caused, even if the offending act were utterly devoid of racial motivation, so long as the target community perceived the act to be racially motivated. There is no justification for an application of strict liability principles in the criminal context.

Accordingly, the criminal law should not focus on the results of a perpetrator's actions when deciding whether he has committed a bias crime. Rather, the law should focus on the accused's culpability. Society refuses to punish a person who has caused an accidental death, but it does punish the murderer, even though both persons' actions have caused a loss of life. Nor would this outcome change if the victim's family firmly, but incorrectly, believed that the accused acted intentionally. Similarly, the guilt or innocence of a person accused of a bias crime should turn on his culpability, not on the results of his actions.

### The Clever Bias Criminal, the Unconscious Racist, and the Unknowingly Offensive Actor

Our focus on culpability presents us with three problem cases that warrant further analysis: the cases of the Clever Bias Criminal, the Unconscious Racist, and the Unknowingly Offensive Actor.

The Clever Bias Criminal is aware of the centrality of culpability in establishing guilt in a bias crime. He therefore articulates a nonbias motivation for an assault that was in fact motivated by his bias. In Massachusetts, for example, prosecutors have observed a tendency among some white bias criminals to plead guilty to the parallel crime in order to avoid being charged with the bias crime. Their behavior, we may presume, is based on their fear of being incarcerated with a disproportionately minority prison population for a charge of racially motivated violence.[3] If such individuals were forced to go to trial, we would expect them to articulate a nonbias motivation for a crime that was in fact motivated by bias.

The Unconscious Racist commits an interracial assault that, although unconsciously motivated by bias, is without conscious racial motivation. He asserts, for example, that the victim improperly strayed into his neighborhood and that he would have attacked the victim regardless of ethnicity in order to defend his "turf." Unlike the Clever Bias Criminal, the Unconscious Racist consciously believes this assertion. For example, the white youths in Bensonhurst, New York, who assaulted Yusef Hawkins, a black teenager, in November 1988 claimed to be motivated not by Hawkins's race but by the fact that he was an outsider to their community. The Bensonhurst case will be discussed in more detail shortly.

The Unknowingly Offensive Actor seeks to shock or offend the community generally, but chooses to do so in a manner that is particularly threatening to a certain racial or ethnic group. Nonetheless, he does so without any bias motivation. There are numerous cases of young offenders in particular who have defaced public property with a swastika for the "thrill" or in order to shock adults. They do not specifically seek to offend the local Jewish community, and are unaware that their conduct has this effect. They know that this public use of a societal taboo will shock people in general, but they neither intend to offend Jews in particular nor are even aware of the fact that the swastika has this effect on the Jewish community.

The least problematic of our three cases is that of the Clever Bias Criminal. This case presents strictly an evidentiary problem. The prosecution will have to demonstrate bias motivation beyond a reasonable doubt. This will often be difficult. The proof problems raised by bias motivation, however, closely resemble those raised by any proof of motivation. Suppose that a state adopts murder for profit as one of the aggravating circumstances in its capital-sentencing process.[4] Profit motivation will involve many of the same evidentiary problems as does bias motivation. To some extent, the prosecution can prove each using circumstantial evidence. For example, evidence that the defendant was paid is certainly probative of profit motivation. But proof of murder for gain requires more. The prosecution must prove not only that the defendant was compensated for committing the murder but also that monetary gain provided the motivation for the act. A combination of such factors as the timing and nature of the payment along with the payment itself may, however, prove profit motivation. Similarly, the circumstances of the Clever Bias Criminal's interracial assault may give rise to a strong inference of racial motivation. Those circumstances, combined with the nature of the assault and statements made by the accused during the assault, may prove bias motivation. The bias crime prosecution of Todd Mitchell, upheld by the Supreme Court in *Wisconsin v. Mitchell,* provides a helpful illustration. The prosecution in that case successfully demonstrated Mitchell's racial motivation through evidence of the circumstances surrounding the assault (just prior to the crime, Mitchell and his cohorts were discussing a scene from the movie *Mississippi Burning* in which a white man beat a young black boy who was praying) and evidence of Mitchell's statements (Mitchell said to the others, "Do you all feel hyped up to move on some white people?" and "There goes a white boy; go get him.").[5]

The Clever Bias Criminal, therefore, presents neither a unique problem nor an insolvable one. Although proof of the defendant's motivation will often present a serious challenge for the prosecution, this fact alone does not justify a result-oriented approach to bias crimes.

The case of the Clever Bias Criminal does raise one additional problem that warrants brief examination. Suppose that the Clever Bias Criminal successfully articulates his pretextual nonracial motivation not to the jury but rather to the victim and the victim's community. Put differently, what should be the result when the victim and the target community of a racially motivated assault are unaware that the attacker was motivated by bias? In such a case, no one might even suspect that it was a bias crime. One might argue that under these circumstances, the actor is not guilty of a bias crime because he has not caused the objective harms associated with bias crimes.

This requirement of actual harm for guilt, however, is misconceived. As I discussed earlier, actual harm has never been a sine qua non for guilt, and there is no reason that bias crimes should be an exception to this rule. Consider a would-be assassin who places what he believes to be a lethal quantity of poison in his victim's drink. Unbeknownst to him the dosage is quite harmless. The intended victim is left alive, unaware of the unsuccessful attempt, and completely unaffected by the events. The actor has thus caused no objective harm. He is guilty, however, of attempted murder. His guilt is grounded either in his future dangerousness[6] or in his moral blameworthiness for this unsuccessful attempt.[7] Under either understanding, it is irrelevant that the intended victim emerged unscathed. Similarly, it is irrelevant to the guilt of the Clever Bias Criminal that he did not cause the harm ordinarily associated with bias crimes. He is guilty of an attempted bias crime.

The case of the Unconscious Racist raises a far more complex problem than that of the Clever Bias Criminal. Unlike the Clever Bias Criminal, the Unconscious Racist does not offer reasons for his conduct that are consciously pretextual.[8] Recall the racially charged incident in Bensonhurst,

New York, in which Yusef Hawkins was assaulted.[9] Many residents of Bensonhurst insisted that the area had no racial problems, reasoning instead, "It's not your color. It's whether they know you or not."[10] Suppose that a jury hearing evidence of this "turf motivation" is fully persuaded that

(1) the defendants were consciously motivated by a desire to protect their neighborhood from outsiders;

(2) the defendants' unconscious motivation was to keep African-Americans out of their neighborhood; and

(3) the defendants were honestly unaware of their unconscious motivation.

These defendants, as described, are Unconscious Racists. Should the Unconscious Racist be found guilty of an "unconscious" bias crime? In other words, is guilt of a bias crime sufficiently established by a *mens rea* of unconscious bias motivation combined with conduct that in fact causes the resulting harm ordinarily associated with bias crimes?

The answer must be "no." For several reasons, the Unconscious Racist is not guilty of a bias crime. First, in general, punishment based upon a person's unconscious motives runs afoul of the principle of voluntariness that underpins the criminal law: a person may be punished only for that which he did of his own volition.[11] Michael Moore has described this as the "principle of consciousness": "[I]n order to ascribe fairly responsibility to a person for causing a harm, he must have *consciously* acted intentionally, and to ascribe fairly responsibility to a person for attempting to cause a harm, he must have acted with that harm as his *conscious* reason."[12] It is one thing to punish the Unconscious Racist for assault; he intentionally acts to attack his victim, and his conscious reason for doing so is to hurt the victim. It is quite another thing to punish the Unconscious Racist for a bias crime; he did not consciously attack his victim *for racial reasons,* nor is his conscious reason for doing so to inflict the particular harms associated with a bias crime. With respect to the bias element of his crime, the Unconscious Racist resembles the paradigmatic case of the sleepwalker who is not criminally liable for acts committed while in that condition because they are not considered his acts at all.[13]

The second reason the Unconscious Racist should not be deemed guilty of a bias crime concerns the evidentiary problems that would arise relative to the determination of the precise nature of a defendant's consciousness. These problems would be extremely difficult and perhaps insolvable. Earlier,

I dismissed the evidentiary questions raised with respect to the Clever Bias Criminal because these questions are not different from similar proof problems that occur in various areas of the criminal law. The same cannot be said of these questions when they concern the problem of the Unconscious Racist. Nowhere in the criminal law is there an established need to determine the unconscious, either as an element of a crime or as an aspect of a defense.[14]

Finally, the need for reliance upon theories of unconscious racism in order to prosecute bias crimes may not be as great as it first appeared. Consider a hypothetical case based on the Bensonhurst case. Suppose that, in addition to the proof outlined above, the prosecutor of Unconscious Racist II could show that

(1) the assault was motivated by the victim's status as "outsider"; and
(2) to the defendants, "outsider" is identical to blacks, and indeed a pretext for racial bias—that is, they regard all African-Americans, and only African-Americans, as outsiders.

Under these circumstances, the prosecution has proven a bias crime. In fact, Unconscious Racist II is not really unconscious about his racist motives at all. He stands in virtually the same moral position as the Clever Bias Criminal. Although his use of a pretext for race is not necessarily driven by a desire to avoid prosecution, Unconscious Racist II articulates a pretext that masks what is in fact a bias motivation. Indeed, there is very strong evidence that Unconscious Racist II is the best description of what actually took place in Bensonhurst the night that Yusef Hawkins was killed.[15]

Unconscious Racist II does not, however, comprise all cases of the Unconscious Racist. For Unconscious Racist II, "outsider" meant blacks and only blacks. Suppose that instead, "outsider" meant all nonwhites and that the victim was assaulted not as an African-American per se but rather as a nonwhite. The difference here is not strictly semantic, but it does not require an answer different from the one we reached for Unconscious Racist II. "Outsider" is still a pretext for race, or more accurately, now a pretext for race, color, ethnicity, and possibly national origin.

But suppose that to the Unconscious Racist, "outsider" includes blacks, all nonwhites, and a sizable number of whites who do not "look familiar" to the actor. Now it appears that "outsider" is not strictly a pretext for race but in fact a more complex concept that correlates strongly but not perfectly with race. It would be too dangerous an invasion into the subconscious to try to separate out precisely the role that race plays in this concept of "outside" and thus construct a case of bias motivation. Under this variation of the Unconscious Racist hypothetical, there is no bias crime.

We should turn to the hypothetical of the Unconscious Racist one last time. What about Unconscious Racist III, who has some reason to know of his unconscious racism; for example, he knows that he feels exceedingly uncomfortable around people of races other than his own. Suppose he puts himself in a position where this unconscious racism is likely to come to the surface. He spends time at a bar frequented by a violent racist gang. On one occasion, a racist assault is committed by the gang. He joins in the attack, claiming afterwards that he shared the gang's purpose to assault, but not their racism. He thus claims not to be guilty of a bias crime.

Unconscious Racist III's defense is flawed. Earlier, we compared the Unconscious Racist to the sleepwalker who harms but is innocent because his harm is not consciously intentional. The sleepwalker who knows that he is prone to cause harm to others while sleepwalking, however, may pose a very different situation. If the recidivist sleepwalker fails to take precaution and then does in fact cause harm, he may well be guilty. The recidivist sleepwalker is comparable to Unconscious Racist III. Unconscious racism is not an absolute defense to a bias crime in all instances. Both Unconscious Racist II and Unconscious Racist III may be found guilty of a bias crime, the former because his animus toward "others" in fact masks a bias motivation, and the latter because he recklessly places himself in a situation in which his racism, albeit not conscious, may turn violent.

The last of the three special cases is that of the Unknowingly Offensive Actor. The Unknowingly Offensive Actor is based upon a growing number of vandalism cases involving the use of swastikas that lack any bias motivation. Young offenders in particular commit these crimes for the "thrill" or in order to shock adults. Perpetrators of these crimes do not specifically seek to offend the local Jewish community, and are unaware that their conduct has this effect. As Jack Levin captured this phenomenon, "Twenty years ago they might have stolen hubcaps. Today they spray-paint a swastika on a building."[16] The Unknowingly Offensive Actor therefore consciously acts intentionally in a manner that

(1) is intended to cause the harm associated with a parallel crime of vandalism; and

(2) in fact causes the additional harm associated with a bias crime; but

(3) is not intended to cause the harm associated with a bias crime.

It is fruitful to take a moment to compare our three hypotheticals with respect to these three elements. The Unknowingly Offensive Actor is like the Clever Bias Criminal and the Unconscious Racist with respect to element 1, similar to the Unconscious Racist but different from the Clever Bias Criminal with respect to element 2, and different from the other two with respect to element 3. The comparisons concerning elements 1 and 3 are relatively straightforward. All three actors are similar with respect to element 1 because all three intend to cause the harm associated with their parallel crime. With respect to element 3, all three actors differ. Unlike the Clever Bias Criminal, the Unknowingly Offensive Actor truly does not intend to cause the harm of a bias crime. (Indeed, the Clever Bias Criminal tries to masquerade as the Unknowingly Offensive Actor.) Unlike the Unconscious Racist, the Unknowingly Offensive Actor does not even unconsciously intend to do so.

Element 2 is somewhat more subtle. The Clever Bias Criminal does not initially cause the harm associated with a bias crime because no one suspects that there was bias motivation behind his conduct. Once his state of mind becomes known, however, he would indeed cause this harm. Conversely, the Unconscious Racist and the Unknowingly Offensive Actor do cause the harm associated with a bias crime initially because everyone believes that there was bias motivation behind their conduct. Once their respective states of mind become known, however, we would expect the harm caused to ease. This easing of harm should certainly occur with respect to the harm caused to the society generally; ultimately the harm to the target community and the individual victims themselves might ease as well, although we would expect the hurt there to heal more slowly. In each of the three hypotheticals, the actual existence of harm is related to the actor's culpability. This connection between the culpability and the resulting harm is not so surprising. In Oliver Wendell Holmes's evocative description, even a dog knows the difference between being tripped over and being kicked.[17]

Let us now return to the question of whether the Unknowingly Offensive Actor has committed a bias crime. Although guilty of the parallel crime of vandalism, the Unknowingly Offensive Actor is not a bias criminal. Most Unknowingly Offensive Actors fall into either of two categories: the Unknowingly Offensive Actor (Unlucky) and the Unknowingly Offensive Actor (Negligent). The Unknowingly Offensive Actor (Unlucky) is a vandal who, by fortuity, selects a means of vandalism that initially creates a harm normally associated with a bias crime. He cannot become a bias criminal merely by the accident of picking a swastika as the mark by which he will deface property if, as we hypothesize, he truly does not know the historical meaning or specific impact of this symbol. All he knows is that this vandalism causes great public upset, and this is his goal. This hypothetical case may be counterintuitive, but it is not counterfactual. Numerous actual cases fit this hypothetical; broad-based ignorance of the Holocaust, Nazism, and the Second World War generally may be shocking, but it does underscore the reality of cases such as Unknowingly Offensive Actor (Unlucky).[18] Punishment of the Unknowingly Offensive Actor (Unlucky) for a bias crime would implicate all the difficulties implicit in a strictly result-oriented punishment scheme, as discussed earlier. In short, we would be blaming him not for acting out of bias but rather for acting out of ignorance. Under this understanding, the Unknowingly Offensive Actor cannot be blamed for his crime beyond the blame that attaches to a case of simple vandalism.

The Unknowingly Offensive Actor (Negligent), by contrast, is not blameless. Even if he did not know the meaning and impact of the swastika, he *should* have known. The blame that attaches to the conduct of the Unknowingly Offensive Actor (Negligent), however, is on a level different and lower from that of the true bias criminal. He is not blameworthy for committing a racially motivated act of vandalism. At most, he has been negligent concerning his awareness of the symbols that he uses. By definition, the behavior of the Unknowingly Offensive Actor (Negligent) does not reach the level of recklessness with respect to the elements of a bias crime. Reckless conduct is that which is taken with a *conscious* disregard of the likelihood of the harm. By hypothesis, the Unknowingly Offensive Actor has not consciously disregarded the possibility that the swastika will have a particularized harm on Jews. At most, he has behaved negligently. A person is criminally negligent with respect to an element of a crime when his failure to perceive a substantial and unjustifiable risk that the element exists "involves a gross deviation from the standard of care that a reasonable person would observe in the actor's situation." The Unknowingly Offensive Actor's ignorance of the swastika's meaning likely constitutes a *gross* deviation from what the reasonable person in his situation would know. Nonetheless, the highest level of culpability that the Unknowingly Offensive Actor exhibits with respect to a bias crime is that of criminal negligence.[19]

This negligence is insufficient culpability to support guilt for the commission of a bias crime. At most, the Unknowingly Offensive Actor (Negligent) could be charged with some low level of bias crime. No jurisdiction with a bias crime law requires only negligence with respect to the element of racial motivation, and for good reason. More is lost through diluting the requirements for a bias crime and the resulting minimization of the gravity of the offense than would be gained through expanding the number of youthful offenders who would in the final analysis be prosecuted less for their conduct than for their ignorance.[20]

Guilt of a bias crime turns on the culpability of the actor—that is, on his bias motivation—and not on the results of his conduct. The problems raised by the Clever Bias Criminal, the Unconscious Racist, and the Unknowingly Offensive Actor require no contrary conclusion. But the question remains: What is the nature of bias motivation? Thus far in the discussion I have not distinguished between bias motivation as racial animus toward the victim's race and bias motivation as discriminatory selection of the victim based on race. It is to this question—the relative merits of the racial animus and the discriminatory selection models of bias crimes—that I now turn.

## Analyzing the Discriminatory Selection Model and the Racial Animus Model

The two models of bias crimes differ with respect to the role racial animus plays, if any, in defining the elements of the crime. As noted, the racial animus model defines these crimes on the basis of the perpetrator's animus toward the racial group of the victim and the centrality of this animus in the perpetrator's motivation for committing the crime.[21] The discriminatory selection model defines these crimes solely on the perpetrator's choice of victim on the basis of the victim's race.[22]

Any case that would meet the requirements of the racial animus model would necessarily also satisfy those of the discriminatory selection model because a crime motivated by animus for the victim's racial group will necessarily be one in which the victim was discriminatorily selected on this basis. The reverse is not true. Cases of discriminatory selection need not be based upon racial animus. Two hypothetical cases will illustrate the point that some cases could fall within a discriminatory selection model statute but outside the racial animus model statute: the Purse Snatcher and the Violent Show-Off.

The Purse Snatcher is a thief who preys exclusively upon women because he believes that he will better achieve his criminal goals by grabbing purses from women than by trying to pick wallets out of the pockets of men. The Purse Snatcher discriminatorily selects his victims on the basis of gender. Nonetheless, he has no animus toward women as a group, and his thefts are not motivated by any attitudes about women other than the manner in which they carry their valuables.

The Violent Show-Off is based on the hypothetical proposed by the Attorney General of Wisconsin during the oral argument to the Supreme Court in *Wisconsin v. Mitchell.* During hiᶜ argument in support of the Wisconsin statute, State Attorney General James Doyle stated that the statute would have applied to Todd Mitchell if his sole motivation in selecting a white victim had been to impress his friends and if Mitchell himself had been otherwise indifferent to the choice of his victim.[23] Suppose that this were an accurate description of Todd Mitchell's motivation. If this were the case, Mitchell's selection of Riddick would have been racially based, but the selection itself would not have been based on any animus toward white people. Has either the Purse Snatcher or the Violent Show-Off committed a bias crime?

As a matter of positive law, both the Purse Snatcher and the Violent Show-Off are guilty under the Wisconsin discriminatory selection model bias crime statute, and both are innocent under the New Jersey racial animus model bias crimes statute. The "innocence" of the Purse Snatcher and the Violent Show-Off, of course, refers only to charges under a bias crime law. Each is guilty of a parallel crime—theft for the Purse Snatcher and assault for the Violent Show-Off.

As a normative issue, the Purse Snatcher should not be deemed a bias criminal, and the Violent Show-Off, depending on the circumstances of his offense, might not be. The discriminatory selection model thus overreaches in instances such as the two cases under consideration.

It is best to begin with the case of the Purse Snatcher because it clearly demonstrates the distinctions between the two models of bias crimes and the shortcomings of a discriminatory selection model. The Purse Snatcher acts with no animus toward his victim's group. From either a retributive or a consequentialist perspective, the Purse Snatcher should not be punished for a bias crime.

Punishing the Purse Snatcher not only for the theft but also for a bias crime places him on the same moral plane as one who targets women as a violent act of misogyny. Even if the harms caused by the two criminals are similar, their culpability is distinct. For a retributivist, the difference in cul-

pability between that of the Purse Snatcher and that of the violent misogynist translates into a difference in blame: the Purse Snatcher is less blameworthy than the violent misogynist and deserves a lesser punishment. Put
differently, the Purse Snatcher deserves to be punished for the theft but not
for a bias crime. The same claim may be maintained from a consequentialist
point of view. The appropriate deterrence for the Purse Snatcher is neither
more nor less than the deterrence appropriate for any other common thief.
If the defendant were a bias criminal, his misogynistic drive to commit his
crime, and that of other would-be misogynistic bias criminals, would hold a
greater probability of future harm, thus requiring greater deterrence and
warranting greater punishment. Under either approach to punishment,
therefore, the culpability of the violent misogynist is directly related to the
factors that make bias crimes more serious than parallel crimes, whereas the
culpability of the Purse Snatcher does not implicate those factors. Because a
discriminatory selection model bias crime statute would punish the Purse
Snatcher as a bias criminal, it must be flawed.

The Violent Show-Off raises a harder set of issues. He has much in common with the Unknowingly Offensive Actor, who, as noted, should not be
held criminally liable for the commission of any bias crime or, at the very
most, whose criminal liability is limited to a very low level appropriate for a
negligent bias crime. The Violent Show-Off's purpose is to assault a victim in
a manner that will impress his friends. To him, it is of no importance that
the manner itself calls for the discriminatory selection of a victim. Although
the racially discriminatory dimension of the Violent Show-Off's act is un-
connected to the *purpose* of his conduct, he does act with *knowledge* of his
friends' prejudice.

This brings us to a distinction between the Violent Show-Off and the Unknowingly Offensive Actor that, under certain conditions, will call for the
former's bias crime liability. Whereas the Unknowingly Offensive Actor was
unaware that his conduct would cause harm to a particular racial group, the
Violent Show-Off knows full well that he is seeking out a member of a particular racial group to do harm. Recall that the Unknowingly Offensive Actor sought to shock everyone; his means of doing so was to draw a swastika.
Suppose that he sought to shock not the general community but the Jewish
community in particular, and that his means of doing so was to deface a synagogue with a swastika. Suppose further that he then claimed he did so only
to impress his friends and not out of any animosity toward Jews. This Focused Unknowingly Offensive Actor has now become the Violent Show-

Off—but is he still innocent of a bias crime? The answer, as we will see shortly, turns on the precise nature of his state of mind.

Why is the answer not simply, "No—under these circumstances he is no longer innocent and is now criminally liable for a bias crime"? The key to understanding why this simple answer is not sufficient lies in understanding why the cause for concern here is not nearly as great as it first appears. The central concern in acquitting the Focused Unknowingly Offensive Actor of a bias crime is quite simple: we do not believe him. When he chooses not only to paint a swastika but also to target a synagogue for his crime, it is hard to accept that he sincerely lacks racial animus. The location of a swastika is often the key to determining whether a particular act of vandalism was racially or religiously motivated, or mere thrill seeking.[24] This tells us that discriminatory selection of a victim is often powerful evidence of racial animus toward the victim's group. When there is proof of animus, albeit circumstantial, then the Focused Unknowingly Offensive Actor or the Violent Show-Off is a bias criminal.

But a Violent Show-Off may truly act without animus. In this case, we must probe further into his mental state before simply saying that he is a bias criminal like any other. We begin again by questioning the supposition that underpins the Violent Show-Off—namely, that he truly acts without racial animus. We must ask whether this is possible. On the surface, the Violent Show-Off could sincerely state that he bears no ill will toward the racial group he selects. Beneath this assertion, however, lies his knowledge that his friends do bear such animus, and his willingness to proceed with the crime under these circumstances. Viewed in this manner, the nexus between the Violent Show-Off and racial animus is sufficiently close to distinguish him from the true Unknowingly Offensive Actor and make him guilty of a bias crime.

We may understand the guilt of the Unknowingly Offensive Actor in either of two ways. First, his knowledge of the animus that ultimately drives his violent act may allow the inference that he has acted purposely in perpetrating the racially motivated attack. Second, his knowledge of the animus and the harm that it will cause may be sufficient to justify his guilt. But the Violent Show-Off is a bias criminal only if he meets the elements of a racial animus model statute. If he is unaware of the racial animus of his friends, then he is identical to the Unknowingly Offensive Actor and similarly not guilty of a bias crime.

Both means of understanding the bias crime guilt of the Violent Show-

Off—inferring purpose from knowledge, and relying upon knowledge alone—are well grounded in criminal law doctrine. The inference of purpose from knowledge finds a rich and appropriate source of support in the law of accomplice liability. An accomplice is a person who aids or attempts to aid another in the planning or commission of a crime.[25] Although he does not directly commit the crime himself, he is nonetheless guilty of that crime. In most jurisdictions, the prosecution must prove that the accused acted with the purpose of aiding in the crime. It is insufficient for the prosecution to show that the accused acted with knowledge that his behavior would provide such aid. The classic statement of the purpose requirement was written by Judge Learned Hand more than half a century ago in *United States v. Peoni,* the facts of which provide a helpful illustration of the doctrine. Peoni sold counterfeit money to Regno, who in turn sold counterfeit money to Dorsey. In this case, Peoni was accused of being Dorsey's accomplice in the possession of counterfeit money. Peoni had plainly sold the counterfeit currency to Regno and had some reason to know that Regno would resell the currency. Hand reversed Peoni's conviction on the accessory charge because the prosecution had been unable to show that Peoni acted with the purpose of helping Regno sell the counterfeit money. Peoni's knowledge that Regno might do so was insufficient. As Hand wrote, accomplice liability requires that

> [the defendant] participate in [the crime] as something that he wishes to bring about, that he seek by his action to make it succeed. All the words used—even the most colorless "abet"—carry an implication of purposive attitude toward it.[26]

In spite of the insistence upon purpose in complicity doctrine, in some instances purpose may be inferred from conduct that is done with knowledge. If a bank security guard, knowing that a person is planning to rob the bank, supplies him with a detailed layout of the bank's security system, we might fairly infer that the guard has acted with the purpose of aiding the robbery.[27] The distinction between purpose and knowledge, however, remains critical. The guard is not an accomplice solely because he acted with knowledge of the robber's plans; he is an accomplice because we may use his knowledge to infer his purpose. Returning to the question of whether the Violent Show-Off is a bias criminal, we ask if his knowledge of his friends' motivation is sufficient to infer purpose and convict him of a bias crime on this basis. This may well be true in the majority of cases of the Violent Show-Off.

Suppose that we are uncertain as to the Violent Show-Off's purpose. This brings us back to the second means of understanding the bias crime guilt of the Violent Show-Off: guilt based on knowledge alone. Here too we find firm support in criminal law doctrine. In virtually all instances of the criminal law, conduct with knowledge of the resulting harm is treated the same as purposeful conduct—indeed the distinction drawn by complicity doctrine is one of the few corners of the criminal law to draw a line between purpose and knowledge. A helpful, if grizzly, hypothetical is often used to illustrate this point to first-year students of criminal law: the hypothetical of the Terrorist and the Assassin. The Terrorist places a bomb on an airplane with the conscious objective of killing all one hundred people on board. This is his purpose. The Assassin, by contrast, places a bomb on an airplane with the conscious objective of killing the person under whose seat the bomb is placed. He is aware that the other ninety-nine people on board will die as a result, though this is not his conscious objective. With respect to the death of one, he acts with the purpose of killing; with respect to the other, he acts with knowledge that he will kill.

Both the Terrorist and the Assassin are guilty of the murder of all one hundred people on the plane. Although they have acted with different culpability with respect to ninety-nine of the victims, for purposes of criminal liability, this is a distinction without a difference. The Assassin's willingness to proceed knowing that his conduct will cause the death of the other ninety-nine is morally indistinguishable from the Terrorist's desire to achieve this result. Indeed, one could argue that ironically, the Assassin is actually the worse of the two. In a macabre way, the Terrorist validates the lives of each of his victims by planning and willing their deaths. The Assassin is callously indifferent to the lives of the ninety-nine.

The Violent Show-Off, if he is fully aware of his friends' racial animus, acts with a similar kind of callous indifference to his victims. He knows that he is furthering his friends' animus, and his willingness to commit the assault in light of this knowledge is an act of reflected animus on his part. This would even be true if the Violent Show-Off had every reason to know of this animus and engaged in a kind of willful blindness so as not to know for certain.[28] In our reliance on his knowledge, just as with our inference of purpose from his knowledge, the Violent Show-Off still must meet the elements of a racial animus model statute. If he is separated from the racial animus of his friends—if he had neither knowledge of their animus nor reasonable basis to suspect it—then he is identical to the Unknowingly Offensive Actor and similarly not guilty of a bias crime. We shall see in Chapter 7 that the conclusions reached concerning the Violent Show-Off apply as well to cases of individual criminals—that is, those not showing off for their friends—who act in the face of certain knowledge that a crime will yield the results associated with racially motivated violence.

The guilt of the Violent Show-Off, however we conceive of it, should finally be contrasted with that of his friends, for they may very well be guilty of bias crimes. Suppose that the Violent Show-Off's friends encourage him to select a victim of a particular race out of animus for that group. They are guilty of solicitation or complicity in the commission of a bias crime.[29] The Violent Show-Off, however, unless he shared the animus-driven purpose of his accomplices or was aware of their animus, does not share their guilt for the bias crime.[30] Lacking purpose or knowledge, he is guilty only of the lesser parallel offense.

The racial animus model of bias crimes more appropriately defines a bias crime than the discriminatory selection model. Many cases of discriminatory victim selection are in fact also cases of racial animus; most cases in which the perpetrator selected his victim on the basis of race may fit comfortably with both models. This demonstrates the continued significance of discriminatory selection in a bias crime regime that embraces the racial animus model. Discriminatory selection may often act as persuasive evidence for racial animus that may not be proven by any other means. A showing of discriminatory selection of a victim will often be powerful evidence for the much more subtle and difficult showing of racial animus. If discriminatory selection of the group can be shown, animus can often be inferred.

Discriminatory victim selection, however, is only evidence of racial animus. If we know that discriminatory selection exists without animus in a particular case, then it ought not be used as a surrogate for racial animus and should not be punished. Alternatively, we might consider discriminatory victim selection, in the absence of racial animus, to be a lower grade of bias crime than true cases of racial animus. Under this approach, discriminatory selection would be seen as a wrong in and of itself but a wrong of less seriousness than that of racial animus.[31] I will return to these alternatives in Chapter 7 and the discussion of a model bias crime law. The central point here is that as we punish bias crimes, we must understand precisely what we are punishing: purposeful or knowing, conscious criminal conduct grounded in racial animus.

## CHAPTER 5

# Are Bias Crime Laws Constitutional?

The punishment of bias crimes and the regulation of racist speech have caused us to focus more on the conflict between First Amendment rights and civil rights than at any time since Nazis threatened to march in Skokie, Illinois, in the late 1970s.[1] I call this the bias crimes–hate speech paradox. How is it possible both to punish the bias criminal and to protect the right of the bigot to express his beliefs?

The paradox has deep roots. On the one hand, we have crimes that are worse precisely because of their racial motivation. As we have seen, bias crimes cause greater harm to their immediate victims and to their target communities than do parallel crimes. Moreover, bias crimes cause a more profound injury to the general community, exciting an extraordinary level of public condemnation and arousing passions that exceed the reaction to other forms of even large-scale violence or human tragedy. On the other hand, we have a fundamental constitutional principle: the right to free expression of ideas, even if distasteful or hateful. The right to free expression, based in the First Amendment to the Constitution, lies at the heart of our legal culture.

The question of how much intolerance a liberal democracy should tolerate has fueled debate for years.[2] Consideration of bias crimes and racist speech focuses this question in a compelling form. The clash between the values underpinning the bias crimes–hate speech paradox has produced an unusual level of explicit ambivalence. Those who argue that bias crime laws and regulations of racist speech unlawfully interfere with the rights of free expression stress their resulting heartache. For example, Justice Antonin Scalia, in his decision in *R.A.V. v. City of St. Paul*,[3] felt obliged to announce, "Let there be no mistake about our belief that burning a cross in someone's front yard is reprehensible."[4] Similarly, the Ohio Supreme Court, in reviewing that state's bias crime law, wrote, "Before undertaking an analysis of the statute . . . we express our abhorrence for racial and ethnic hatred, and especially for crimes motivated by such hatred."[5]

Bias crimes and racist speech have spawned a great deal of scholarly attention.[6] Judicial consideration of this debate initially centered around state university speech codes. Subsequently, the scope of the debate significantly broadened. Chapter 2 looked briefly at the flurry of judicial activity in this area, bracketed by the United States Supreme Court decisions in *R.A.V. v. City of St. Paul* in 1992 and *Wisconsin v. Mitchell* in 1993.[7] In between, several state Supreme Courts wrestled with these questions. In this chapter, we will return to the fray and examine in depth the apparent conflict between the enhanced punishment of bias crimes and the protection of free expression. It is indeed an *apparent* conflict because the so-called paradox of seeking to punish the perpetrators of racially motivated violence while being committed to protecting the bigot's rights to express racism is a false paradox. We can, in fact, do both and we should.

## Distinguishing Bias Crimes and Racist Speech

It is not only possible to maintain a distinction between bias crimes and racist speech, but also imperative that we do so. The problems left unresolved by the decisions in *R.A.V.* and *Mitchell* and within the bias crime–free speech debate are best addressed by establishing this distinction. Among courts and scholars alike there has been a persistent tendency to blur or even ignore the distinction. As a result, they have also mischaracterized the very issue raised by the St. Paul ordinance and bias crime laws generally.

This tendency transcends the ordinary divisions within legal thought. Consider, for example, the understanding of the issue at stake in *R.A.V.* by the conservative Supreme Court Justice Scalia and the liberal legal philosopher Ronald Dworkin. In his opinion for the Court, Justice Scalia treated *R.A.V.* as a pure case of racist speech. Dworkin similarly defined the question in *R.A.V.* as "whether a state may constitutionally make an assault a special crime, carrying a larger sentence, because it is intended to express a conviction the community disapproves of."[8] Both Justice Scalia and Dworkin incorrectly viewed *R.A.V.* as posing solely speech issues. Once *R.A.V.* is framed in this manner, the outcome is largely determined and the constitutional fate of bias crime laws in general is sealed. We naturally invoke "content neutrality," the doctrine that *all* views must be protected and treated equally, particularly those that society detests. Bias crime laws are thus doomed because they target a particular form of violence, that which is motivated by racial bias.

The scholarly debate over racist speech and bias crimes has also failed to explore the distinction. Some scholars argue that racist speech restrictions and bias crimes are both unconstitutional interferences with free expression.[9] At the other end of the spectrum, scholars argue that racist speech is unprotected by the First Amendment.[10] Ironically, these opposing positions share a common premise: that proscription of bias crimes involves regulation of expression and is therefore either (1) impermissible, or (2) requires a justification for suppressing expression. Even those who have sought a middle ground wind up searching for a permissible suppression of speech—albeit a narrowly defined one.[11]

## Searching for a Firm Middle Ground

I wish to probe for a different middle ground, one that provides a framework for upholding and enforcing bias crimes while at the same time protecting racist speech as a form of free expression. I am making an assumption here, and I want to make it clearly. I assume that racist speech is in fact constitutionally protected. There is a hard and a soft version of this assumption. The hard version is a normative argument that a proper jurisprudence of free expression requires the protection of racist speech. Such an argument goes well beyond the scope of this book—indeed, it would be a book unto itself.[12] Nonetheless, for those interested, I have sketched out the argument in the notes.[13] The soft version is the argument that, assuming racist speech is constitutionally protected, we may assert a critical distinction between racist speech and bias crimes, leaving the former protected while enhancing the penalties for the latter. This is the version I adopt here.

This chapter first explores the background to the false paradox of bias crime and hate speech, using *R.A.V.* and related state Supreme Court decisions as points of departure for a consideration of the standard First Amendment challenge to bias crime laws. Then begins the search for a resolution of the paradox, that is, a theory by which bias crimes may be prosecuted while racist speech is protected. I first consider two promising, yet flawed, bases for distinguishing bias crimes and racist speech. The first rests upon the proposed distinction between "expression" and "conduct" discussed briefly in Chapter 2. Although it is tempting to assert that racist speech is "expression" and is thereby protected, whereas bias crimes are "conduct" that may thereby be criminalized, this is a distinction that will not hold.

The second flawed approach rests upon the purported distinction between "pure bias crime statutes" and "penalty-enhancement statutes." *Pure bias crime* statutes proscribe specified racially motivated behavior directed at a person or property. The St. Paul, Minnesota, ordinance that was struck down by the Supreme Court in *R.A.V.* is an example of a pure bias crime law. *Penalty-enhancement laws* increase the criminal sanction—the fine or term of incarceration—for certain crimes when those crimes are committed with racial motivation. A penalty-enhancement law was at issue in *Mitchell*. Although there is a descriptive difference between these categories of bias crimes, it is not one that will bear any normative weight. This proves to be a distinction without a difference. A firmer basis for the distinction between bias crimes and racist speech must be found elsewhere.

The search continues with an exploration of the differences between the nonbias element of bias crimes and racist speech: the parallel crime that is included in the bias crime and the parallel behavior that is part of racist speech. The parallel behavior of racist speech is expression, a form of behavior that, however offensive, is not made criminal in our legal system. The parallel crimes that are included in bias crimes, however, are punishable. This is true even when the parallel crime consists solely of speech. Speech that is intended to frighten another into a state of serious fear is a verbal assault that is criminally proscribable. The concept of verbal assault provides a reworking of the "fighting words" doctrine established half a century ago by the Supreme Court in *Chaplinsky v. New Hampshire*.[14] *Chaplinsky* is best understood today as placing outside the reach of the First Amendment words that are intended to and have the effect of creating fear of injury in the addressee. Words that have the effect or even the intent of hurting the target's feelings, however unfortunate, do not come under this understanding of "fighting words."

I then return to the context of bias motivation. The proposed understanding of "fighting words" is consistent with a distinction between prosecutable bias crimes and protected racist speech that does not rely on the speech-conduct dichotomy. Racially targeted behavior that is intended to create fear in its targeted victim constitutes a bias crime, whether the behavior is primarily verbal or physical. Racially targeted behavior that vents the actor's racism, even if it disturbs the addressee greatly, constitutes racist speech that is protected by the First Amendment.

The final part of this chapter addresses the two prime arguments that have been advanced against the enhanced punishment of bias crimes. The first argument, based on the doctrine of content neutrality, fails because the proposed distinction between bias crimes and racist speech does not run afoul of the requirements of the doctrine. The second argument, resting upon the purported distinction between "intent" and "motivation," asserts that an actor may be punished on the basis of his intent but that his motivation is beyond the reach of the criminal law. There are two flaws in this argument. First, motivation is frequently a basis for criminal punishment. Second, the distinction between motivation and intent is not clear, and these concepts are more properly seen as descriptive points on a continuum whose normative weight must be found elsewhere.

## The Bias Crimes–Hate Speech Paradox

*The Conflict between Two Values*

Bias crime law has been the subject of great controversy precisely because it implicates two of our most cherished values: equal treatment of citizens and free expression. Racism is anathema to the American ideals of freedom and equality. Yet a state may not punish a person for holding an opinion, regardless of how obnoxious the opinion may seem to the general public or how good a predictor it might be for future antisocial conduct. It is striking that Chief Justice Fred Vinson, not renowned as a strong advocate of a robust view of the First Amendment, saw no need to provide any support for his assertion that "one may not be imprisoned or executed because he holds particular beliefs."[15] This is the same Justice Vinson who applied the "clear and present danger" standard to permit the prosecution of leaders of the Communist Party in *Dennis v. United States*.[16] According to Chief Justice Vinson, the teaching of Marxist-Leninist doctrine by the Communist Party from 1948 to 1951 posed a sufficiently clear and present danger of an overthrow of the American government to warrant prosecution of the party's leaders. The noted First Amendment theorist Thomas Emerson justly criticized Vinson's use of the "clear and present danger" test as an interpretation that "virtually abandoned the element of 'clear,' greatly subordinated the element of 'present,' and overemphasized the element of the seriousness of the 'evil.'"[17]

Consider the context of flag-burning, which continues to press the limits of the right to express unpopular views. The Supreme Court, even as it has become more conservative in its approach to numerous areas of the law, has repeatedly upheld the right to burn an American flag. In *Texas v. Johnson*, in which the Texas flag-burning prohibition was struck down, the Court held that "if there is a bedrock principle underlying the First Amendment, it is that the government may not prohibit the expression of an idea simply because society finds the idea itself offensive or disagreeable."[18]

Oliver Wendell Holmes, Jr., was one of the greatest champions of this principle. In 1929, he dissented from an opinion in which the Supreme Court denied citizenship to Rosika Schwimmer. The sole basis on which Ms. Schwimmer's application was denied was her ardent pacifism, which led her to state that she would not bear arms in order to defend the United States. In his pointed dissent, Justice Holmes set out his views as to the scope of the First Amendment:

> Some of her answers might excite popular prejudice, but if there is any principle of the Constitution that more imperatively calls for attachment than any other it is the principle of free thought—not free thought for those who agree with us but freedom for the thought that we hate. I think that we should adhere to that principle with regard to admission into, as well as to life within this country.[19]

This dissent became the law seventeen years later, when the Supreme Court overruled *Schwimmer*, relying extensively on Justice Holmes.

It is thus clear that a racist may not be punished merely for his racist beliefs. But no law has sought to punish mere racist beliefs. Belief is only the "first stage in the process of expression."[20] Regulation of the succeeding stages of expression has, however, occurred. As noted, the contemporary debate over the bias crimes–hate speech paradox began in the context of university speech codes. Concerned over the increase in racial tensions on campuses, many schools adopted policies proscribing the expression of bigotry. These codes received a mixed scholarly reception.[21] None, however, has survived a First Amendment challenge in court. Campus speech codes at public universities have been viewed as prohibitions of speech based solely on the content of that speech. Although sympathetic to the goals of the campus speech codes, the district courts that struck down such regulations as those adopted by the University of Michigan and the University of Wisconsin ruled that they impermissibly interfered with the First Amendment.[22]

University speech codes have no direct analog in general society. There has been no contemporary attempt by any state to apply a racist speech code to the general public. Beginning with *R.A.V.*, however, courts moved beyond the setting of the university and confronted general bias crime laws for the first time since the dramatic legislative activity in this arena. *R.A.V.* thus provides the best point of departure for an examination of the First Amendment issues that underpin the bias crime–hate speech paradox.

### R.A.V. v. City of St. Paul

The Supreme Court unanimously struck down the St. Paul ordinance at issue in *R.A.V.* but agreed about little else. Four members of the Court—Justices White, Blackmun, Stevens, and O'Connor—concurred in the judgment of the Court, but did so solely on the grounds that the ordinance was overly broad, sweeping within its proscription expression that should be protected.[23] It is safe to assume that these justices would have upheld a narrowly drawn bias crime statute. The other five members of the Court, in the majority opinion of Justice Scalia, reached further and found that the St. Paul ordinance—and presumably any bias crime law—was an unconstitutional content-based regulation of speech.[24]

The facts of the *R.A.V.* case, alluded to earlier, require only brief amplification now. Robert Viktora, then a minor, was accused of burning a cross on the lawn of Russell and Laura Jones and their children, an African-American family who had recently moved into the neighborhood. Viktora was charged with violating St. Paul's Bias-Motivated Crime Ordinance, which provides:

> Whoever places on public or private property a symbol, object, appellation, characterization or graffiti, including, but not limited to, a burning cross or Nazi swastika, which one knows or has reasonable grounds to know arouses anger, alarm or resentment in others on the basis of race, color, creed, religion or gender commits disorderly conduct and shall be guilty of a misdemeanor.[25]

In moving to dismiss the indictment, Viktora asserted both that the ordinance was overbroad and that it was an unconstitutional, content-based restriction on speech. The Minnesota Supreme Court rejected the overbreadth challenge because that court construed the language "arouses anger, alarm or resentment in others" in the ordinance to apply only to "fighting words," and therefore not to any expression protected by the First Amendment.[26] Although a minority of the Supreme Court held that this limiting construction by the Minnesota court did not save the ordinance from overbreadth, Justice Scalia was prepared to accept that all of the expression reached by the ordinance was proscribable.[27] He thus had to reach the content-based challenge.

Justice Scalia utilized a limited categorical approach to the First Amendment that assigns certain forms and types of expression to categories that receive less protection than general expression.[28] Acknowledging that "fighting words," along with other categories of expression such as obscenity and defamation, are not entitled to full First Amendment protection, Justice Scalia asserted that these forms of expression nevertheless enjoy some limited protection and are not "entirely invisible to the Constitution."[29] Within any of these categories, expression may be proscribed only on the basis of its categorical nature and not on the basis of its content. Fighting words are "analogous to a noisy sound truck": the state may regulate or even altogether ban this form of expression, but not on the basis of its content.[30] According to Justice Scalia, expression operates either in the full light of the First Amendment or in the shadow of that amendment, but never wholly outside of its protection. Regardless of the First Amendment status of a category of expression, however, content-based regulations are the greatest evil and are "presumptively invalid."[31]

I suggest below that Justice Scalia's approach in *R.A.V.* is thoroughly flawed in the context of bias crimes because it misconceives the requirements of the content-neutrality doctrine.[32] But it is important to recognize at this point precisely what Justice Scalia's approach to the content-neutrality doctrine is—or, of greater significance, what it claims *not* to be—about. His approach purports not to require the state to proscribe either all forms of proscribable speech or none at all. Rather, Justice Scalia identified several exceptions to the general unacceptability of content-based restrictions on expression. Under the first set of exceptions, choices may be made as to which forms of speech to proscribe so long as these choices do not address the content of the expression. For example, the regulations upheld in *Sable Communications* restricted obscene communications when the medium of communication is the telephone.[33] According to Justice Scalia, the provisions at issue in *Sable* permissibly regulated the medium but not the message.[34]

Under the second set of exceptions, Justice Scalia would also exempt from the content-neutrality rule, regulations that address content for the "very reason the entire class of speech at issue is proscribable" in the first place. Justice Scalia provided two examples of this type of exception. First, a regulation prohibiting only obscenity "which is the most patently offensive *in its prurience*" would be permissible.[35] Second, and somewhat more curious, threats of physical violence directed at the President of the United States would be permissible.[36]

Justice Scalia found that the St. Paul ordinance fell within neither exception. Instead, when he applied his approach to the St. Paul ordinance, he concluded that the city had established a regulation aimed directly at racist speech and biased beliefs rather than at "fighting words" generally or at a subgroup of "fighting words" selected for reasons other than the content of those words. He thus held that the ordinance impermissibly chose sides in the debate over racial prejudice. In perhaps the most famous sentence in the *R.A.V.* opinion, Justice Scalia wrote: "St. Paul has no such authority to license one side of a debate to fight freestyle, while requiring the other to follow Marquis of Queensbury Rules."[37]

Justice Scalia's majority opinion thus does not permit any distinction between racist speech and bias crimes. The impermissible attempt to suppress racist speech unavoidably infects the state's effort to punish bias crimes. This view was adopted, with some modification, by the state Supreme Courts in *Wisconsin v. Mitchell*[38] and *Ohio v. Wyant*.[39]

The facts of each case may be briefly summarized or, in the case of *Mitchell,* resummarized. In the Wisconsin case, as noted, the defendant was Todd Mitchell, a nineteen-year-old black man convicted of aggravated battery for his role in the severe beating of Gregory Riddick, a fourteen-year-old white male. Under Wisconsin law, this crime carries a maximum sentence of two years.[40] Wisconsin's penalty-enhancement law, however, provides that the maximum possible penalty for a racially motivated aggravated battery is seven years.[41] In addition to his conviction for battery, Mitchell was found to have acted out of racial bias in the selection of the victim. Facing a possible seven-year prison term, he was sentenced to four years' incarceration.[42]

*Wyant* arose out of a series of cases commenced under Ohio's ethnic intimidation law. The charges brought against David Wyant, a white male, were based upon his use of vulgar and threatening language directed at a black couple, Jerry White and Patricia McGowan, at a campsite. The Ohio statute is a penalty-enhancement law applicable to a number of personal and property crimes which, if committed "by reason of the race, color, religion, or national origin of another person or group of persons," are elevated to the next grade of offense.[43] Wyant was convicted of aggravated menacing, predicated upon the racial motivation behind his conduct, and sentenced to one and one-half years' incarceration.

The Wisconsin State Supreme Court decision in *Mitchell,* announced the day after *R.A.V.* was decided by the United States Supreme Court, adopted much the same approach as did Justice Scalia. The Wisconsin court held that the penalty-enhancement law "punishes the defendant's biased thought . . . and thus encroaches upon First Amendment rights."[44] Because Todd Mitchell's conduct—regardless of motivation—was punishable as an aggravated battery, the court held that the only basis for the enhanced sentence was Mitchell's beliefs. "The hate crimes statute," the court held, "enhances the punishment of bigoted criminals because they are bigoted."[45] This would not only constitute an impermissible interference with Mitchell's right to his ideas, the court held, but would also keep others from holding and expressing similar ideas for fear of providing evidence for a future bias crime charge.[46]

The Ohio Supreme Court in *Wyant* tracked the Supreme Court holding in *R.A.V.* and the state court decision in *Mitchell*. The Ohio court bolstered its conclusion with an additional argument that, though rooted less in First Amendment jurisprudence than in criminal law doctrine, still addressed concerns of free expression. The court argued that punishing motive was the equivalent of thought control: "The same crime can be committed for any of a number of different motives. Enhancing a penalty because of motive therefore punishes the person's thought, rather than the person's act or criminal intent."[47]

A common thread runs through Justice Scalia's opinion in *R.A.V.* and the state court opinions in *Mitchell* and *Wyant*. All conclude that bias crimes inevitably represent an unconstitutional regulation of racist speech and thought. It therefore appears to be impossible to separate racist speech from bias crimes. Because the former must be protected under the First Amendment, the latter may not be punished.

## Resolving the Bias Crime–Hate Speech Paradox

The search for a distinction between protected racist speech and proscribable bias crimes begins with a brief consideration of two unsuccessful approaches: the purported distinctions between (1) speech and conduct and (2) pure bias crimes and penalty-enhancement laws.

### Speech vs. Conduct

It is tempting to distinguish bias crimes from racist speech by describing bias crimes as conduct and racist speech as strictly expression. This approach was explored by Thomas Emerson, among others.[48] Despite substantial scholarly criticism, the purported dichotomy and its role as a tool in constitutional analysis has a remarkable sticking quality.[49] In his *R.A.V.* opinion, for example, Justice Scalia distinguished impermissible content-based restrictions from other restrictions, such as laws against treason, that are "directed not against speech but against conduct."[50] Similarly, the Supreme Court of Oregon upheld that state's bias crime law because it was a law "directed against conduct not a law directed against the substance of speech."[51]

As noted in Chapter 2, the United States Supreme Court in *Wisconsin v. Mitchell* also based its decision on a speech-conduct distinction. Indeed, this was precisely the basis of the Court's distinction between the St. Paul ordinance that was struck down in *R.A.V.* and the Wisconsin statute that was upheld in *Mitchell*. Writing for a unanimous Court, Chief Justice William Rehnquist wrote that "whereas the ordinance struck down in *R.A.V.* was explicitly directed at expression (i.e., 'speech' or 'messages') the statute in this case is aimed at conduct unprotected by the First Amendment."[52]

The speech-conduct distinction is tempting because it promises a predictable and logical solution to the hate speech–bias crimes paradox. Once we can differentiate speech from conduct, we can effectively protect the former and punish the latter. The Supreme Court in *Mitchell* made this promise. Unfortunately, the promise is ephemeral because the speech-conduct distinction does not work.

Emerson's work is the best place to begin. Emerson did not, in fact, suggest that a perfect distinction could be drawn between speech and conduct. He conceded that "[t]o some extent expression and action are always mingled; most conduct includes elements of both."[53] Nonetheless, he proposed that there exists a sufficiently workable division between speech and action, and that this dichotomy permits a judicial inquiry into which element is "predominant" in any particular behavior.

Although the Supreme Court never explicitly adopted Emerson's proposal, long before the *Mitchell* case it did draw on the distinction between speech and conduct in an effort to place certain behavior beyond the protected bounds of "expression." For example, the Court relied on this distinction when it upheld a federal statute that punished the destruction of a draft card. The Court stated that it "cannot accept the view that an apparently limitless variety of conduct can be labeled 'speech' whenever the person engaging in the conduct intends thereby to express an idea."[54]

In application, however, the speech-conduct dichotomy is far too brittle. Emerson himself noted that efforts to apply the distinction will to a great extent "be based on a common sense reaction."[55] Therein lies the problem.

Speech and action are not merely intermingled; they are inextricable. Thus the dialectic encompassing speech and conduct precludes not only a neat separation of the two, but even Emerson's efforts to determine whether act or expression is the "predominant element" in certain behavior. Consider two examples used by Emerson himself: laws punishing the burning of a draft card and laws enhancing the punishment for the assassination of the President, both of which have been explicitly upheld by the Supreme Court.[56] To Emerson, "it is quite clear" that, as to the burning of a draft card, "the predominant element . . . is expression,"[57] but, as to the assassination of the President, the predominant element is proscribable conduct.[58] It is obvious to Emerson not only that assassination must be conduct, but also that what distinguishes an assassination of the President from a case of ordinary murder must also be "conduct."

The slipperiness of the speech-conduct distinction is apparent. One could easily argue that a Presidential assassination differs from, and is punished more severely than, other murders precisely because it manifests the expression of a deeply held opinion. Such may very well have been the case in the assassinations of, at least, Presidents Lincoln and McKinley. There is strong support for the idea that John Wilkes Booth's predominant motivation in the assassination of Abraham Lincoln was to protest the conduct of the Civil War and the treatment of the Southern states by Union troops, and that Leon Czolgosz's predominant motivation in the assassination of William McKinley was to further the goals of anarchism.[59]

Although it is harder to contend that the major part of burning a draft card is the conduct of burning, it is at least plausible that, both in terms of the actor's own understanding of the card burning and in terms of the state's concern with punishing this behavior, the "conduct" of no longer having a draft card predominates in the act. As John Hart Ely wrote in his classic article on the draft card–burning case,

> burning a draft card to express opposition to the draft is an undifferentiated whole, 100% action and 100% expression. It involves no conduct that is not at the same time communication, and no communication that does not result from conduct.[60]

Perhaps we could even say the same of assassination. While murder is usually motivated by hatred or other feelings about the victim, a Presidential assassination may be motivated by political, not personal, animus. Public action is the most direct and dramatic means of communicating this political animus. The act demonstrates, albeit in a sociopathic manner, depth of conviction in a way that words alone probably could never communicate.

The point here is that the purported distinction between speech and conduct will not add rigor to any attempt to distinguish bias crime from racist speech. Robert Viktora's cross-burning on the lawn of the Jones family certainly constitutes an "undifferentiated whole." It is 100 percent action directed against the Jones family and 100 percent expression of deeply felt racism. Even the simple flying of a swastika flag from one's home cannot be objectively described as expression alone. It is action as well. Accordingly, applying the distinction between conduct and expression requires a process that assumes its own conclusions. That which we wish to punish we will term "conduct" with expressive value, and that which we wish to protect we will call "expression" that requires conduct as its means of communication. The critical decision—which behavior may be punished and which should be protected—is wholly extrinsic to this process. As a result, if a meaningful distinction between bias crimes and racist speech exists, we must find it elsewhere.

## Pure Bias Crimes vs. Penalty-Enhancement Laws

The distinction between pure bias crime laws and penalty-enhancement laws has been presented as an argument for the constitutionality of certain bias crime laws. According to this argument, pure bias crime laws are unconstitutional, but penalty-enhancement laws are constitutionally permissible. Pure bias crime laws proscribe specified racially motivated behavior such as cross-burning or racially motivated assault. Penalty-enhancement laws "piggy-back" on other criminal laws, increasing the criminal penalty for certain crimes when those crimes are committed with racial motivation.

Unlike the argument based upon the speech-conduct distinction, the argument based upon the distinction between pure bias crimes and penalty-enhancement laws is of recent origin. This distinction figured prominently in testimony before the House of Representatives Subcommittee on Crime and Criminal Justice in support of H.R. 4797, the "Hate Crimes Sentencing Act of 1992,"[61] the precursor to the federal penalty-enhancement law ultimately enacted two years later.[62] Both Laurence Tribe and Floyd Abrams stated that the proposed legislation was constitutional because it sought to use bias motivation only as a factor in sentencing and not as an element of a crime itself.[63]

We must return to definitions in order to evaluate the usefulness of the distinction between pure bias crimes and penalty-enhancement laws. Penalty-enhancement laws explicitly rely upon some other criminal provision, such as assault, and increase the sentence if the crime is committed with bias motivation. Penalty-enhancement laws may increase the sentence by adding a specified length of time to the underlying sentence,[64] or by increasing the "level" of the crime, for example, increasing a misdemeanor to a felony or a lower-grade felony to one of greater severity.[65] Moreover, penalty-enhancement crimes may mandate an enhancement of the sentence or may provide discretion to the sentencing judge to increase the penalty if she deems it appropriate to do so.[66] All penalty-enhancement laws thus derive from some other criminal law. Pure bias crime laws, by contrast, create a free-standing prohibition of some bias-motivated conduct. On the surface, this appears to be a distinction with significance. As Tribe stated:

> Enhancing a criminal sentence for any "hate crime" . . . in no way creates a "thought crime" or penalizes anyone's conduct based upon a non-proscribable viewpoint or message that such conduct contains or expresses. In this crucial respect, the trigger for enhanced punishment [laws] differs completely from the constitutionally problematic trigger for punishment under the St. Paul ordinance struck down by the Supreme Court in the *R.A.V.* case.[67]

Pure bias crime laws, however, are free-standing in appearance only. If there is any distinction between pure bias crime laws and penalty-enhancement laws, it is that the former rely upon other criminal statues implicitly whereas the latter rely explicitly. The insignificance of this distinction flows from the very idea of a bias crime.

Recall that a concept of two tiers is inherent in bias crimes and that every bias crime contains within it a "parallel" crime against person or property. In *R.A.V.*, for example, the parallel crimes of trespass and vandalism existed alongside the bias crime charged in the case.[68] The bias crime consisted of a parallel crime with the addition of bias motivation.

A pure bias crime law, therefore, derives from some other criminal provision in the same manner that a penalty-enhancement law does. The distinction is strictly a matter of form. The nature of the derivative relationship is made explicit in the instance of the penalty-enhancement law. For pure bias crime laws, the derivation, although implicit, is no less real. If we conclude, therefore, that pure bias crime laws impermissibly punish ideas and expression, surely so do penalty-enhancement laws. In each case, the criminal act has already been punished through the imposition of a sentence for the predicate offense (for a penalty-enhancement law) or the parallel crime (for a pure bias crime law). Alternatively, if there exists a constitutional basis for imposing an increased sentence under a penalty-enhancement law, this same basis will justify the imposition of a sentence under a pure bias crime law. The distinction between the descriptions of the two types of bias crime laws, therefore, cannot provide the constitutional basis for the punishment of bias crimes.

Before moving on to a proposed resolution of the bias crimes–hate speech paradox, I should make one final observation about the distinction relied upon by Tribe and Abrams. Their congressional testimony represented a project very different from that of this book. In their testimony, Tribe and Abrams took the Court's decision in *R.A.V.* as a given and attempted to argue that H.R. 4797 was nonetheless constitutional. This was particularly true of Tribe, who did not endorse *R.A.V.* as much as he accepted it. Abrams, both in his testimony and elsewhere, explicitly embraced the position of the majority in *R.A.V.* He testified that "I appear before you as someone who welcomed and publicly praised the Supreme Court's recent ruling in *R.A.V. v. City of St. Paul* . . . Justice Scalia's ruling for the Court . . . seemed to me not only correct but admirable."[69]

I press the more fundamental questions concerning the strength of *R.A.V.,* particularly in light of the subsequent decision by the Supreme Court in *Mitchell.* Although I share with Abrams and Tribe a pragmatic interest in an expanded federal role in bias crime law enforcement, I nonetheless maintain that the distinction between pure bias crimes and penalty-enhancement laws is, in the final analysis, untenable.

## Bias Crimes and Parallel Crimes

### *The* Mens Rea *of Bias Crimes and Racist Speech*

Bias crimes and racist speech cannot be distinguished by differentiating speech from conduct or pure bias crime laws from penalty-enhancement laws. The distinction, however, can be maintained.

My proposed distinction begins with the recognition that, even without the actor's racial motivation, his commission of a bias crime may be proscribed and may, in turn, be punished. The same cannot be said of racist speech. Without racial content, there is no suggestion that speech could be or should be prohibited.

We must return to the concept of the bias crime as a two-tiered crime in order to develop fully the implications of this observation. As noted in earlier chapters, the distinction between parallel crimes and bias crimes looks both to the resulting harm of the criminal act and to the culpability of the criminal actor. A racially motivated assault, in addition to causing the general harm that any assault might cause, frequently also causes an additional harm. The victim suffers for being singled out on the basis of her race, and the general community of the target racial group suffers harm as well. The harm caused by bias crimes thus exceeds that caused by parallel crimes. This is why bias crimes warrant enhanced punishment.

When we focus on individual guilt, however, the distinction between bias crimes and parallel crimes rests on the actor's state of mind. To establish a bias crime, the prosecution must prove two essentially unrelated mental state, or *mens rea*, elements. The first of these is the *mens rea* that is applicable to the parallel crime, for example, the specific intent to commit an assault. In addition to this "first-tier" *mens rea*, the prosecution must demonstrate that bias motivated the accused in the commission of the parallel crime. This second-tier *mens rea* for bias crimes involves motive and ordinarily serves a function similar to a required *mens rea* of purpose. As we saw, in certain circumstances, purpose may not be required in cases where the accused knew that his conduct reflected the bias of others. This was the case of the Violent Show-Off, who knew of his friends' animus and chose his victim to further that animus.

Now we may return to the distinction between bias crimes and racist speech. The perpetrator of each has the requisite second-tier *mens rea* of bias motivation. As to first-tier *mens rea*, however, the two perpetrators are critically different. Consider first the perpetrator of a bias crime such as the racially motivated assault in *Wisconsin v. Mitchell*. The requisite *mens rea* for the parallel crime will generally be "recklessness" (that is, conscious disregard of a substantial and unjustifiable risk of causing harm to another), "knowledge" (that is, awareness of the virtual certainty that this harm will occur), or "purpose" to assault another (that is, conscious desire to cause this harm).[70] But if first-tier *mens rea* is absent, there can be no overall culpability for the bias crime.

Consider the speaker of racist speech. He lacks the first-tier *mens rea* for any parallel crime. When it comes to his "parallel behavior," his *mens rea*,if this is even the proper term here, is strictly one of expressing himself. This is not to suggest that the speaker's act of expressing himself is purely deontological. To the contrary, all expression has ramifications. As Oliver Wendell Holmes wrote in his celebrated dissent in the *Gitlow* case, "every idea is an incitement."[71] The speaker of racist speech, however, does not seek to cause injury to a particular victim and thus lacks the *mens rea* associated with a parallel crime of assault or a similar personal crime.

This distinction, though keyed to first-tier *mens rea,* does not resurrect the overly simplistic speech-conduct distinction that, as we saw, largely assumed its own conclusions. The "perpetrator" of racist speech lacks the first-tier *mens rea* for a parallel crime whether his "speech" takes the form of thinking, talking, flying a flag, or painting a sign. His behavior—which we, along with Ely, may assume is 100 percent action and 100 percent expression—does not constitute a parallel crime.

The facts of *R.A.V., Mitchell,* and *Wyant* provide a helpful means of testing this framework for distinguishing bias crimes and racist speech. These cases cover a broad sweep of potential bias crimes. We begin with *Mitchell* because the facts of this case best illustrate the dichotomy between bias crimes and racist speech. As noted, prior to the beating of Riddick, Mitchell and a group of about ten others were discussing the movie *Mississippi Burning,* particularly a scene in which a white man beat up a young black child who was praying. Mitchell asked the group, "Do you all feel hyped up to move on some white people?"[72] Plainly, Mitchell's comments reflected "bias motivation," but just as plainly he had not yet committed any parallel crime. Had he stopped at this point, his actions would have constituted racist speech but not a bias crime. Unfortunately, he did not stop there. Mitchell intentionally directed and encouraged the group to attack Riddick and thus was a party to the beating. This conscious desire constitutes the first-tier *mens rea* for the parallel crime of battery, or, more specifically, complicity in the crime of battery. Additionally, Mitchell purposely chose the victim because he was white. The victimization of Riddick based on his race constitutes the second-tier *mens rea.* Mitchell's parallel crime of battery merits punishment. The animus underlying his choice of a victim is an aggravated form of that parallel crime. In effect, Mitchell was punished not for his earlier racist statement, but only for his later criminal conduct that would have violated a discriminatory selection bias crime statute or a racial animus statute. Mitchell thus committed a bias crime and did not engage in merely unpunishable racist speech.

The case of Robert Viktora is slightly more complex. Viktora acted with the first-tier *mens rea* of purpose when he intentionally trespassed upon the lawn of his victims and committed acts of vandalism on their property. He also acted with the requisite second-tier *mens rea* owing to the racial animus that led him to target the Jones family. One of Viktora's accomplices in the cross-burning, Arthur Morris Miller, 3rd, who, prior to the Supreme Court's opinion in *R.A.V.*, pleaded guilty to a violation of the St. Paul ordinance, subsequently also pleaded guilty to a charge under federal housing law, for conspiring to interfere with the Jones family's right of access to housing by intimidation and the threat of force. In his federal plea, Miller acknowledged that he and his accomplices burned the crosses with the intention of frightening the Jones family into moving because they were African-Americans.[73]

What makes Viktora's case more complicated than Mitchell's is that Viktora did not merely commit a racially motivated trespass. He burned a cross. Whereas we might be tempted to address *Mitchell* by resurrecting the expression-conduct distinction and asserting that Mitchell's assault of Riddick was utterly devoid of expressive content, there is no such way out when considering *R.A.V.* Certainly Viktora's conduct carried a strong communicative content. As a result, more than the straightforward assault in *Mitchell*, it triggers unavoidable First Amendment concern. Because his cross-burning was 100 percent action and 100 percent expression, we must ask precisely what is the parallel crime Robert Viktora committed in burning a cross on the Jones's lawn. Put somewhat differently, suppose that Viktora had burned the cross just outside the Jones's property line, and further suppose that in St. Paul there is no local ordinance banning the burning of nontoxic materials on a public street. Is Viktora innocent of all relevant parallel crimes, and thus also innocent of a bias crime?

The question is more clearly focused when we turn to the case of David Wyant, who was convicted of ethnic intimidation solely on the basis of using words in an offensive and threatening manner. Wyant and his family had rented adjoining campsites. They released one of the sites, which thereafter was leased by Jerry White and Patricia McGowan, both of whom are black. Wyant tried unsuccessfully to re-rent the adjoining site and, when unsuccessful, rented the next site over. During the evening, White and McGowan complained to park officials about the loud music from Wyant's campsite. Wyant at first complied with an official's request to turn the music down, but fifteen or twenty minutes later he turned the music up again. In a loud voice, Wyant was heard to say, "We didn't have this problem until those niggers moved in next to us," "I ought to shoot that black mother fucker," and "I ought to kick his black ass." White and McGowan complained and then left the park.[74]

Did Wyant commit a bias crime, and if so, what is the parallel crime here?

If indeed there was not a parallel crime, then Wyant's words constituted protected racist speech. Wyant's actions pose difficulties for categorization because they seem to involve only the speaking of words. On the surface, there is only the expression of a racist message and no parallel crime for expression of some other message.

But this surface understanding is wrong. It overlooks the fact that words alone can sometimes constitute a parallel crime. Behavior designed to instill serious fear certainly may be criminalized, and it does not matter whether it takes the form of spoken words alone, physical conduct alone, or some combination of the two. Many states have some form of assault law that proscribes the creation of fear or terror in a victim.[75] These laws, variously enacted as "menacing," "intimidation," and "threatening" statutes, may be violated through the defendant's use of words alone.[76]

Reviewing courts have upheld various forms of verbal assault statutes, if sufficiently narrow in focus. Intimidation statutes, which criminalize words used to coerce others through fear of serious harm, are constitutional so long as it is clear that they apply only when the words are purposely or knowingly used by the accused to produce fear and that the threat is real.[77] Menacing statutes differ from intimidation statutes. Whereas intimidation statutes focus upon coercion, the gravamen of menacing is the specific intent to cause fear.[78] Finally, "terroristic threatening" statutes are similar to intimidation laws in that they criminalize the use of fear to achieve specific results.[79] In each case, verbal assault statutes make words alone the basis for a criminal charge when those words are used purposely or knowingly to create fear in another.

Returning to Wyant's case, our attention is refocused on his first-tier *mens rea*. If Wyant intended his abusive language to create fear in White and McGowan, or if Wyant knew that his language would do so, he committed a parallel crime of verbal assault. Accordingly, if he did so with racial motivation, he committed a bias crime. If, by contrast, Wyant lacked the requisite first-tier *mens rea* for a verbal assault, then, rather than committing a bias crime, Wyant expressed a racist message. By saying "expression of a racist message," I am not invoking the rejected speech-conduct distinction. Again, it does not matter whether the racist speech takes the form of a racial epithet or burning a cross on one's own property. Analogous behavior is a crime only when the actor's purpose is to put his victim in a state of fear of imminent serious harm. When he does so with racial motivation, such behavior is a bias crime. Thus the epithet, when screamed at the victim in a menacing manner, or the cross, when burned on or near the lawn of a black family to terrorize them, is no longer just racist speech; it is a bias crime.

## A New Understanding of "Fighting Words"

We can now place the understanding of verbal assaults in general, and verbal bias crimes in particular, within the broader context of First Amendment law. Far from being dissonant with contemporary First Amendment doctrine, the identification of the verbal assault, as distinct from protected speech, provides a firm basis for a reworking of the long-established but thinly constructed "fighting words" doctrine. In the half-century since the United States Supreme Court introduced the term "fighting words" into First Amendment jurisprudence in *Chaplinsky v. New Hampshire*,[80] the definition and scope of the fighting words doctrine have remained unclear at best.[81]

Before proposing a reformation of the fighting words doctrine, we should review the creation of the doctrine in *Chaplinsky* and its difficulties since then. Over time, the Supreme Court reinterpreted *Chaplinsky*, both directly and indirectly, so that the fighting word exception as originally understood lacks coherence as First Amendment doctrine.

In 1942, Walter Chaplinsky was convicted of violating a New Hampshire ordinance that made it illegal to "call . . . [anyone] by any offensive or derisive name." The ordinance under which Chaplinsky was convicted provided:

> No person shall address any offensive, derisive or annoying word to any other person who is lawfully in any street or other public place, nor call him by any offensive or derisive name, nor make any noise or exclamation in his presence and hearing with intent to deride, offend or annoy him, or to prevent him from pursuing his lawful business or occupation.

This law still exists in New Hampshire with only slight modification. Although *Chaplinsky* enjoys an illustrious history as the source of the fighting words doctrine, there are no other reported New Hampshire cases prosecuted under the disorderly conduct statute for the use of fighting words.[82]

Chaplinsky, a Jehovah's Witness, had been distributing religious literature on the streets of Rochester, New Hampshire, on a busy Saturday afternoon. A resentful crowd gathered around Chaplinsky, and a city marshal arrived at the scene, telling the crowd that Chaplinsky was permitted to pass out his leaflets but warning Chaplinsky that the crowd was "getting restless and that he should better go slow." Some time later, a disturbance did occur and Chaplinsky was escorted by a police officer toward the police station. En route, Chaplinsky encountered the city marshal and said, "You are a God damned racketeer . . . a damned fascist and the whole government of Rochester are Fascists or agents of Fascists."[83] Such words today might barely be enough to raise an eyebrow. At the time, however, Chaplinsky's behavior was considered outrageous.

In a brief opinion for a unanimous Court, Justice Frank Murphy upheld Chaplinsky's conviction. Citing only Zechariah Chafee's *Free Speech in the United States*[84] for support, Justice Murphy embraced the categorical approach to First Amendment jurisprudence and asserted that there are

> certain well-defined and narrowly limited classes of speech, the prevention and punishment of which has never been thought to raise any Constitutional problem. These include the lewd and obscene, the profane, the libelous, and the insulting or "fighting" words.[85]

In the course of the opinion, Justice Murphy proffered two largely overlapping definitions for the term "fighting words." The first definition itself had two parts: "fighting words" are "those which [1] by their very utterance inflict injury or [2] tend to incite an immediate breach of the peace."[86] The second definition, which came from the construction placed upon the New Hampshire law by that state's highest court, was restricted to clause 2: "The statute's purpose was to preserve the public peace. The direct tendency of [the proscribed] conduct . . . is to provoke the person against whom it is directed to acts of violence."[87]

The first definition provided two possible meanings: (1) words that *inflict injury* and (2) words that tend to incite an immediate breach of the peace. The New Hampshire court's construction contained only the breach-of-the-peace concept. Justice Murphy incorporated this construction into his conclusion. The prosecution of Chaplinsky and the law under which it was brought were upheld because the "statute [was] narrowly drawn and limited to define and punish specific conduct lying within the domain of state power, the use in a public place of words likely to cause a breach of the peace."[88]

Thus, the fighting words exception that emerged from *Chaplinsky* was limited to words so insulting as to threaten a breach of the peace. The only defendant whose conduct the Supreme Court has ever found to constitute the use of fighting words was Walter Chaplinsky himself; the Court narrowed the standard each time it applied it. In *Cohen v. California,* for example, the Court upheld the right of Paul Robert Cohen to wear his now-famous "Fuck the Draft" jacket in a Los Angeles courthouse.[89] Cohen had been convicted under a California breach-of-the-peace statute for "offensive conduct" that was defined as "behavior which has a tendency to provoke *others* to acts of violence or in turn disturb the peace."[90] Though the Court reasserted its holding in *Chaplinsky,* thus allowing states "to ban the simple use, without demonstration of additional justifying circumstances, of so-called 'fighting words,'" and also recognized that the phrase used by Cohen "is not uncommonly employed in a personally provocative manner," the Court nonetheless refused to uphold the defendant's conviction for use of fighting words.[91] The Court held that to be guilty of using fighting words, an individual must direct "personally abusive epithets" at a specific individual. Ely observed that, after *Cohen,* "'fighting words' are unprotected, but that category is no longer to be understood as a euphemism for either controversial or dirty talk but requires instead an unambiguous invitation to a brawl."[92]

Three years after *Cohen,* in *Lewis v. New Orleans,* the Court concluded that even profanity and "abusive epithets," allegedly directed at a police officer by the mother of a young man who had just been arrested, did not constitute "fighting words" absent an actual fist fight.[93] Supporting the Court's *per curiam* opinion that the Louisiana statute at issue in *Lewis* was overbroad on its face, Justice Powell stated that

> words may or may not be "fighting words," depending upon the circumstances of their utterance. It is unlikely, for example, that the words said to have been used here would have precipitated a physical confrontation between the middle-aged woman who spoke them and the police officer in whose presence they were uttered.[94]

In effect, "fighting words" can only be uttered to those individuals who are predisposed to fight.[95]

Once the Court abandoned a reading of fighting words as "[words] which by their very utterance inflict injury" in favor of those that "tend to incite an immediate breach of the peace," the fighting words doctrine was doomed to virtual insignificance. Reading "fighting words" as those likely to inspire violence by the addressee has several problems. First, taken literally, this would provide precisely the kind of "heckler's veto" that the Supreme Court properly rejected more than twenty years ago. While recognizing the need to preserve public safety,[96] the Court has refused to allow suppression of speech solely because the crowd was offended or violent.[97] Heckling necessitates added protection for the speaker; it certainly does not warrant his being silenced.

There is a second problem with interpreting fighting words strictly as those likely to inspire violence. This interpretation "protects" those addressees who need it least: those inclined and able to fight back. The problem is not merely that the standard of the reasonably pugilistic addressee is probably androcentric.[98] The problem is that the most severely injured victim of fighting words—the person who is reasonably and sincerely placed in great fear of imminent serious bodily harm—is the person least likely to fight back.

In light of these problems, the fighting words doctrine finds a much firmer footing in the concept of verbal assault developed above. If *Chaplinsky* is to maintain any contemporary vitality, it must be understood to place outside the First Amendment's reach those words that are intended to and have the likely effect of creating fear of injury in the addressee. Words that have the intent to hurt the addressee's feelings, even those that also have that effect, however unfortunate, do not come under this understanding of fighting words.

We can now return to the context of bias motivation. The proposed understanding of fighting words is consistent with the distinction between prosecutable bias crimes and protected racial speech. The theory does not rely on the speech-conduct dichotomy. Racially targeted actions that are intended to create fear in the addressee and that are likely to do so may be treated as bias crimes whether the behavior is primarily the use of words or a physical act. Conversely, racially targeted behavior that vents the actor's racism is racial speech that is protected by the First Amendment, even if it disturbs the observer greatly.

## The Role of Content Neutrality and the Intent-Motivation Distinction

Two sets of arguments have been advanced in opposition to the constitutionality of bias crime laws. The first returns us to Justice Scalia's argument in *R.A.V.* that the St. Paul ordinance impermissibly regulated speech based on its content. Writing for the majority in *R.A.V.*, Justice Scalia accepted the

Minnesota Supreme Court's construction of the St. Paul ordinance as a regulation applying only to fighting words.[99] He held, however, that the ordinance violated principles of content neutrality because it applied only to bias-motivated fighting words.

> Those who wish to use "fighting words" in connection with other ideas to express hostility, for example, on the basis of political affiliation, union membership, or homosexuality are not covered. The First Amendment does not permit St. Paul to impose special prohibitions on those speakers who express views on disfavored subjects.[100]

Thus, Justice Scalia held that fighting words could "be regulated because of their constitutionally proscribable content," but they could not be further regulated based on the content of the offensive message.[101]

At a certain level, Justice Scalia is correct: content neutrality places certain restrictions upon the state's ability to proscribe fighting words. Surely, a state could not criminalize only those fighting words that are addressed toward members of a particular political party. To do so would be to establish a plain legislative preference for one political party and against another or all others. Such approval and disapproval of a set of political ideas by the state is anathema to basic First Amendment principles.

To accept some role of content neutrality, however, does not require Justice Scalia's all-or-nothing-at-all approach. It is not necessary to prohibit either all fighting words or none. Were that the case, virtually all criminal laws would raise issues of content neutrality. But a state may properly make a judgment that, within the universe of assaults, some are worse than others. For instance, an assault with a deadly weapon is, in most states, some form of aggravated assault.[102] The crime is more serious than unarmed assault because the defendant has exposed society to greater risk—even if the weapon is not actually used—and has presumably caused greater fear in the victim. These differences justify an increased penalty for the crime. Similarly, a state may determine that assaults based on race are worse than comparable assaults, because these racially motivated assaults cause greater societal harm and injury to the individual and community victims.

The initial response to this argument is that the actor who assaults with a deadly weapon has not sought to "express" anything. Hence, the state makes no content-based determination when it seeks to punish this actor more severely than one who commits a simple assault. This response, however, is flawed in that it relies on the discredited speech-conduct distinction. Once it is recognized that any public act contains elements of both expression and conduct, it is impossible to rationalize certain legislative determinations as implicating only conduct and others as implicating only expression.

The recognition that expression and conduct are analytically inseparable does not deprive the First Amendment of vigor. It does, however, strongly suggest that the traditional content-neutrality inquiry poses the wrong question. The proper inquiry is that articulated by the Court in the draft card–burning case, *United States v. O'Brien:*[103] "[A] governmental regulation is sufficiently justified . . . if it furthers an important or substantial governmental interest [that] is unrelated to the suppression of free expression."[104] In *O'Brien*, the Court concluded that regulations prohibiting the destruction of draft cards furthered the important governmental interest of maintaining selective service records, an interest unrelated to the suppression of expression.

In effect, the *O'Brien* test requires more than a mere articulation of some legitimate interest by the state. A state could always claim an interest. As Ely observed, "[r]estrictions on free expression are rarely defended on the ground that the state simply didn't like what the defendant was saying."[105] The state must therefore advance a nonpretextual justification for the distinctions drawn in its criminal law, a justification that stands independent of any effort to suppress the expression of ideas.

Consider the example of the federal criminal law that explicitly defines the assassination or threatened assassination of the President of the United States as a crime that is unlike any other murder.[106] In *R.A.V.*, Justice Scalia expressly stated that this statute satisfied the requirements of content neutrality because the distinction "consists entirely of the very reason the entire class of speech at issue is proscribable."[107] This reasoning warrants closer analysis. According to Justice Scalia, the reasons threats of physical violence are exempt from First Amendment protection in the first place are: "protecting individuals from the fear of violence, from the disruption that fear engenders, and from the possibility that the threatened violence will occur."[108] These three reasons, he held, "have special force when applied to the person of the President."[109] The government could not, however, "criminalize only those threats against the President that mention his policy on aid to inner cities."[110]

Justice Scalia's analysis thus constructs three levels of specificity at which threats might be criminalized:

(1) all threats of physical violence against another person;

(2) all threats of physical violence against the President of the United States; and

(3) all threats of physical violence against the President of the United States because of a particular policy.

Whereas both 1 and 2 are permissible, 3 is not. Although I share these conclusions, Justice Scalia's own reasoning in *R.A.V.* provides insufficient support for them. Format 2 is "content-neutral" because threats are outside the scope of the First Amendment. But a threat against the President could be better described as consisting of two components. The first is a simple threat against a person. The punishment of this component of the threat against the President is fully covered by format 1. The second component of the threat against the President is a particularly virulent opposition to the President. This opposition might stem from a single policy of the President's or from an array of causes. Seen in this light, 2 is no more content-neutral than is 3. Formats 2 and 3 differ only in their level of specificity, not in their "neutrality" as to content.

We can better understand the acceptability of 1 and 2 and the impermissibility of 3 through application of the *O'Brien* test as developed above. The state can articulate numerous reasons for format 1 other than the suppression of expression. The following, in fact, are the reasons set out by Justice Scalia: the need to protect the populace from the fear of violence, from the negative consequences of this fear, and from the possibility that the threatened violence may occur. Similarly, there are legitimate reasons for format 2. The federal government reasonably fears that violence directed against the President will cause serious injury to the nation. This avenue of expressing opposition to the President is therefore foreclosed. Finally, format 3 may not be justified by legitimate reasons. By criminalizing threats against the President only insofar as they manifest an opposition to a particular policy, the government would express a preference for certain policies as against others and act to suppress only opposition to those policies. Under the *O'Brien* standard, this is not allowed.

I now return to the context of bias crimes. The critical question is similarly not whether bias crime laws are, in some technical sense, content-neutral. Clearly they are not. Bias crime laws select a subset from the universe of parallel crimes. They do so on the basis of the actor's racially based selection of a victim under discriminatory selection statutes and on the basis of his animus under the racial animus model. Similarly, we saw that the government may select a subset from all threats of violence on the basis of the actor's motivation when that motivation leads to the selection of the President as the victim.

We must then subject bias crime statutes to the same test that explained the permissibility of laws punishing threats directed against the President. We must ask whether bias crime statutes further an important interest unrelated to the suppression of racist speech. The evidence is compelling that they do. The state interests served by laws specifically targeting bias crimes include many of the issues that we have addressed: the need to deter generally a rapidly increasing form of crime and to deter specifically a perpetrator with a high degree of potential dangerousness, and the desire to address a crime that has a particularly injurious effect on the victim, the targeted group, and the society at large.

Bias crime statutes thus stand on grounds wholly independent of efforts to suppress racist speech. Hence the standard articulated in *O'Brien*, which ought to inform the inquiry as to the constitutionality of these criminal prohibitions, is satisfied.

### The Punishment of Racially Motivated Violence

There is an additional argument against the constitutionality of bias crime laws, drawn from a blend of First Amendment doctrine and substantive criminal law, that was advanced by the Wisconsin and Ohio Supreme Courts, in *Mitchell* and *Wyant* respectively, and that was argued to the Supreme Court in both *R.A.V.* and *Mitchell*. The state courts in *Mitchell* and *Wyant* held that bias crime laws impermissibly strayed beyond the punishment of act and purposeful intent and went on to punish motivation. As the Wisconsin Supreme Court in *Mitchell* held:

> Because all of the [parallel] crimes are already punishable, all that remains is an additional punishment for the defendant's motive in selecting the victim. The punishment of the defendant's bigoted motive by the hate crimes statute directly implicates and encroaches upon First Amendment rights.[111]

These holdings, however, are not required by a careful analysis of the relevant doctrines. We begin with the positive law, the approach taken by the Supreme Court in *Wisconsin v. Mitchell*, and then turn to normative argument.

Purely as a matter of positive law, concern with the punishment of motivation is misplaced. Motive often determines punishment. In those states with capital punishment, the defendant's motivation for the homicide stands prominent among the recognized aggravating factors that may contribute to the imposition of the death sentence. For instance, the motivation of profit in murder cases is a significant aggravating factor adopted in most capital sentencing schemes.[112]

Bias motivation itself may serve as an aggravating circumstance. In *Barclay v. Florida*,[113] the Supreme Court explicitly upheld the use of racial bias as an aggravating factor in the sentencing phase of a capital case. The Court reaffirmed *Barclay* in 1992 in *Dawson v. Delaware*.[114] The prosecution in *Dawson* sought to use the defendant's membership in the Aryan Brotherhood as an aggravating circumstance. The Court rejected the prosecution argument but only because the defendant had been convicted of a same-race murder, not a bias-motivated murder, and because the prosecution did not argue that the defendant's relationship with the Aryan Brotherhood indicated a propensity for future violence. In this case, therefore, the evidence was deemed irrelevant and thus inadmissible. But in reaching that holding, the Court reaffirmed the holding in *Barclay* that evidence of racial intolerance and subversive advocacy was admissible when such evidence was relevant to the issues involved in sentencing.[115] Moreover, several federal civil rights crime statutes explicitly make racial motivation an element of criminal liability.[116]

Finally, racial motivation is the *sine qua non* for a large set of civil antidiscrimination laws governing discrimination in employment[117] and housing,[118] among others. In most states, for example, unless an employment contract or collective bargaining agreement provides otherwise, an employer may fire an employee for any reason at all or for no reason whatsoever. Under federal (and often state) civil rights laws, however, this same firing becomes illegal if it is motivated by the employee's race or a number of other protected characteristics. Thus the only way to determine whether such a firing is legal or not is to inquire at some level into the motivation of the employer. If bias crime laws unconstitutionally punish motivation as a matter of First Amendment doctrine, then this argument should apply with equal weight to those statutory schemes that authorize civil damage awards for otherwise permissible actions such as discharging an at-will employee. No one has seriously challenged civil antidiscrimination laws on this basis, nor would any court uphold such a challenge. Bias crime laws do not raise a different issue in any relevant manner.

The second flaw with the argument that motive may not be a basis for punishment is somewhat more abstract. The argument against the punishment of motive is necessarily premised on the assertion that motive can be distinguished from *mens rea,* that is, that motive can be distinguished from intent. Plainly, an actor's intent is a permissible basis for punishment. Indeed, as shown, intent serves as the organizing mechanism of modern theories of criminal punishment. Specifically, intent concerns the mental state provided in the definition of an offense for assessing the actor's culpability with respect to the elements of the offense.[119] Motive, by contrast, concerns the cause that drives the actor to commit the offense.[120] On this formal level, motive and intent may be distinguished. The state Supreme Courts in both *Mitchell* and *Wyant* relied upon this formal distinction.[121]

The distinction between intent and motive does not hold the weight that the *Mitchell* and *Wyant* state courts placed upon it because the decision as to what constitutes motive and what constitutes intent depends on what is being criminalized. Criminal statutes define the elements of the crime, and a mental state applies to each element. The mental state that applies to an element of the crime we will call "intent," whereas any mental states that are extrinsic to the elements we will call "motivation." The formal distinction, therefore, turns entirely on what are considered to be the elements of the crime. What is a matter of intent in one context may be a matter of motive in another. Consider the bias crime of a racially motivated assault upon an African-American. There are two equally accurate descriptions of this crime, that is, two different ways in which a state might define the elements of this bias crime: one describes the bias as a matter of *intent;* the other, as a separate matter of *motive.* The perpetrator of this crime could be seen as either

(1) possessing a *mens rea* of purpose with respect to the assault, along with a *motivation* of racial bias; or
(2) possessing a first-tier *mens rea* of purpose with respect to the parallel crime of assault and a second-tier *mens rea* of purpose with respect to assaulting *this* victim because of his race.

Either description accurately describes that which a state could criminalize by a bias crime law. Moreover, either description is valid regardless of whether a state has adopted the racial animus model or the discriminatory selection model for its bias crime law. The defendant in description 1 "intends" to assault his victim and does so *because* the defendant is a racist. The defendant in description 2 "intends" to assault an African-American and does so with both an intent to assault and a discriminatory or animus-driven intent as to the selection of the victim.

Because both descriptions are accurate, the formal distinction between intent and motive fails. Whether bias crime laws punish motivation or intent is not inherent in those prohibitions. Rather, the distinction simply mirrors the way in which we choose to describe them. The decision by a state to enhance the punishment of racially motivated violence, therefore, raises neither pragmatic nor practical problems concerning a punishment of motivation. Properly understood, bias crime laws punish motivation no more than do criminal proscriptions generally.

## CHAPTER 6

# What Is the Federal Role
# in Prosecuting Bias Crimes?

Bias crimes, as stated at the outset, occur at the intersection of three fundamental values of the American polity: equality, free expression, and federalism. We have now come to the third of the three fundamental questions spawned by these values. The answer to each of the first two questions has been "yes." A society that is dedicated to equality must treat bias crimes differently from other crimes, and must enhance the punishment of these crimes; a society that is also dedicated to freedom of expression and belief may do so. The third question raises issues of intergovernmental allocation of authority: Is a prominent federal role in the prosecution and punishment of bias crimes consistent with the proper division of authority between state (and local) government and the federal government in our political system? If this question is not uniquely American—Australia, Canada, and Germany, for example, have federal systems of government—it is still a peculiarly American question to be asking. The following true story illustrates the issues raised.

On May 29, 1980, in Ft. Wayne, Indiana, an assassin attempted to kill Vernon Jordan, then president of the National Urban League. Fortunately, the attempt was unsuccessful—Jordan survived, and is now a prominent Washington, D.C., lawyer and Presidential advisor. Within a day or so of the shooting, national news carried a story that the FBI had commenced an investigation to determine whether the assassination attempt constituted a violation of Jordan's civil rights.[1] Shortly thereafter, I received a phone call from a nonlawyer who is fascinated by legal issues and delights in calling with strange legal puzzles that arise from current events. He wanted to know why anyone would question seriously whether Jordan's civil rights had been violated; someone had, after all, tried to kill him.

The answer to this question begins with the deceptively simple fact that murder, the most serious crime of all, is not a federal crime. Certain murders—those in which specific federal issues are implicated—are federal crimes. For example, it is a federal crime to murder the President of the United States[2] or certain other federal officials,[3] or foreign officials and official governmental guests.[4] But as a general matter, murder is a state-law crime. Thus, while the state of Indiana and the Ft. Wayne law enforcement community had an attempted murder to investigate, the Federal Bureau of Investigation and the United States Department of Justice would have no jurisdiction at all, unless there had been a violation of Vernon Jordan's federal civil rights.

The proper role for federal law enforcement in civil rights crimes generally and bias crimes in particular occupies a significant place in the study of American bias crime law. More than any event in the recent past, the videotaped beating of Rodney King and the subsequent trial and acquittal of the officers charged with the attack focused the nation on federal civil rights crimes. Even as post-acquittal rioting enveloped Los Angeles, attention was turned to the potential for a federal civil rights prosecution of those who beat King.[5]

The beating of King on March 3, 1991, by officers of the Los Angeles Police Department riveted public attention in an extraordinary way. It is not altogether clear, however, which aspects of the beating gave rise to this focus. The King incident may be seen as a case of police brutality, an extreme excessive use of official force that transcends the race of both the officers and the victim. Alternatively, the King incident may be seen as a case of racially motivated violence, a beating that occurred because the victim was black. In fact, the beating of Rodney King may well have involved aspects of both. Consideration and analysis of these alternative formulations, however, are critical to understanding what took place on March 3, 1991, and what the proper response of federal law enforcement should have been.

Up to this point, we have been concerned exclusively with bias crimes. Although this chapter, too, will ultimately focus attention on federal bias crime law, we must first broaden the study to those crimes—bias crimes and police brutality included—that have historically been grouped together as "civil rights crimes." A review of the development of federal civil rights crimes since the Civil War demonstrates that the federal government has a significant role to play in the investigation, prosecution, and punishment of bias crimes.

First we must frame the "federalism problem." We begin with a brief examination of the questions posed by federalism for criminal law generally. Federalism, for our purposes, concerns the respective roles of state and federal criminal law enforcement. At its core, it is the search for appropriate limits on federal criminal jurisdiction over civil rights violations. Given the broadest possible construction, federal civil rights crimes could expand federal criminal law into all or virtually all areas of traditional state criminal law. The federalism problem is not strictly about the limits of constitutional authority for federal criminal jurisdiction. Clearly these constitutional boundaries play some role here; the starting point for judicial or legislative analysis of the federalism problem is often determining the limits of federal authority under the Reconstruction-era amendments to the Constitution. The federalism problem, however, goes beyond locating constitutional boundaries. It also considers prudential issues concerning the optimal allocation of the criminal enforcement function in our federal system.

The balance of the chapter focuses on federalism in the context of civil rights crimes and, more particularly, bias crimes. I outline the development of federal civil rights crimes through the first century of civil rights crimes enforcement. This century is bracketed by the two great periods of congressional enactment of civil rights legislation, the "First Reconstruction," during the 1860s and 1870s, and the "Second Reconstruction," during the 1960s. The Historical Appendix to this book presents a comprehensive history of the federal legal response to racial violence in America. The text addresses the history of the role that the federalism problem has played in the development of the federal legal response to racial violence in America.

A common thread runs throughout the discussion of the first seventy-five years following the Civil War—from the origins of the federalism problem during the Civil War, to the legislative and executive commitment to vigorous civil rights enforcement during the First Reconstruction, to the judicial retrenchment that followed and the ultimate abandonment of civil rights enforcement by all three branches of the federal government. The First Reconstruction-era Congresses that passed the first civil rights statutes saw criminal sanctions as a critical part of the civil rights enforcement arsenal. Sanctions were aimed at private perpetrators of racially motivated violence and public perpetrators of violence generally. Through this legislation, Congress sought to protect newly freed blacks and to guard against politically motivated violence directed at Southern Unionists. The general intent behind the criminal civil rights laws called for vigorous enforcement to address a compelling social ill.

Analysis of the federal judiciary's role over the following century, as well as that of the federal executive branch, reveals a much narrower view of civil rights crimes than was intended by the drafters of those laws. From the beginning, the development of federal criminal civil rights law—the potentially broad language of the statutes, the congressional debates about those statutes, and the increasingly narrow interpretation of their scope by the Supreme Court and the Department of Justice—has been driven in large part by a concern with federalism. I do not question the legitimacy of federalism as an issue that requires resolution for a coherent theory of federal criminal civil rights enforcement. But present doctrine has failed to address these problems adequately.

The exploration of the federalism problem continues with *Screws v. United States,* which warrants in-depth discussion for several reasons.[6] *Screws* is the most significant criminal civil rights case decided by the Supreme Court since the end of the First Reconstruction. It still represents the touchstone for current federal criminal civil rights doctrine. The discussions of the federalism problem in both the plurality and the main dissenting opinion in *Screws* demonstrate both the complexity of the issues involved and the flaws in the approaches that have been advocated. The decades following *Screws* saw federal recommitment to civil rights enforcement, culminating in the enactment of federal civil rights crimes law during the Second Reconstruction.

Finally, I will bring the discussion up to the present by examining three interrelated issues of contemporary significance: first, as a matter of constitutional authority, whether a federal bias crime law is authorized; second, as a matter of public policy, whether such legislation is warranted; and third, returning to one of the problems raised by the Rodney King beating trials, what the relationship ought to be between federal and state law enforcement authorities in enforcing civil rights generally and bias crime laws in particular.

## The Federalism Problem in Criminal Law Enforcement

Chief Justice Earl Warren observed, "It is essential that we achieve a proper jurisdictional balance between the federal and state Court systems, assigning to each system those cases most appropriate in the light of the basic principles of federalism."[7] His was the more optimistic view of this challenge. Roughly a century earlier, Frederick Douglass had said:

While there remains such an idea as the right of each State to control its own local affairs,—an idea, by the way more deeply rooted in the minds of men of all sections of the country than perhaps any one other political idea,—no general assertion of human rights can be of any practical value.[8]

The concept of federalism has a long history. The founding generation of our government believed in a system of checks and balances whereby no one within the government would have too much power. To accomplish this, the founders divided the federal government into three separate branches so that each branch could keep a check on the others. Additionally, in order to keep a check on the federal government, states maintained considerable power over the daily operations of society. In particular, under the structure of government created by the Constitution, the states were charged with the responsibility to maintain law and order.[9]

The Constitution gave Congress little power to regulate criminal conduct. In fact, the Constitution grants the federal government jurisdiction over only four types of crimes: counterfeiting,[10] piracy on the high seas,[11] crimes committed on federal property,[12] and treason.[13] The underlying principal is that the federal government is one of limited powers: the Tenth Amendment to the United States Constitution provides that all "powers not delegated to the United States by the Constitution, nor prohibited by it to the States, are reserved to the States respectively, or to the people."[14] States, by contrast, are governments of general powers: unless precluded by the Constitution, state governments, as sovereign entities, may exercise authority. Generally speaking, therefore, the power to regulate criminal conduct, to fight crime, and to maintain law and order was constitutionally left to the states or to local law enforcement.[15]

Through the time of the Civil War, therefore, federal criminal power was very limited. The federal criminal law that did exist was limited to crimes against the existence of the federal government, misconduct of federal officers, crimes against the operation of federal courts, and interference with federal governmental programs.[16] The first expansion of federal criminal jurisdiction occurred with the creation of civil rights crimes during the First Reconstruction. More will be said about this later in this chapter. For now, however, we turn to an outline of the continued development of the federalism problem generally in the area of criminal law enforcement.

The tradition of federalism, as understood by the founding generation, underwent significant transformation as Congress began federalizing criminal law in the nineteenth century. Since then, Congress, with the Supreme Court's approval, has enacted more than 3,000 federal offenses. What is more, these offenses have dealt with traditional state crimes. Congress successfully trumped the original, strict version of federalism on the basis of its constitutional power to "make all laws . . . necessary and proper" for carrying out federal powers, including the powers under the "Commerce Clause" of Article I of the Constitution "to regulate Commerce . . . among the several States."[17] As will be shown, Congress was somewhat less successful utilizing its enforcement power under the Thirteenth and Fourteenth Amendments, although this authority was used as a constitutional basis for certain civil rights legislation.

At the same time the federal government began legislating civil rights, it also began to expand the scope of its criminal law generally, beginning in 1872 with the Post Office Act, the first federal mail fraud statute. This law prohibited committing the act of fraud through the federal post offices. Congress justified the law on its constitutional right to establish post offices. Arguably, therefore, although this statute expanded federal criminal authority, it did not intrude upon the states' traditional prerogative in the area of criminal law.[18]

As Lawrence Friedman has shown, the real growth of federal criminal law came with the American "culture of mobility" in the late nineteenth century and, even more so, during the early twentieth century.[19] It was during this time that Congress reached out to criminalize interstate transportation of a woman for "illicit purposes," and the interstate transportation of such items as stolen motor vehicles, lottery tickets, and obscene literature.[20] Indeed, Prohibition itself is an example of this kind of expansion of federal criminal authority.

Congressional reliance on the Commerce Clause to expand federal jurisdiction was upheld even by pre–New Deal Supreme Courts. For example, in 1925 the Court upheld congressional authority over the interstate transportation of such items as stolen motor vehicles in *Brooks v. United States*.[21] By the time of the New Deal, federal criminal authority was seen as part and parcel of the expansion of federal authority generally. In the early 1940s, the Supreme Court routinely used the Commerce Clause as the basis for upholding increased congressional authority, including in the area of criminal law. The watershed case was a noncriminal suit, *Wickard v. Filburn*.[22] In *Wickard*, the Court upheld a statute regulating wheat produced for personal consumption by holding that Congress has the power to regulate acts that "affect interstate commerce." In the criminal context, as elsewhere, the Court limited the expansive nature of the "affect" test by requiring that federal criminal offenses prosecuted under the Commerce Clause have a nexus to interstate commerce. The *Wickard* test continued to provide Congress with the constitutional justification for the federalization of criminal offenses.

In 1971, the Supreme Court further expanded Congress's Commerce Clause power in *Perez v. United States*.[23] The Court upheld a federal loan-shark statute without any showing of a specific interstate nexus. Congress had made a determination that loan-sharking could "affect" interstate commerce because its proceeds could be used to finance interstate crime. The Court accepted this finding and held that Congress could regulate such activity under its Commerce Clause power. The *Perez* decision gave Congress substantial authority to regulate areas that have traditionally been left to the states. At the time, it was hard to imagine which issues, if any, lay beyond the reach of federal criminal authority, a belief that Congress appeared to share. After *Perez*, Congress passed legislation that made federal crimes of such traditional state offenses as arson,[24] disruption of a rodeo,[25] sale or receipt of stolen livestock,[26] and wrongful disclosure of videotape rentals.[27]

Perhaps the most well known example of the power of Congress to legislate criminal offenses is the Anti–Car Theft Act of 1992, the "federal carjacking statute."[28] The law made armed automobile theft a federal offense. Congress passed the law in response to the nationally publicized tragic death of Pamela Basu, who died trying to rescue her two-year-old daughter from two carjackers.[29]

Congress based its authority to legislate carjacking on its Commerce Clause power. The requirement that the carjacker possess a firearm provided the "interstate nexus" because firearms often are brought across state boundaries. Even this attenuated nexus, however, was ultimately deemed unnecessary. Some members of Congress felt that the firearm requirement limited the utility of the statute, and in 1994 Congress removed the firearm requirement, making even unarmed carjacking a federal offense.[30]

With the passage of the carjacking statute, it was tempting to ask whether the federalism problem even exists anymore except as a historical artifact. Here was a statute of questionable interstate impact dealing with a crime for which most states already had a law. Is there still a federalism problem?

In the spring of 1995, the Supreme Court said "yes." In *United States v. Lopez*, the Court struck down the Federal Gun-Free Zones Act,[31] which prohibited the possession of a firearm "at a place that the individual knows, or has reasonable cause to believe, is a school zone."[32] In a 5-4 opinion, the Supreme Court held that, because the act neither regulated a commercial activity nor contained a requirement that the possession be connected to interstate commerce, it exceeded Congress's authority under the Commerce Clause.

Several arguments were advanced to support the proposition that the possession of a firearm in a school zone sufficiently affected interstate commerce to justify federal jurisdiction over this crime. Guns pose a threat to the educational process, which in turn hampers the national economy. Moreover, guns increase crime, which harms the national productivity, and thus "affects commerce." The majority of the Court rejected both these arguments. Chief Justice Rehnquist asserted the federalism problem, contending that the congressional justifications would allow federalization of virtually any criminal offense, because all crime conceivably "affects interstate commerce" by damaging the national productivity. Giving Congress this much power, according to Rehnquist, would disrupt the delicate balance of power between the federal government and the states.

> To uphold the Government's contentions here, we would have to pile inference upon inference in a manner that would bid fair to convert congressional authority under the Commerce Clause to a general police power of the sort retained by the States. Admittedly, some of our prior cases have taken long steps down that road, giving great deference to congressional action . . . The broad language in these opinions has suggested the possibility of additional expansion, but we decline here to proceed any further. To do so would require us to conclude that the Constitution's enumeration of powers does not presuppose something not enumerated . . . and that there never will be a distinction between what is truly national and what is truly local . . . This we are unwilling to do.[33]

The reach of *Lopez* is not yet clear. One court has followed the Supreme Court's lead and struck down a federal criminal law for exceeding federal jurisdiction, the Violence Against Women Act.[34] By contrast, numerous lower courts have upheld such federal criminal laws as the 1992 Federal Carjacking Act, the Child Support Act of 1992, the Freedom of Access to Clinic Entrances Act, and the Migratory Bird Treaty Act in the face of challenges that, under *Lopez*, these laws exceeded federal jurisdiction.[35] Moreover, the majority opinion in *Lopez* itself commanded only the slimmest of majorities.

Justice Breyer, in a vigorous dissent joined by Justices Stevens, Souter, and Ginsburg, argued that the majority opinion ignored decades of precedent that allowed Congress to regulate expansively activity that "affects interstate commerce." Citing such cases as *Wickard* and *Perez,* Justice Breyer stated that the Court should defer to Congress when Congress has made a rational determination that the activity it is seeking to regulate affects interstate commerce and that departing from these settled precedents would create legal uncertainty that would "restrict Congress' ability to enact criminal laws aimed at criminal behavior that . . . seriously threatens the economic, as well as social, well-being of Americans."[36]

There is a slender aspect of agreement between the *Lopez* majority and dissent. Chief Justice Rehnquist and Justice Breyer do in fact agree on the question to be asked even if, quite obviously, they would answer that question differently. Both agree that there is a distinction between that which is national and that which is local, and further, that this distinction, wherever it falls, marks the boundary beyond which federal criminal jurisdiction may not cross. For more than 125 years, we have struggled to assess on which side of this boundary civil rights crimes generally and bias crimes in particular fall.

## The Federalism Problem in the First Century of Prosecuting Bias Crimes

Although the prime focus of most studies of civil rights enforcement has been on civil remedies, the seven civil rights statutes enacted during the First Reconstruction period all utilized criminal sanctions as a critical element in the protection of civil rights.[37] There are three categories of federal civil rights crimes: (1) bias crimes, our prime concern, (2) "rights interference crimes," interference by nonstate officials with the exercise of certain political or civil rights, and (3) "official crimes," unjustifiable use of force under color of law such as police brutality. All are present from the very beginning. The federalism problem that has plagued modern interpretation of the federal civil rights crimes statutes has its roots in the very origins of these laws.

### *The Origins of the Problem*

The federalism problem can be seen in the very birth of civil rights legislation. Indeed, we can trace the problem's origins even earlier, to the debates that occurred among Union policy-makers during the Civil War.

It is obvious that the Civil War reordered the federal-state balance in the governing of the republic. The nature of the reordering, however, is difficult to articulate with precision.[38] There was hardly unanimity concerning the precise nature of the breach represented by the secession of the Southern states. Nor was there agreement about whether the aftermath of a Union victory should bring about a return to *status quo ante,* or the birth of a new federal Union. As early as 1863, the lines of dispute were drawn even within Republican ranks concerning the nature of the Confederate states' relationship to the Union. President Lincoln saw secession as illegal; thus the Southern states were still "states" and restoration of the Union required only the restoration of lawful governments. The radical Republicans, typified by Congressman Thaddeaus Stevens, saw the Confederate states as rebels who had formed a new entity with which the Union was at war. At the war's end, these states would attain the status of "conquered provinces." Readmission to the Union was thus an open matter, justifying full Reconstruction, both of the states and of their relationship with the Union.[39]

The distinction between these two views of secession was, in part, a question of separation of powers among the federal branches of government, rather than division of powers between the federal and the state governments. If the states required only lawful leadership to continue as states within the Union, then the matter could be handled by the Executive Branch. If, by contrast, readmission to the Union was necessary, only Congress possessed the power to set the terms of the readmission.[40] In addition, there was also an issue of division of powers. Lincoln's view (or the moderate view attributed to him in 1863) did not appear to call for a fundamental restructuring of the relationship of the federal government to the states. The view held by Stevens and other Radical Republicans did.

The course ultimately taken along the moderate-radical spectrum began to emerge with the ratification of the Thirteenth Amendment, the constitutional abolition of slavery. The abolition of slavery by means of constitutional amendment did not involve the federal government directly in the running of state affairs. Indeed, it is revealing that the "United States" in the Thirteenth Amendment takes the plural pronoun "their" in the final clause of the first section (the common usage prior to the Civil War), rather than the singular "its" of contemporary usage.[41] Nonetheless, the Thirteenth Amendment represented a federal regulation of what had previously been an issue of state law.[42] Thus the seeds of the federalism problem were planted at the very beginnings of the First Reconstruction.

Initially there was some dispute over the scope and purpose of the Thir-

teenth Amendment. Narrowly, the amendment could act as a formal statement of emancipation—largely already accomplished. Alternatively, it could
serve as a broad proscription of the "badges" of slavery. In practice, it was
the narrow interpretation of the Thirteenth Amendment that described its
effect. Southern states soon enacted the infamous "Black Codes," and there
were widespread incidents of violence against the newly freed slaves. The
federal response to this violence brought the federalism problem to the
fore.[43]

The policies associated with President Andrew Johnson's "Presidential
Reconstruction" were clearly inadequate to address the postwar violation of
the newly won citizenship rights of freed slaves. The very failure of these
policies, however, reveals the inevitability of the federalism problem in any
realistic civil rights enforcement policy. Johnson's goal as President was to
restore the Union to antebellum status as quickly as possible. He had no intention of allowing a re-formation of the Southern states, radical or otherwise. He thus opposed black suffrage and resisted black property ownership
as well. Johnson recognized the strong resistance to change in the South and
viewed the Civil War as a rebellion by traitors who must be punished but not
as a rebellion by states that required reconstruction of their way of government or of life. Finally—and here Johnson differed greatly from Lincoln—
he simply "was convinced of the inferiority of the black race," and he never
changed that opinion. The essence of Presidential Reconstruction was an effort to avoid the federalism problem by allowing the antebellum relationship
between the Southern states and the federal Union to remain essentially unchanged.[44]

Congressional Reconstruction, which began with the convening of the
Thirty-ninth Congress in December 1865, was based on a very different
view of federal-state relations, one that made the federalism problem unavoidable. The contrast with Presidential Reconstruction was sharp: on the
opening day of the Thirty-ninth Congress, the clerk of the House of Representatives omitted the names of the representatives elected by the Southern
states that had undergone readmission pursuant to Presidential Reconstruction (and in fact even denied living expenses to those seeking to serve as
representatives).[45] The battle between the executive and the legislative
views of federal-state relations came to a head over the enactment of the
Civil Rights Act of 1866.

The act was supported by a broad if somewhat unsteady consensus of
moderate and radical Republicans in Congress.[46] It is thus difficult to define

a single legislative intent behind the statute. Nevertheless, two points are clear with respect to the 1866 act. First, the consensus that allowed passage of the legislation was based on a commitment to serious and substantial federal involvement in issues that previously had been matters solely of state authority. Second, the debate between this majority and its opposition can best be understood in terms of the primary role of the federalism problem.

One group supporting the Civil Rights Act of 1866 was the moderate wing of the Republican party. The primary author and sponsor of the bill was the Senate Judiciary Committee's moderate chair, Senator Lyman Trumbull. According to Trumbull, the law was to have broad application, applying to "white men as well as black men," protecting all persons in the United States in their civil rights, and furnishing the means of vindicating these rights.[47] The 1866 act established citizenship for "all persons born in the United States" regardless of race or prior condition of servitude, required equal protection under state laws, and set up enforcement mechanisms. Trumbull met frequently with President Johnson as the bill was being drafted, and he believed, as did almost all congressional Republicans, that the President intended to approve it. (Contrary to Trumbull's perceptions, however, Johnson had always intended to veto the civil rights bill.) Moderates thus saw the bill as narrow in scope, directed primarily at combating the recently enacted Black Codes.[48]

The radical Republicans saw the statute as an important first step toward a fundamental reordering of the federal-state relationship. They sought a powerful, centralized federal government that could enforce and protect a broad panoply of national rights. Ultimately, the bill drew support from both wings of the Republican party, receiving the votes of all but three Republicans in the Senate and all but four in the House of Representatives.[49]

A significant reordering of the federal-state relationship—radical or otherwise—was inherent in congressional Reconstruction, and this was not lost on President Johnson. Seeking to maintain the nature of the prewar Union, Johnson vetoed the Civil Rights Bill of 1866. In his veto message, the President explicitly raised the federalism problem, asserting that the bill would "stride towards centralization and the concentration of all legislative powers in the national Government."[50] It was Johnson's veto of the bill that led to the split between the President and his party in Congress. Until that time, most Republicans had no desire for the split, and it had been the radicals who were relatively isolated.[51] With the veto, President Johnson had "declared war on Congress." This was evident to all, including the moderates.

For the first time in American history, on April 6 (in the Senate) and April 9 (in the House of Representatives), the Congress overrode a Presidential veto of a major statute.[52]

## Congressional Reconstruction and the Focus on Criminal Civil Rights Sanctions

The atmosphere surrounding the early civil rights statutes, even after the enactment of the 1866 act, was one of violence toward both the freedmen and the Southern unionists. In the Southern states, freedmen were at best second-class citizens and at worst subject to harassment, intimidation, and murder. In addition to the Black Codes and other restrictive measures, there were numerous incidents of routine beatings and several large-scale massacres such as those that took place in New Orleans and Memphis in 1866.[53] In response to this pervasive lawless violence, radicals in Congress were determined to expand protection for the freedmen beyond suffrage. Their efforts resulted first in the Enforcement Act of 1870. The act was intended primarily to guarantee the rights of due process of law and equal protection of the law guaranteed by the Fourteenth Amendment, and, particularly, the right to vote established by the Fifteenth Amendment. It provided civil and criminal remedies against state officials who failed to allow an equal opportunity to vote or to qualify to vote and federalized all state-law crimes that were committed in the course of any violation of the act.

Despite the enactment of the Enforcement Act, the violence directed at blacks in the Southern states continued and may even have increased. Congress was inundated with reports of violence from the South rivaling the reports of violence in 1866. President Grant issued a statement calling upon Congress to enact legislation to combat the violence in the Southern states.[54] In response, Congress enacted the Ku Klux Klan Act of 1871.

The debate over the criminal provisions of the Ku Klux Klan Act was among the most dramatic early expositions of the federalism problem. The legislation as originally proposed would have made federal offenses of a long litany of common law crimes such as murder, manslaughter, robbery, assault, or arson.[55]

As a result of the debate centering on the federalism problem, the Klan Bill was amended. It still provided criminal sanctions for numerous conspiracies but narrowed the grounds for federal criminal prosecution to conspiracies to violate an enumerated set of civil rights, each of which implicated an explicitly federal issue, such as intimidation of federal office-holders or of a witness at a federal trial. The legislation as amended preserved the effort to apply criminal sanctions to the violence in the South but stepped back from the federalization of all or most crimes of violence in the Southern states. As opposed to a broad federal bias crime law, the Ku Klux Klan Act was restricted to rights interference crimes.

The Department of Justice's enforcement of the 1870 Enforcement Act and the 1871 Ku Klux Klan Act raised many of the basic federalism problems that confronted Congress. Amos T. Akerman was Attorney General during the first phase of civil rights enforcement by the Grant administration. Akerman initially believed that criminal prosecutions should be left to state and local authorities. With the continued growth of the Ku Klux Klan, however, Akerman became radicalized and sought to develop a more aggressive federal role in the prosecution of both official crimes and rights interference crimes. Under Akerman, the Department of Justice searched for a federalism position that would permit active federal involvement in what had previously been a state domain.

The limited success of this effort was due less to a rejection of the position on federalism by the Grant administration than to a number of other factors that conspired against Akerman's attempts. The Department of Justice's efforts to enforce the Enforcement Act of 1870 and later the Ku Klux Klan Act of 1871 were hampered by problems of both resources and politics. Enforcement Act cases, involving numerous witnesses, many of whom needed protection from marshals or other legal officers, were unusually complex for federal criminal cases of the day. They required resources well in excess of those available to local United States Attorneys. Requests for additional funds had to be made to an increasingly skeptical Congress. The cost and difficulty of bringing Enforcement Act cases were such that, with the exception of the notable successes of North Carolina United States Attorney D. H. Starbuck, federal enforcement of criminal civil rights laws was already a relatively ineffective tool when Akerman left office in 1871. These criminal statutes remained largely unenforced by the Department of Justice until the modern period.[56]

## The Path of Criminal Civil Rights from 1872 to 1883

From Grant's second inauguration until the Supreme Court decision in *The Civil Rights Cases*, which struck down the criminal enforcement provisions of the Civil Rights Act of 1875, federal criminal civil rights enforcement virtually ground to a halt.[57] Congress continued to create civil rights crime legislation in enacting the Civil Rights Act of 1875, but, as will be shown in the Historical Appendix, this was less a matter of creating new legislative remedies than a matter of passing a memorial to a period and its leader. By the time the bill was enacted into law, the consensus that accompanied the 1870 and 1871 acts was all but gone, and the tide was running against Radical Reconstruction policies at virtually every level of government. In the few years between the passage of the Ku Klux Klan Act in 1871 and the Civil Rights Act of 1875, Presidential support for Reconstruction reached a low unseen since the Johnson administration, the Republican party lost control of one of the houses of Congress for the first time since the Civil War, and the Supreme Court began to undercut the Reconstruction-era statutes with a grudging response to the federalism problem.[58] By the end of this decade, the future course of federal criminal civil rights enforcement was set until well into the twentieth century.

We begin with the Supreme Court, which in *The Slaughter-House Cases*[59] had its first opportunity to interpret both the Thirteenth and the Fourteenth Amendments. The Court's decision had an enormous bearing on its evolving views as to the federalism problem and the Reconstruction amendments.[60] *Slaughter-House* was brought by a group of butchers in Louisiana who challenged the creation of a state-chartered monopoly over cattle-slaughtering facilities in New Orleans. Their Thirteenth Amendment claim—unanimously rejected by the Court—asserted that the monopoly created a condition of involuntary servitude because it restricted the ability of local butchers to work.[61] Of particular relevance here is their Fourteenth Amendment claim, challenging the monopoly as a violation of a right to work, which, the butchers argued, was one of the privileges or immunities protected by the amendment.[62]

In the narrowest sense, Justice Samuel F. Miller for the majority rejected the butchers' Fourteenth Amendment claims because the Reconstruction-era constitutional amendments were designed primarily to aid the newly freed slaves and not to protect white butchers in Louisiana. But Justice Miller did not completely restrict the protection of the amendments to blacks. He saw the Thirteenth Amendment, for example, as a prohibition not only against slavery of black citizens but also against "Mexican peonage" and "Chinese coolie labor systems" as well.[63] He did, however, restrict this protection to rights of "national citizenship" as opposed to those of "state citizenship." The rights asserted by the butchers were seen as strictly state matters with which the Fourteenth Amendment had "nothing to do."[64] Rights pertaining to *national* citizenship, according to Justice Miller, were limited to such matters as access to ports and navigable waterways, the ability to run for federal office and to travel to the seat of government, and the right to protection on the high seas or abroad.

The implication of Miller's opinion in *Slaughter-House* for the federalism problem with respect to civil rights crimes, although not fully appreciated at the time, is now clear. Rights interference crimes, as defined in the Ku Klux Klan Act, were nothing more than state-law crimes made federal by Congress because of the relationship between the crime itself and a federally protected right. If the well of national citizen rights created by the Fourteenth Amendment was exceedingly shallow, the basis for rights interference crimes would be as well.

In articulating his position, Miller explicitly rejected the more far-reaching view of national rights proposed by the dissenting justices. Justice Stephen Field, for example, explicitly described the Fourteenth Amendment as a tool by which a fundamental reordering of federal-state relations was worked. For Justice Field, the first clause of the Fourteenth Amendment "recognizes in express terms, if it does not create, citizens of the United States." National citizenship, according to Field, conferred upon the citizen "[t]he fundamental rights, privileges, and immunities which belong to him as a free man and a free citizen . . . and are not dependent upon his citizenship of any state. [These rights] do not derive their existence from [a state's] legislature, and cannot be destroyed by its power."[65] Field's position would have provided the constitutional underpinning for a solution to the federalism problem that would broaden federal criminal jurisdiction into areas formerly left to state competence. Federal criminal jurisdiction would be based on the nature of the injury inflicted and its relationship to matters of national interest. This approach was rejected by the majority.

By the time of the decision in *Slaughter-House,* the administration had become far less aggressive in enforcing the criminal provisions in the Enforcement Acts and the Ku Klux Klan Act. Although the number of prosecutions continued to increase through 1872, the new Attorney General, George H. Williams, under the guise of fiscal concerns, began to signal a cutback in administrative support for civil rights enforcement. United States Attorneys were instructed to bring Enforcement Act cases only if necessary to protect the public peace. It is ironic that this administrative retreat was sounded just as criminal civil rights enforcement attained its greatest successes. By the end of 1872, the war against the Ku Klux Klan was largely won and the Klan was essentially destroyed. The end of the Klan, however, did not mark the end of violence in the South. By 1873, the administration's battle against terrorism had become one of threat rather than deed, with the Department of Justice hoping that the threat of prosecution would be sufficient to deter renewed Klan activity.[66]

As prosecution gave way to mere threat of criminal enforcement, so threats gave way to executive clemency. With the dismantling of administration efforts to enforce the criminal civil rights laws, the federalism problem ceased to seem pressing. As the federal government gradually abandoned enforcement of both official crimes and rights interference crimes, the prosecution of these offenses was left to the states themselves. Because states failed to enforce criminal laws to protect African-Americans, the protections offered by civil rights criminal statutes virtually disappeared for half a century.[67]

The implications of Justice Miller's majority opinion in *Slaughter-House* for interpretation of criminal civil rights statutes became explicit in *United States v. Cruikshank,* the first Supreme Court case to review a conviction for a civil rights crime.[68] *Cruikshank* arose out of the Colfax massacre, the most violent single episode of the Reconstruction period.[69] The village of Colfax, Louisiana, was the county seat of Grant Parish. Both the village of Colfax and Grant Parish (named for the Vice President and President, respectively) were established by the Reconstruction government in Louisiana.[70] Colfax became one of the battlegrounds after Louisiana's intensely disputed 1872 state elections. Two rival camps—those supporting William P. Kellogg, a Republican originally from Illinois, and supporters of the local Democrat John McEnery—each claimed victory. They established two parallel governments in the state. Kellogg and McEnery each commissioned a sheriff and a judge for Grant Parish. Kellogg's appointees, along with a group of freedmen concerned with the possibility of a Democratic use of force to seize local authority, sealed off Colfax and held the village during early April 1873. On April 13, Easter Sunday, a group of whites, armed with rifles and a small canon, took Colfax by violent and particularly brutal means. Even those sympathetic to the local Democratic effort to assert control reported a scene of rampant slaughter and the murder of many innocent and unarmed blacks. As many as 280 blacks died during the Colfax massacre.[71]

Within days of the massacre, Attorney General Williams directed the

United States Attorney for Louisiana, James R. Beckwith, to commence an investigation and seek indictments of those responsible for the events in Colfax—the notoriety of the Colfax massacre was such that the Department of Justice had little choice but to respond.[72] The ultimate response, however, was negligible: of the ninety-seven defendants ultimately indicted by the federal grand jury, only nine ever came to trial, and of these, six were acquitted of all charges. Three were convicted under the Enforcement Act of 1870 for conspiring to deprive two of the victims of the Colfax massacre of various constitutionally protected rights, including the rights to assemble peacefully, to bear arms, to vote, and not to be deprived of life, liberty, or property without due process of law. All three convictions were thrown out by the Supreme Court in *Cruikshank*.[73]

The legal challenges to the convictions in *Cruikshank* called for the first full explication of the federalism problem, asking whether such crimes as the mayhem in Colfax, Louisiana, could be prosecuted by federal authorities. The case first came before Justice Joseph P. Bradley, sitting as Circuit Justice on the trial bench.[74] Bound by the Court's decision in *Cruikshank*, Justice Bradley read the Fourteenth Amendment to apply only to instances of state action and not to private conduct. In the context of criminal law, Bradley believed that the Fourteenth Amendment authorized federal action only if a *state* has violated some recognized right; otherwise, "the interference of [C]ongress would be officious, unnecessary, and inappropriate."[75]

When it came to the Thirteenth Amendment, however, Justice Bradley was far more expansive.[76] He had begun to explore the constitutional abolition of slavery as a basis for broad congressional authority over common law crimes in his dissenting opinion two years earlier in *Blyew v. United States*.[77] In *Cruikshank*, Bradley anticipated the modern development of bias crime law, reading the Thirteenth Amendment as a font of federal authority for all crimes committed with racial animus. According to Justice Bradley, for federalization of an otherwise common law crime

> there must be a design to injure a person, or deprive him of his equal right of enjoying the protection of the laws, by reason of his race, color, or previous condition of servitude. Otherwise it is a case exclusively within the jurisdiction of the state and its courts.[78]

Ironically, Bradley's sweepingly broad view of federal bias crimes contrasts sharply with his actual application of this legal doctrine to the facts of the Colfax massacre. According to Bradley, each count of the *Cruikshank* indictment failed as a matter of law because each count failed to show any underlying racial animus. Justice Bradley did not doubt that racial animus had in fact driven the Colfax massacre, but he focused upon an extremely technical reading of the indictment and concluded that its counts failed to allege racial motivation. There were two counts in the *Cruikshank* indictment where the accusation of racial motivation was undeniably present. Bradley dismissed these counts on a different ground. He concluded that because each was "such a general and sweeping charge . . . [it] does not amount to the averment of a criminal act."[79] Justice Bradley thus never applied his own intriguing theory of federal criminal jurisdiction over all racially motivated violence.

Following Bradley's decision as Circuit Justice in *Cruikshank,* Attorney General Williams suspended all prosecutions under the Enforcement Act—whether arising out of the Colfax massacre in particular or criminal civil rights cases in general—pending Supreme Court review. In spite of the dramatic increase in violence by Southern whites upon blacks and Republicans in 1874 and 1875, the Department of Justice under Williams and his successor, Edwards Pierrepont, maintained this moratorium on civil rights prosecutions. As a conservative former Democrat, Pierrepont was even less prepared than his predecessor to order federal enforcement of the criminal civil rights laws.[80] When the Supreme Court did decide *Cruikshank* two years later, Justice Bradley's attempt to draw the focus of civil rights crimes to the mental state of the accused and the issues of racial motivation was lost in an opinion that followed only his narrow reading of the indictment.

Chief Justice Morrison R. Waite's opinion for a near unanimous court in *Cruikshank* tracked Bradley's views on each count of the indictment.[81] These counts purportedly suffered either from federalism problems because of a failure to allege racial motivation or from a failure to set forth the grounds of the accusation with sufficient specificity. In one of the greatest examples of judicial understatement, Chief Justice Waite observed that the Court "may suspect that race was the cause of the hostility." Nonetheless, these counts of the indictment were fatally flawed because they failed to allege this with sufficient explicitness.[82]

The most significant impact of the decision in *Cruikshank* was the formal application of the limited *Slaughter-House* view of federalism to civil rights crimes. The federal government's role with respect to the protection of constitutional rights and privileges was strictly to safeguard individuals from state encroachment. The duty to protect the individual rights of all citizens "was originally assumed by the States; and it still remains there. The only obligation resting upon the United States is to see that the States do not deny the right . . . The power of the national government is limited to the enforcement of this guarantee."[83] Nowhere did Chief Justice Waite even broach the idea raised by Justice Bradley of using the Thirteenth Amendment as a basis for recognizing federal bias crimes.

Chief Justice Waite also wrote the Court's opinion in *United States v. Reese,* which was handed down the same day as *Cruikshank.*[84] *Reese* struck down the indictment of several election inspectors in Lexington, Kentucky, under the Enforcement Act of 1870 for interfering with the voting rights of black citizens.[85] What *Cruikshank* did to criminal civil rights enforcement of Fourteenth Amendment rights, *Reese* did to Fifteenth Amendment voting rights enforcement. The Fifteenth Amendment guaranteed not a positive right to vote, but only a negative right to be free from "discrimination in the elective franchise on account of race, color, or previous condition of servitude"; there was no federal criminal jurisdiction over general infringements on the franchise. Chief Justice Waite thus held that the relevant sections of the Enforcement Act of 1870 were unconstitutional.[86]

The limitation that began to emerge in *Slaughter-House* now applied with full force to the criminal civil rights statutes. According to *Cruikshank* and *Reese,* federalism needed a strict state-action requirement for Fourteenth and Fifteenth Amendments claims. This left the responsibility and authority for criminal enforcement almost exclusively with the states, and allowed for a federal role only in cases of demonstrable state default. There could be little, if any, middle ground. Robert Kaczorowski has described the Supreme Court's fear as based on "a recognition [that] Congress's concurrent authority over civil rights would destroy the states and change the nature of American federalism beyond recognition."[87] Federalism was a virtually incurable problem.

The *Civil Rights Cases* were among a series of decisions that, applying the view of federalism developed in *Slaughter-House* and *Cruikshank,* struck down most of the Reconstruction-era criminal civil rights laws.[88] In the *Civil Rights Cases,* the Court held that the 1875 Civil Rights Act was unconstitutional because of its regulation of private conduct. The main thrust of the act was the prohibition of discrimination based on race in public accommodations such as inns and theaters.[89] The Court's conclusion could hardly have been surprising after *Cruikshank* and *Reese.* What is surprising, however, is that the author of the *Civil Rights Cases* was Justice Bradley. Bradley, who a decade earlier had raised the possibility that the Thirteenth Amendment might provide constitutional authorization for a general federal criminal jurisdiction over bias crimes, concluded in the *Civil Rights Cases* that the Thirteenth Amendment "has respect, not to distinctions of race or class or color, but to slavery."[90] Justice Bradley believed that the time for special legislation to protect freedmen was now past, and that federal intervention on behalf of African-Americans was no longer necessary. In perhaps the most frequently quoted language of his opinion, Bradley wrote:

> When a man has emerged from slavery, and by the aid of beneficent legislation had shaken off the inseparable concomitants of that state, there must be some stage in the progress of his elevation when he takes the rank of mere citizen, and ceases to be the special favorite of the laws, and when his rights, as a citizen or a man, are to be protected in the ordinary modes by which other men's rights are protected.[91]

As a matter of federalism, therefore, the right of access to public facilities should be protected "in the ordinary modes," that is, under state law and state law alone.[92]

By 1883, the Supreme Court had cut back severely on Reconstruction efforts to expand federal criminal jurisdiction. Congress had long since abandoned the enterprise of attempting to do so. Over the following decades, the Court continued to eviscerate civil rights crimes provisions.[93] The federal civil rights prosecutions that were successfully brought by the government and upheld by the courts constituted a very narrow range of cases. The federalism problem narrowly circumscribed federal criminal jurisdiction. Specifically, the federalization of bias crimes, suggested by Justice Bradley in his *Cruikshank* opinion, was never recognized by the Court.

The fifty years that followed saw no aggressive federal criminal civil rights enforcement. Congress passed no civil rights crimes legislation during this time, the enforcement policies of the Department of Justice were modest at best, and the courts generally were unsympathetic to those prosecutions that were brought. The few successful prosecutions during this period involved rights interference crimes. Interference with election-related rights was by far the most prominent source for those criminal civil rights cases. Direct interference with federal elections, whether committed by private persons or by state officials, was deemed to be within the circumscribed areas of federal criminal jurisdiction that satisfied even the Court's crabbed view of federalism. Thus the federal government brought and the Supreme

Court upheld a prosecution of an Oklahoma county election official for conspiring to prevent filing of accurate election returns in a federal congressional election.[94] Moreover, where the federal interest was patent, the federal government could prosecute what was in essence a bias crime. In *Ex Parte Yarbrough*, for example, the Supreme Court, just one year after the *Civil Rights Cases*, upheld the conviction of nine white men who were indicted under the Enforcement Act of 1870 for beating a black man because he had voted in a federal congressional election.[95] Although cases were brought for violations of rights unrelated to voting, they were limited and prosecutions under them were relatively rare.[96] The recognition of voting rights as a solid basis for federal civil rights enforcement culminated in *United States v. Classic*, in which criminal jurisdiction was extended to interference with voting in a primary election.[97]

The relative lack of federal civil rights prosecutions and the complete lack of such legislation between the First and the Second Reconstructions illustrate that the federalism problem had political as well as legal dimensions. The most significant item on the civil rights community's legislative agenda during this period was federal antilynching legislation. Lynchings demonstrated that the subjugation of African-Americans through violence continued long after the legal abolition of slavery. Lynching not only involved horrific violence at the hands of the mob, but also pointedly illustrated the lack of protection that blacks could expect from local law enforcement. Indeed, local law enforcement was often complicitous.[98]

Efforts to enact some form of federal antilynching legislation were not ultimately successful. The NAACP pushed hard for such legislation, and some members of Congress responded by proposing several forms of antilynching legislation. Southern Democrats strongly opposed the new legislation and asserted federalism in support of their efforts. They argued that the federal government should allow the states to resolve local lynching incidents without federal interference.

The congressional debates over the antilynching law turned on the issue of federalism and the federal government's power to punish lynching. The proposed antilynching legislation had four basic components. First, it gave the Department of Justice the power to investigate lynchings wherever there was evidence of delinquency on the part of local officials. Second, it allowed the Department of Justice to prosecute local officials who failed to restrain mob violence or pursue lynching cases. Third, it provided a civil remedy so that victims of mob violence could sue the county or city whose peace officers either aided in a lynching or failed adequately to control the mob. Fourth, it outlawed any assemblage of three or more persons who unlawfully attempted to use violence in order to punish any citizen charged with a crime.[99]

The views expressed by some of the principals in the debate over the federal antilynching legislation provide the best illustration of the elements of that debate. Representative Hatton W. Sumners' arguments reflected the general sentiment among the law's opponents. Sumners contended that states should bear the burden and responsibility of preventing lynching and that the proposed legislation violated the principles of federalism because it allowed the federal government to disrupt the states' natural sphere of influence and power. Sumners claimed that lynchings had become less common and that this was attributable to "a constantly developing public sentiment in the communities of the States . . . the growth of which has been stimulated by the greatest of all stimulants, the sense of exclusive responsibility."[100] For Sumners, federal legislation took away that "responsibility" from the states and further indicated a federal distrust of state capacity to solve the problem. Federal authority in areas traditionally left to the states is appropriate only insofar as it fosters cooperation between the federal government and the states. The antilynching law, to Sumners, had "no spirit of helpful respectful cooperation" because it authorized "direct intervention of the Federal Government . . . as a governmental overlord approaching the State as governmental vassals."[101]

Advocates of the antilynching legislation also recognized that the federalism problem played a significant role in the debate over the legislation. They advanced three main arguments for its passage. The first two arguments accepted the opponent's federalism concerns and advanced the federal nature of the crime of lynching by way of rebuttal. The third, and more radical, argument, challenged the federalism premise altogether.

The first argument looked to the Reconstruction-era constitutional amendments and asserted that the federal government had authority to intervene when states failed to protect their citizens' constitutional rights. Federal authority over lynchings was grounded in state default and even complicity. Senator Van Nuys, for example, argued that the law's purpose was "to enlist the aid of the Federal Government within its constitutional province to supplement the efforts of the States in stamping out lynching." To Van Nuys, the states had the initial obligation to combat lynching without federal involvement. The federal government, however, would have the prerogative to intervene in the investigation and prosecution of state officials who had participated in the lynching or failed to prevent it. This prerogative was limited: the federal government "will not and cannot intervene in any case in which State agents . . . have been diligent in attempting to prevent and punish mob violence."[102]

The second argument in favor of antilynching legislation also accepted the federalism problem as a starting point and found a basis for the law in the inherently interstate nature of mob violence. Charles H. Tuttle, an attorney who played an active role in support of the antilynching law, argued that the "time . . . has come when the Nation should defend itself against this national evil which has assumed colossal proportions." Tuttle argued that the problem of mob violence mandated federal intervention because it "destroy[s] the security of the national investment . . . and undermine[s] the strength of the national credit and of the national institutions." Mob violence crosses state borders and ultimately affects the entire nation.[103]

Only the third argument advanced by supporters of the antilynching legislation rejected the seriousness of the federalism problem, arguing that, while traditional notions of federalism were still important, they should give way to the pragmatic changes of increased cooperation and interdependence between the federal and state governments that characterized much of the New Deal. Representative Emanuel Celler argued that the "National Government . . . should not be denied an interest and voice in preventing . . . recurrence of mob insurrection."[104] Celler responded to charges that the bill destroyed states' rights by arguing that the boundaries between states were becoming less clear owing to "social development, to science and invention, and rest[ed] upon the closer relations of trade and amity which exist[ed] between communities and the different states."[105] Charles Tuttle also believed that the growing interdependence and cooperation between state and federal government justified the latter's increased role in the area of civil rights. "Does it seem fair," Tuttle asked, "that where the National Government is, on solicitation of State and local communities, making ever-increasing investment among them, that they should deny to the National Government an interest and a voice in preventing in their own midst recurrences of mob insurrection?"[106]

The failure of antilynching legislation ultimately resulted not from technical debates over federalism but from harsh political realities. The House of Representatives passed antilynching legislation in 1922, 1937, and 1940, but each time the legislation failed in the Senate. President Franklin Roosevelt's position on the issue was ambiguous. In the late 1930s and early 1940s, Roosevelt spoke out against lynching and supported the passage of the antilynching law. Southern Democrats, however, were the law's biggest opponents, and Roosevelt needed their support on other pieces of New Deal legislation. Recognizing the dilemma, Roosevelt decided to compromise on the antilynching law as an appeasement to the Southern Democrats. Without the President's support, the law died in the Senate in 1941.[107]

### *Where Racially Motivated Violence Meets Police Brutality:* Screws v. United States

What Franklin Roosevelt believed he was unable to do legislatively, he attempted to do executively. In July 1942 the President instructed the Department of Justice to investigate all mob killings of African-Americans to determine if there was a basis for federal prosecution.[108] Roosevelt had other concerns in addition to protecting his support among Southern Senate Democrats. Service, as well as casualties, among black soldiers and sailors had strengthened black political will. Moreover, the axis powers made effective use of lynchings in their propaganda.[109] When local federal officials and a local black newspaper brought the killing of Robert Hall to the attention of the Department of Justice, the department became actively involved in investigating the circumstances of the case.

The best short description of the murder of Robert Hall was captured in the opening sentence of the resulting Supreme Court opinion two years later: "This case involves a shocking and revolting episode in law enforcement."[110] Hall was killed in Newton, Georgia, in Baker County, late in the evening of January 29, 1943, or the early morning hours of January 30. M. Claude Screws, the sheriff of Baker County, Special Deputy Sheriff Frank Edward Jones, and Jim Bob Kelley, a police officer from the city of Newton, were charged with the killing.

Screws, along with Jones and Kelley, sought to arrest Robert Hall, a thirty-year-old African-American, on a warrant charging Hall with the theft of a tire. Screws had a grudge against Hall and was out to get him, undoubtedly owing to Hall's reputation in Baker County as a "troublemaker" because of his militancy on behalf of black causes. During the federal investigation, Screws told an agent of the FBI that he had known Hall all of Hall's life, that he had experienced "considerable trouble" with him for the two years prior to his death, and that Hall was a "biggety Negro" who "considered himself a leader among the colored people in the community."[111]

Several days before the arrest of Hall, Jones and Screws had taken Hall's pistol without any apparent justification. Hall had gone before a state grand jury in Baker County to obtain an order directing the return of his pistol. Although the grand jury did not provide Hall with the relief that he sought, it did a remarkable thing for the time: the grand jury summoned Sheriff Screws to testify on the basis of allegations made by a black man. Moreover, after Hall failed to receive any satisfaction from the grand jury, he retained a local lawyer, Robert Culpepper, who wrote to Screws, requesting the return of the pistol. Screws received this letter from Culpepper on the day the arrest took place. After having received the letter, but prior to the arrest, Screws said that "he was going to go and get the black son-of-a-bitch and going to kill him, and that he had lived too long then."[112]

Jones and Kelley went to Hall's house shortly after midnight to arrest him. Screws waited at the well in front of the Newton Courthouse. When Hall was arrested, his shotgun was taken from his home, again with no supporting legal basis. The seizure did not occur during a search of Hall and was conducted without warrant. Hall was handcuffed and taken by car to the courthouse. Upon arriving at the courthouse and leaving the car, the three men severely beat Hall with their fists and a blackjack that was about eight inches long and weighed approximately two pounds. Hall, handcuffed throughout the entire incident, was beaten for between fifteen and thirty minutes until he was rendered unconscious. He was then dragged feet first along the courthouse square, into the courthouse, and to a jail cell, where he was left, already dying. Hall was subsequently taken to a hospital, where he died in less than one hour, never having regained consciousness.[113]

The murder of Robert Hall was both a case of police brutality and a bias crime. It thus provided the vehicle for the department of Justice to accomplish two goals. First, the department wished to establish the applicability of the federal criminal civil rights jurisdiction beyond explicit constitutional provisions such as federal supervision of federal elections, to the broader terrain of deprivations of liberty without due process.[114] Second, as we have just seen, President Roosevelt had increasingly pressured the department to become involved in the prosecution of racial violence in the South.

Nonetheless, the Department of Justice tread slowly, even in a case as egregious as this one, trying to persuade local law enforcement authorities in Georgia to bring charges against Sheriff Screws, Deputy Sheriff Kelley, and Officer Jones.[115] No such state charges were ever brought against any of them. There are at least two sets of explanations for the Georgia authorities' failure to press criminal charges in this matter. The narrowest explanation flows from the systemic difficulties in commencing a criminal investiga-tion against members of law enforcement, namely, the impossibility of self-prosecution. The local district attorney blamed his inability to prosecute Sheriff Screws on the fact that he had no substantial independent investiga-tive facilities and thus had to rely upon local sheriffs and policemen to con-duct investigations.[116] Clearly the Newton, Georgia, police were unlikely candidates to develop a criminal case against their sheriff, deputy, and fel-low officer.

The systemic explanation exists on a more general level as well. Even if the district attorney had not been placed in the impossible situation of rely-ing upon Screws to investigate and bring charges against himself, he would have had to rely upon local police officers and deputy sheriffs in counties very much like Baker County. Such officers, although not facing a strict conflict of interest in the investigation, would likely show an excessive will-ingness to view events from the suspects' perspective. This general "there but for luck go I" syndrome serves to minimize the effectiveness of investi-gations by local law enforcement officers.

In addition to the systemic explanations for the local authorities' failure to bring a case against Screws, there is a social and political explanation as well. Even if law enforcement agents were prepared to investigate such cases vig-orously, a serious question exists regarding the willingness of authorities, particularly elected law enforcement, to pursue politically unpopular causes. It is worth noting that several years after the conclusion of the fed-eral case, Claude Screws was elected to the Georgia state senate.[117]

Four months after the killing of Robert Hall, with no local prosecutorial action having been taken, the Department of Justice brought the case to a federal grand jury in Georgia. The grand jury returned a three-count indict-ment as to each of the three defendants. Each was charged under what are now sections 241 and 242 of the Federal Criminal Code. Section 242 prohib-its "deprivation . . . of any rights, privileges or immunities secured or pro-tected by the Constitution and laws of the United States," under color of law, that is, deprivation of rights by a state official acting in an official capacity with the pretext of lawful authority, and section 241 punishes conspiracies to interfere with the exercise of "any right or privilege secured . . . by the Constitution or laws of the United States."[118]

The indictments charged the defendants with acting under color of the laws of Georgia and willfully causing Robert Hall to be deprived of his rights under the Fourteenth Amendment. The indictment specified Hall's right not to be deprived of life without due process of law, his right to be immune from illegal assault and battery, his right to be tried before being subjected to any punishment, and his right not to be punished except in accordance with the laws of the state of Georgia.[119]

One additional aspect of the indictment deserves special attention. The indictment also charged Screws, Kelley, and Jones with subjecting Hall to a different punishment by reason of his race, in violation of section 242.[120] This aspect of the indictment, however, did not figure prominently in the trial and conviction of the defendants. The government did not press the racially discriminatory punishment aspect of the case because, as subsequently explained by Victor Rotnem, the chief of the Civil Rights Section of the Department of Justice at the time, "[i]t would be very hard . . . to find an officer who could not demonstrate that at some time in his official career he had used towards white men the same methods which he customarily uses towards Negroes."[121]

Although United States District Judge Bascom S. Deaver did include the allegation of racially discriminatory punishment in his charge to the jury, he minimized the racial aspect of the case. For example, he told the jury that, although they had a charge of disparate punishment on the basis of race to consider, "it is not a question, gentlemen of the jury—and I want to make this clear to you—it is not a question of race prejudice." Judge Deaver explained that a juror's view of "any race question" should not affect his judgment as to whether there had been a violation of a statutory prohibition on "imposing any punishment, that would not be imposed on any other citizen, or any inhabitant because of his race or color."

In the final analysis, therefore, Judge Deaver's instructions to the jury deemphasized the race issues in *Screws*. This emphasis is similar to the government's presentation and formulation of the case. Significantly, the charge of disparate imposition of punishment on the basis of race was only briefly mentioned by the Court of Appeals in its review of the case, and the charge was not even mentioned by the Supreme Court in its decision.[122]

*Screws* was thus treated as a police brutality case in which racial motivation was the obvious and dominant background but not an element of the crime. Accordingly, the defendants were charged with acting under color of state law in such a way as to deprive Hall of his constitutional rights.[123] Following a three-day trial, the jury convicted each defendant on each count. Judge Deaver fined each man $1,000 and sentenced each to three years in prison.[124]

The convictions of the *Screws* defendants were affirmed by a divided panel of United States Court of Appeals for the Fifth Circuit.[125] The Supreme Court produced four separate opinions in *Screws*, none of which commanded the support of a majority of the Court. I will focus on the two main opinions— the plurality opinion of Justice Douglas, which commanded the votes of four justices, and the dissenting opinion of Justice Felix Frankfurter, which was joined by two others—and analyze the manner in which each addressed the federalism problem.[126] Before doing so, we should briefly consider the outcome of *Screws* and its impact on future federal civil rights prosecutions.

In addition to the federalism problem, the Court was also deeply concerned with what I have described elsewhere as the "vagueness problem."[127] Criminal statutes must provide clear ascertainable standards of guilt for the crimes they proscribe. The vagueness problem in the context of civil rights crimes asks whether a criminal prohibition of violations of unenumerated constitutional rights is so vague as to run afoul of this well-established requirement. So long as the violation at the heart of an alleged civil rights crime was a specific and enumerated constitutional right—for example, the right to vote—this tension could be largely overlooked. *Screws*, however, presented a nonenumerated constitutional right to be free from police brutality.

The plurality opinion concluded that, if properly interpreted, section 242 was not unconstitutionally vague. Specifically, the plurality read section 242 to require a showing of willful constitutional violation by the perpetrator of a "right which has been made specific either by the express terms of the Constitution or laws of the United States *or by decisions interpreting them.*"[128] The problem here rests not with the requirement of the specificity of the right, but with the requirement of "willfullness."[129]

The plurality held that the defendants were entitled to a new trial with a new instruction concerning "willfulness" and thus reversed the convictions. Justice Felix Frankfurter's dissent would have reversed the convictions—resulting not in a new trial but in the dismissal of the indictments altogether.

There are numerous problems with the approach articulated by the plurality in *Screws*.[130] It is enough here to mention just one. *Screws* greatly reduced the ability of the Civil Rights Section of the Department of Justice to prosecute civil rights crimes.[131] Perhaps the most immediate proof of this assertion is also the most dramatic. On retrial, the *Screws* defendants were acquitted. Although numerous factors could plausibly explain the different outcome from the first to the second trial, the attorney who tried the second

*Screws* case believed that the prosecution had been "handicapped by the necessity of proving 'willfulness.'"[132] The jury, instructed on constitutional willfulness by the judge, focused on the personal nature of the quarrel between Screws and Robert Hall. The government was thus unable to persuade the jury that the defendants had willfully violated Hall's *constitutional* rights. The chief of the Civil Rights Section described the outcome:

> [T]he judge's charge, while . . . proper under the *Screws* case, was clearly very damaging . . . In short, the burden that the Government now has under the general theme of the *Screws* case in proving the necessary willful intent in such cases is going to continue to build up very high hills to climb.[133]

As briefed to the Supreme Court by the parties, *Screws* was a case about the limits of federalism. Significantly, the *Screws* defendants framed the question presented solely in terms of whether the district court had jurisdiction over state officers whose conduct violated state law.[134] The federalism problem presented itself in *Screws* with a special urgency. Federalizing the punishment of misconduct by state officials—whether or not that misconduct was authorized by state law—had been well established by the time of *Screws*.[135] The scope of misconduct that might be federalized, of course, was restricted to violations of *federal* law. So long as the basis of civil rights crimes was a specific and enumerated constitutional or statutory federal right, this issue of scope presented no conceptual difficulties.

The very significance of *Screws* lies in the fact that it did not involve an enumerated federal right. Rather, *Screws* concerned a nonenumerated constitutional right to be "free from police brutality" that is derived from rights protected by the Fourteenth Amendment. Once the creation and expansion of a federal criminal civil rights law left the safe port of expressly stated federal predicates, it was not self-evident where the limits of federal criminal jurisdiction would be set. *Screws* placed precisely this issue before the Supreme Court.

The dissent of Justice Frankfurter most pointedly discussed the federalism problem. Justice Frankfurter concluded that the federalism problem posed by section 242 was insolvable and that the statute was therefore unconstitutional. Frankfurter grounded his exposition of the federalism problem primarily in the legislative history of the criminal civil rights statutes but also in the policy of "maintaining the delicate balance 'between the judicial tribunals of the Union of the states.'"[136] Frankfurter found the legislative history of section 242 amply clear on the issue of prosecuting state officials in federal court for conduct that violated state law. He concluded that the Fourteenth Amendment may well have provided the power for Congress to authorize such federal prosecutions but that in this statute, Congress had not done so.[137]

Justice Frankfurter went further than merely reviewing and seeking guidance from legislative history. He indicated that broad expansion of federal criminal jurisdiction through the vehicle of criminal civil rights enforcement, even if constitutional, would not comport with his conception of federalism. Frankfurter believed that common law crimes, such as murder, were properly left to the authority of the state to prosecute and adjudicate. This conclusion was grounded not only in his general conception of federalism, but also in the belief that this limitation was necessary to *strengthen* the protection of civil rights. If federal criminal authority were to be applied broadly to violations of the due process rights of citizens, as the federal government sought in *Screws,* the victims would turn to Washington for help and state governments would not be held accountable. With rhetorical flourish, Justice Frankfurter described the "practical question" in *Screws* as "whether the States should be relieved from responsibility to bring their law officers to book for homicide, by allowing prosecution in the federal courts for a relatively minor offense carrying a short sentence."[138]

The most pronounced flaw in the Frankfurter dissent is its attempt to derive a clear and singular lesson from what is among the most muddled of legislative histories. According to the notes kept by Justice Murphy, at the Supreme Court's private conference session at which *Screws* was discussed, one of the justices said that if "we go to the legislative history it will go bad for us." More pointedly, another justice commented that the legislative history might well reveal that, contrary to Frankfurter's constrained view of federalism, the Congresses that enacted the civil rights statutes sought a broad expansion of federal criminal authority and "to hell with state courts."[139] Justice Douglas put it somewhat more delicately in the plurality opinion when he wrote that the pieces of legislative history relied upon by Justice Frankfurter were "inconclusive on the precise problem involved . . . in the present case."[140]

The dissent's utter inability to confront the reality that underlay cases such as *Screws* is an equally serious defect. The concern that expansion of federal authority would relieve state authorities of their obligation in this area ignored the obvious fact that state authorities had no such interest in the first place: no state case was brought, nor were local authorities even willing to investigate the events.

The dissent's core treatment of the federalism problem, however, reflected a valid concern. Certainly the federal civil rights crimes statutes were not designed to make federal all crimes that hitherto had been strictly of state concern. The plurality endeavored to address this federalism problem.

The initial answer to the broadest formulation of the federalism problem is that section 242 itself expressly applies only to conduct "under color of law." Accordingly, this civil rights crimes statute could not federalize all state criminal law, but rather only those crimes that occurred under "color of law" and resulted in the violation of a federally protected right. This was, in essence, the argument made by the plurality of the Court, which held that section 242 "should be construed so as to respect the proper balance between the States and the federal government in law enforcement . . . Congress . . . did not undertake to make all torts of state officials federal crimes."[141] The discussion must then move to a definition of the scope of "color of law," and it is here that the plurality is less than clear.

The plurality seized upon certain quirky aspects of the facts in *Screws* to demonstrate that Claude Screws's conduct, along with that of Frank Jones and Jim Bob Kelley, took place under "color of law." Of greatest import was the fact that the defendants were in the process of arresting Robert Hall. Justice Douglas's opinion is thus based upon the following syllogism:

(1) "It was [the defendants'] duty under Georgia law to make the arrest [of Hall] effective";
(2) "[b]y their own admissions they assaulted Hall in order to protect themselves and to keep their prisoner from escaping";
(3) "[h]ence, their conduct comes within the statute."[142]

Justice Douglas relied on a proposition that had been established for some time: a state official might still be acting under "color of" state law even if his conduct itself violated state law.[143] Douglas coined the term "under 'pretense' of state law" to mean actions taken under authority granted by the state albeit in contravention of state mandate, and the term is still commonly used in jury instructions in federal criminal civil rights cases.[144] Justice Douglas viewed "color of law" far more broadly than did Justice Frankfurter. Yet the actual scope of "color of law" in Douglas's consideration of the federalism problem is not easy to identify with precision. There is reason to

read Douglas broadly: he distinguished acts committed by state officials under "pretense" of law from the "act of officers in the ambit of their personal
pursuits."[145] If "personal pursuits" are restricted to conduct that occurs in an
official's private life, then Justice Douglas's "pretense" of law would be a
sweeping concept.

It is not at all clear that Douglas's opinion embraces this broad interpretation, however, and that reveals the difficulty in this proposed resolution of
the federalism problem. Justice Douglas's finding that the assault and murder of Robert Hall had taken place under color of law rested on the underlying arrest of Hall by the *Screws* defendants: "Acts of officers who undertake
to perform their official duties are included whether they hew to the line of
their authority or overstep it."[146] The plurality's approach, however, ignored
the fact that the performance of "duties" by Screws, Jones, and Kelley was
virtually irrelevant to the events that transpired. Screws was angered at
Hall's assertive behavior: Hall's questioning the seizure of his pistol and having Screws brought before a local grand jury. Screws plotted his revenge
against Hall by effecting an arrest that was of specious foundation at best and
persuading Kelley and Jones to join him in this scheme. Once Kelley and
Jones detained and handcuffed Hall, they brought him to the courthouse
where Screws was waiting.

Suppose that Screws's plot had been slightly different. Suppose that he
had directed Kelley and Jones simply to kidnap Hall, without benefit of any
arrest warrant, even one of questionable validity, and to bring him to Screws
at the well in front of the courthouse. The rest of the facts are the same: Hall
is beaten at the well by the three defendants and subsequently dies from the
injuries he sustains at the hands of a sheriff and two police officers, and no
state investigation or prosecution follows. Justice Douglas could not say of
this hypothetical what he said of *Screws:* "[T]he state officers were authorized to make an arrest and to take such steps as were necessary to make the
arrest effective. They acted without authority *only in the sense* that they used
excessive force in making the arrest effective."[147] The hypothetical *Screws*
defendants would have acted without authority, not in the sense of using
excessive force to effect an arrest, but in the sense of kidnapping a private
citizen in order to inflict serious physical harm. The need and justification
for federal civil rights jurisdiction in our hypothetical case are just as great as
they are in *Screws,* but Douglas's approach to the federalism problem would
be unavailing in recognizing such jurisdiction.

Douglas's proposed middle ground between (1) federalization of all state crimes (or at least all criminal behavior by state officials) and (2) Justice Frankfurter's restriction of federal criminal civil rights jurisdiction to those cases, if any, in which the state itself is directly complicitous, cannot hold. The solution to the federalism problem does lie in the center that Douglas sought, and I will return to this problem at the end of the chapter.

### Federal Civil Rights Crime Law from the 1950s through the Second Reconstruction

Our examination of the federalism problem comes full circle with the resurgence of the civil rights movement during the late 1950s and the 1960s, culminating in the Second Reconstruction era. The assertion of federally based civil rights by and on behalf of African-Americans met with widespread racial violence. While the majority of such incidents occurred in the South, the North often proved no safer.[148] This violence took the form of numerous murders, as well as hundreds of shootings, bombings, beatings, and church burnings.[149] Generally, state law enforcement was unequal to the task of preventing or punishing these crimes. For its part, the federal government sought to diffuse situations as they arose rather than to use federal prosecutions as means to stem racial violence. The celebrated federal response to the desegregation of schools in Little Rock, Arkansas, is an early example of this approach to crisis management.

Pursuant to the Supreme Court's landmark 1954 decision in *Brown v. Board of Education*, the Little Rock School Board announced that it would begin a program of gradual desegregation of its schools beginning in the 1957–58 school year. Six days before the scheduled start of school, a white citizen of Little Rock sought a state court injunction prohibiting the integration of the schools.[150] Partly on the basis of Governor Orval Faubus's testimony that violence was likely to occur if desegregation went forward, the state court enjoined the requirement that white children attend school with black children, and barred black children from attending schools maintained for white children. Although this injunction was vacated by a federal district judge, Governor Faubus called on the National Guard to prevent the enrollment of black children.

The scene that followed is well known. The nine black students who attempted to enroll at the white high school were met by a jeering mob and the National Guard. In response to the federal court desegregation order, Faubus recalled the National Guard; this had the effect of letting loose a violent mob. A crisis of national proportion quickly developed, and President Eisenhower reacted by sending in federal troops.

Once peace was restored in Little Rock, a number of options were available. Given the involvement and complacency of local officials, federal authorities could have sought individual indictments under sections 241 and 242. This would have sent a strong message, both in Little Rock and elsewhere, that racial violence would not be tolerated by the federal government. Indictments, however, were never brought. Federal troops were required to remain in Little Rock for the rest of the school year to maintain the peace.

Another well-known example of the federal response to racial violence during this period involves the Freedom Rides of 1961. The Freedom Rides were part of an effort to breathe life into the Supreme Court decisions barring segregation on all interstate buses and trains and in transportation terminals.[151] To draw attention to the continuing segregation of bus terminals in the South, the Congress of Racial Equality (CORE) organized a racially mixed group of travelers who volunteered to board buses in the North and attempt to travel to New Orleans.[152]

The buses met with violence almost immediately upon entering the South. Five days after beginning their journey, riders were assaulted in South Carolina. Even as the violence level heightened, the federal response was tepid. When the bus pulled into Montgomery, Alabama, it was met by a mob of 1,000 that attacked the riders with pipes, sticks, and clubs and inflicted severe beatings, even knocking unconscious a special assistant to the attorney general who was serving as the President's representative. Local law enforcement officials stood by silently. Despite his misgivings about providing federal protection for civil rights activists, Attorney General Robert Kennedy felt forced to dispatch 600 federal marshals to Montgomery.[153]

Events forced the hand of federal law enforcement. Soon after the original violence, Martin Luther King, Jr., flew to Montgomery to lend support to the riders. He quickly found himself trapped in a church with other civil rights workers by a mob that seemed intent on violence. Not until the federal marshals employed tear gas and billy clubs did the mob dissipate. As a result of the severity of the situation, the Justice Department sought and received a sweeping federal injunction from Judge Frank Johnson enjoining the Ku Klux Klan and others from interfering with interstate travel. The Attorney General also spoke with Senator Eastland of Mississippi, who offered his personal assurance of safety for the riders while in his state. This combination of measures successfully brought an end to the immediate threats of physical violence to the Freedom Riders.[154]

In the aftermath of the 1961 Freedom Rides, the Kennedy administration, like the Eisenhower administration before it, opted against pursuing indictments for civil rights crimes. Instead, a more limited course was followed. Robert Kennedy began discussions with the Interstate Commerce Commission (ICC), an independent federal agency, to ban segregation at interstate transportation facilities. The Department of Justice went so far as to provide the ICC with a complete course of action to follow. While the plan initially met with resistance, the ICC was eventually persuaded to adopt it. In addition, to avoid similar situations in the future, the Attorney General began discussions with various leaders of the civil rights movement to convince them to change their tactics from provocation to voter registration drives. The focus was on preventing similar incidents in the future, not on utilizing federal criminal sanction to hold individuals accountable for their actions.[155]

The federalism problem was at the heart of the Justice Department's reluctance to become involved in racial violence cases. Both Robert Kennedy and Burke Marshall, the Assistant Attorney General in charge of the Civil Rights Division, firmly believed that it was improper to expand federal jurisdiction in the area of civil rights. The violence that was occurring in the South, although clearly racially motivated, was also clearly the type that had traditionally been investigated and prosecuted at the local level. Murder and assault are not federal crimes, and therefore there was no federal jurisdiction. Broadly expanded federal criminal jurisdiction, Kennedy and Marshall feared, would be tantamount to creating a national police force, a substantial threat to civil liberties.

The federalism problem was the basis on which the Justice Department in the Kennedy administration justified its decisions whether to establish a federal presence during the violence surrounding the civil rights movement. Federal marshals were sent to Montgomery in 1961 to protect the right to interstate travel. A year later, marshals (and even soldiers) were sent to the University of Mississippi campus to enforce a federal court order and to aid James Meredith's admission to 'Ole Miss. But federal officers were not sent to Birmingham, Alabama, in May 1963 or to Philadelphia, Mississippi, in July 1964 because there was no similar federal responsibility.[156] Robert Kennedy was well aware of the grave difficulties raised by the administration's view of the federalism problem. Describing the nature of the dilemma he faced in 1964, he wrote:

But the intricacies of our federal system and the distinctions between when and how the federal government can act are difficult to explain to a nation sickened and aroused by photographs and news accounts of a police dog at the throat of a Negro woman and of a fire hose knocking over a Negro child . . . Accordingly, there is an increased demand on the part of our people for federal protection of our Negro citizens in some areas in the South, as well as protection for those working with them on behalf of civil rights. At the same time, there is a reluctance to start down the path that would lead inevitably to the creation of a national police force.[157]

To be sure, there were more ominous reasons as well for the federal government's limited response to racial violence in the South. The FBI's policy during this time was not to get involved with racial violence unless absolutely necessary. Agents were to take notes of events that transpired but not to get involved. Some have suggested that it was J. Edgar Hoover's racism that prevented him and the FBI from taking a more active role.[158] Two somewhat less nefarious reasons suggest themselves as well. The first reason we have observed before: the FBI, under Hoover, depended upon the cooperation of Southern law enforcement officers for help in solving numerous crimes and could not afford to alienate them. The second reason stemmed from Hoover's famous concern with the FBI's crime statistics. He did not tolerate low conviction rates and sought to restrict investigations to those crimes likely to result in convictions. Hoover recognized that white juries in the South were unlikely to indict, let alone convict, other whites for violence against blacks generally and against civil rights workers in particular. The result was that FBI agents became famous for observing horrific acts of violence and standing by while victims were attacked. As Hoover was fond of saying, the agency was only allowed to investigate, not get involved.[159] The FBI's refusal to help victims, even when agents were on the scene, added to many civil rights groups' distrust of the government. This distrust was exacerbated as an increasing number of voter-registration workers were attacked and no federal response came. The focus on registration was in part a response to government's request after the Freedom Rides that the civil rights movement concentrate its efforts in this area. Many in the civil rights movement began to lose their faith in the federal government.[160]

During the Second Reconstruction, Congress passed what is today codified as section 245 of the Federal Criminal Code.[161] Section 245 was the first federal criminal civil rights legislation since the Civil Rights Act of 1875. Because this statute deals with federalization of crimes committed by private individuals—as opposed to state officials—it is the perfect place to conclude this historical discussion of the federalism problem. Two Supreme Court decisions in 1966 interpreting the scope of the First Reconstruction statutes, sections 241 and 242, provide the necessary backdrop for understanding the Second Reconstruction legislation.

*United States v. Price* presented the Court with a case that had garnered national attention, the brutal incident that would forever link the names of three young civil rights workers: Michael Schwerner, James Chaney, and Andrew Goodman.[162] On June 21, 1964, Schwerner, Chaney, and Goodman were detained by the deputy sheriff of Neshoba County, Mississippi. They were placed in jail, released later that night, and then shortly thereafter again intercepted by the deputy, who made all three get into the police car, and then abandoned them on an unpaved road. Once deposited, the three were attacked and killed by a group of eighteen men, including deputy sheriffs from the Philadelphia, Mississippi, Police Department. Their bodies were dumped into a dam at a construction site.

The incident set off a national outcry, as the three were missing for an extended period of time. The FBI was directed to find the men and began a massive search that ultimately led agents to the bodies. The Department of Justice abandoned its usual reluctance to bring federal criminal charges and sought indictments against numerous defendants under sections 241 and 242. The federal district court dismissed the indictments because the majority of defendants were private citizens, not law officers.[163]

The Supreme Court addressed each of the two counts of the indictment in *Price.* With respect to the indictment under section 242—the deprivation of rights under color of law—the Court focused on the "under color of law" requirement in the statute. A unanimous Court held that actions by private individuals when "jointly engaged with state officials" constitute state actions themselves.[164] Given the involvement of state officials in the release, recapture, and murder of Schwerner, Chaney, and Goodman, the Court had more than enough evidence to sustain the indictments against all the defendants. The Court next turned its attention to the indictment of all eighteen defendants under section 241. The district court had interpreted the general language of section 241, prohibiting all conspiracies to deprive persons of the rights guaranteed under the Constitution and laws of the United States, not to apply to rights secured under the Fourteenth Amendment. The *Price* Court, in accordance with the holding in *Screws,* disagreed with the district court and held that Fourteenth Amendment rights, specifically due process rights, were secured by the Constitution, and thus a willful violation of such rights was punishable under section 241.

The decision in *United States v. Guest*,[165] handed down the same day as *Price*, addressed the question of whether section 241 applied to the Equal Protection Clause of the Fourteenth Amendment, specifically an alleged violation of the right to equal access of public facilities "owned, operated, or managed by or on behalf of the State of Georgia."[166] Because *Price* fully resolved that section 241 covered violations of rights secured by the Fourteenth Amendment, the real question in *Guest* was whether state action was necessary; the indictment contained no allegation of any person's acting under color of law. Historically, the Court had held that the Fourteenth Amendment was a protection only against state discrimination, not private conduct. Justice Potter Stewart wrote an opinion that, with respect to most issues in the case, commanded the majority of the Court. Justice Stewart "solved" the state action problem through reliance on a quirky fact in the case: the defendants had filed false reports in order to have their victims arrested. This he found was sufficient state action to withstand dismissal. Justice Stewart also concluded that the defendants had interfered with the victims' right to travel, an independent basis for the indictment that required no state action. Justice Stewart's opinion, however, never reached the question of whether the Constitution authorized Congress to punish discrimination by individuals in the absence of any state action.

The issue of punishing purely private discrimination drew the direct attention of Justices Tom Clark and William Brennan, each of whom wrote a separate opinion. These two opinions together represented the views of six of the nine justices on the Supreme Court and thus a kind of majority of their own. Justice Clark wrote briefly to emphasize the Court's lack of opinion on the question of whether Congress could proscribe individual private action, concluding that Congress indeed has such authority.[167] Justice Brennan took the Court's silence on the issue to imply that Congress could not legislate if it so chose, a conclusion he, like Justice Clark, rejected. He thus wrote to argue affirmatively that section 241 did prohibit private conspiracies and that this reach of the law was constitutional under the Fourteenth Amendment.[168] Combined, the six votes of the Clark and Brennan opinions were a clear "invitation to legislate."

Congress accepted the invitation in 1968 when, as part of the Civil Rights Act of 1968, it enacted the statute codified today as section 245. Section 245 was designed to address the racial violence arising out of the civil rights movement.[169] While acknowledging the centrality of local law enforcement in punishing crime, Congress noted the unwillingness of local governments to fulfill their obligations where African-Americans were concerned and the resulting need for federal action to compensate.[170] Section 245 thus allowed federal law enforcement to prosecute and punish private people for violations of federal rights, such as interstate travel or voting in federal elections, and violations of state rights, such as attending public school or voting in state elections, with racial motivation.

The statute has been sparsely used, perhaps even underutilized. In the first ten years following passage of section 245, for example, only sixteen prosecutions were undertaken for acts in the South.[171] If, however, there is to be an active federal role in the prosecution of racial violence under present law, section 245 is the statutory basis.

## The Federalism Problem Today

All federal criminal legislation faces the federalism problem. As a matter of legal doctrine, this is certainly true since the Supreme Court decision in *United States v. Lopez.* In the area of civil rights crimes generally, and bias crimes in particular, it has always been true.

As noted, a civil rights crime consists of a parallel crime with the addition of bias motivation, rights interference, or official misconduct. Parallel crimes, by themselves, are state crimes only. As a matter of federal criminal jurisdiction, the distinction between the parallel crime and the civil rights crime is therefore critical. (In a broader context, we have seen that the distinction between a parallel crime and a bias crime exists even when federal jurisdiction is not an issue and when the concern is enhanced punishment for the bias crime.) Official crimes and rights interference crimes raise the fewest problems with respect to federalism, once we set aside the fanciful objections such as those in Justice Frankfurter's dissenting opinion in *Screws.*

Federal criminal jurisdiction of official crimes is limited to criminal acts committed by state officials. This is a circumscribed body of cases that avoids the concern that federal criminal enforcement will be imposed in all matters of state law. Moreover, these are precisely the cases in which federal enforcement will be most required. The reluctance of state law enforcement to investigate and prosecute state officials is one of the prime justifications for federal criminal civil rights jurisdiction. Finally, as a constitutional matter, when the defendant is a state official, the constitutional authority for federal criminal jurisdiction is at its highest, even according to the most limited interpretations of the Reconstruction-era amendments.

Under a federal rights interference crime statute, the accused may be punished only if he acted with the purpose of interfering with the right concerned. The limit created by this fully addresses the federalism problem. By limiting federal criminal jurisdiction to those instances in which the accused seeks to violate the victim's federal rights, the law protects the jurisdictional boundaries. Consider a perpetrator who intentionally commits an assault that, unbeknownst to him, keeps his victim from being able to vote. He stands in the same position as anyone who commits a simple assault, governed by state law. The lack of intent to violate the victim's federal rights precludes federal involvement in such a case. Only the defendant who purposely precludes his victim from voting is brought within the reach of federal criminal jurisdiction.

A federal bias crime law, however, meets the federalism problem head-on. It is partially for this reason that, at the present time, there is no pure federal bias crime statute. Bias motivation is an element of certain federal civil rights crimes. As was seen in the discussion of *Screws,* there is a little-used clause in section 242 that punishes the official crime of imposing excessive punishment on racial minorities or aliens.[172] A litany of rights interference crimes, if committed because of the victim's race, color, religion, or national origin, is proscribed by section 245.[173] Moreover, in 1994 Congress directed the United States Sentencing Commission to promulgate guidelines enhancing the penalties for any federal crimes in which there is racial motivation.[174] These statutes, however, cover only a small range of cases involving bias motivation. The inquiry for the balance of this chapter is whether there could and should be a federal criminal statute reaching bias crimes generally.

Because bias crimes are distinguished from ordinary state law crimes solely by the actor's racial motivation toward the victim, we confront three sets of questions concerning federal bias crimes and the federalism problem:

(1) The constitutional question: Is there a constitutional basis for federal criminal jurisdiction over bias crimes?

(2) The prudential question: Assuming a constitutional basis for federal criminal jurisdiction over bias crimes, is there a sufficient federal interest here to warrant such legislation?

(3) The pragmatic question: Assuming both a constitutional basis and a

prudential need for federal bias crime laws, how should federal and state jurisdiction over these crimes work together?

## The Constitutional Question

On some level, the federalism problem is an issue of constitutional authority. As shown, federal criminal jurisdiction, as originally understood, was quite limited. The constitutional authority for most of the expansion of federal criminal jurisdiction has been congressional power over interstate commerce. This is easy to understand in areas such as federal laws dealing with organized crime and the distribution and sale of narcotics. It is also an obvious basis for asserting federal jurisdiction over carjacking. What is more surprising is that interstate commerce has been the constitutional predicate for all Second Reconstruction–era civil rights statutes. The more obvious choice for this constitutional authority would have been the post–Civil War amendments to the Constitution, particularly the Thirteenth Amendment, which abolished slavery, and the Fourteenth Amendment, which, among other things, provided federal guarantees of due process of law and equal protection of the laws. We saw, however, that in cases such as the *Slaughter-House Cases, Cruikshank,* and *The Civil Rights Cases,* the Supreme Court limited the scope of criminal jurisdiction supported by these amendments. Specifically, due process of law and equal protection of the laws were held to be rights that could be asserted only against the state, and not against private individuals.

When Congress enacted civil rights legislation that would provide rights against private individuals during the Second Reconstruction, these statutes were thus grounded in federal authority to regulate interstate commerce. This was the basis upon which the Supreme Court upheld the legislation. The classic source for this development is the pair of civil rights cases that the Supreme Court decided in 1964, upholding the public accommodations provisions of the Civil Rights Act of 1964: *Heart of Atlanta Motel v. United States*[175] and *Katzenbach v. McClung.*[176] In *Heart of Atlanta Motel,* an Atlanta, Georgia, hotel owner refused to serve black travelers, while in *McClung,* the owner of Ollie's Barbecue in Birmingham, Alabama, refused to serve black customers. Each claimed that the Civil Rights Act of 1964, in barring discrimination in public accommodations, exceeded constitutional authority to regulate private conduct. The Civil Rights Act as applied in these two cases was deemed to be constitutional, because the Heart of Atlanta Motel served interstate travelers, and because Ollie's Barbecue, though it served primarily local customers, bought a substantial quantity of food products that had moved through interstate commerce. Two Justices, William O. Douglas and Arthur Goldberg, wrote separate opinions, arguing that the civil rights legislation could be constitutionally grounded in the Fourteenth Amendment's Equal Protection Clause. The other seven justices expressly declined to rule on this point, and the federal government did not argue either case on this basis.[177]

The Commerce Clause could be used as constitutional authority for public accommodation nondiscrimination laws or for laws barring discrimination in housing and employment. But the Commerce Clause is a poorer fit with federal civil rights crime laws. Official crimes, rights interference crimes, and bias crimes do not always interfere with interstate commerce, even an expansive view of interstate commerce. Indeed, they generally do not. Constitutional authority for federal laws prohibiting official crimes and rights interference crimes is clear. Official crimes such as police brutality, at least since *Screws*, are understood to involve sufficient state action to fall within the Fourteenth Amendment—the official crime is a denial of due process of law. Rights interference crimes, by definition, implicate a constitutionally created federal right, such as the right to vote in federal elections. Thus the official crimes and rights interference crimes aspects of sections 241 and 242 raise no constitutional problems—the problems arise with respect to federal bias crimes.

Upon the occasion of creating the Civil Rights Unit of the Department of Justice, then–Attorney General Frank Murphy expressed the constitutional limits of the federal government's ability to enforce civil rights against private defendants:

> It must be borne in mind that the authority of the Federal Government in this field [of civil rights enforcement] is somewhat limited by the fact that many of the constitutional guarantees are guarantees against abuse by the Federal Government itself or by the State Government, and are not guarantees against infringement by individuals or groups of individuals.[178]

As a matter of constitutional authority, therefore, may the federal government punish bias crimes?

The answer lies in the post–Civil War constitutional amendments. We saw that when the Civil Rights Act of 1964 regulated private conduct, with the civil antidiscrimination provisions governing, among other things, employment, education, housing, and access to public accommodations, Congress, the Department of Justice, and the Supreme Court itself all looked to the Commerce Clause of the Constitution and not to the post–Civil War amendments. But for the criminal provisions in the Civil Rights Act of 1968, section 245, covering criminal violation of certain federal rights, and racially motivated violation of certain state rights, Congress expressly relied, in part, upon the Fourteenth and Fifteenth Amendments.[179] Such constitutional authority for federalization of racially motivated deprivation of state rights was hardly a new idea in 1968. It may be found at least as early as Justice Bradley's opinion in *Cruikshank*.[180]

Our question goes beyond what Justice Bradley wrote in 1874 or what Congress did in 1968. Not all bias crimes deprive the victim of the ability to exercise some right under state law. Thus not all federal bias crime prosecutions could be authorized by the Fourteenth or Fifteenth Amendments, no matter how generous the understanding of state action. The Thirteenth Amendment, however, does provide constitutional authority for a federal bias crime law.

The Thirteenth Amendment states that "[n]either slavery nor involuntary servitude . . . shall exist within the United States" and further provides Congress with the power to enforce the amendment "by appropriate legislation."[181] In the nineteenth and early twentieth century, the Court interpreted the scope and purpose of the amendment narrowly, viewing it as a formal statement of emancipation, which was largely already accomplished. For example, in *Hodges v. United States*, the Court dismissed an indictment that had charged a group of white defendants with conspiring to deprive black workers of the right to make contracts, because the violation of the right to make a contract was not an incident of slavery.[182] The modern view of the Thirteenth Amendment is much broader. Indeed, in a series of cases, the Supreme Court has articulated a theory of the Thirteenth Amendment as a source of broad proscription of all the "badges and incidents" of slavery. Moreover, this proscription applies to the conduct of private individuals, not just to state actions.

The path-breaking case was *Jones v. Alfred Mayer Co*,[183] in which the Court held that private racial discrimination in the sale of property violated section 1982, a civil First Reconstruction statute that guarantees to all citizens the "same right . . . as is enjoyed by white citizens . . . to inherit, purchase, lease, sell, hold and convey real and personal property."[184] In this regard, *Jones* expressly overruled *Hodges*. Several years later, in *Runyon v. McCrary*,[185] the Court similarly held that section 1981, a statute of the same period providing all persons with "the same right . . . to make and enforce contracts . . . as is enjoyed by white citizens," prohibited private racial discrimination in any contractual arrangements.[186] *Runyon* itself involved discrimination in education. In *Jones* and *Runyon,* the Court held that the Thirteenth Amendment provided the constitutional authority for the regulation of private discriminatory conduct. Just as the first section of the amendment had abolished slavery and all "badges and incidents" of slavery, so the second section empowered Congress to make any rational determination as to that conduct which constitutes a badge or incident of slavery and to ban such conduct, whether from public or private sources.

The abolition of slavery in the Thirteenth Amendment, although clearly grounded in the enslavement of African-Americans, has always been understood to apply beyond the context of race. As noted, as early as the *Slaughter-House Cases,* Justice Miller saw the Thirteenth Amendment as a prohibition not only against slavery of black citizens but also against "Mexican peonage" and "Chinese coolie labor systems."[187] Modern cases have extended the protection of the amendment to religious and ethnic groups as well.[188]

As a matter of constitutional authority, Congress may enact a federal bias crime law so long as it is rational to determine that racially motivated violence is as much a "badge" or "incident" of slavery as is discrimination in contractual or property matters. This determination is surely rational. Racially motivated violence, from the First Reconstruction on, was in large part a means of maintaining the subjugation of blacks that had existed under slavery. Violence was an integral part of the institution of slavery, and post–Thirteenth Amendment racial violence was designed to continue *de facto* what was constitutionally no longer permitted *de jure.*

The broad reach of the Thirteenth Amendment as understood today goes beyond a prohibition of re-enslavement of those who have been previously enslaved. By protecting ethnic, religious, and national-origin minority groups, the Thirteenth Amendment is now more consonant with a positive guarantee of freedom and equal participation in civil society.[189] Violence, directed against an individual out of motive of group bias, violates this concept of freedom. The Congress, in determining which groups to include in a federal bias crime statute, engages in precisely the same process as do state legislatures or local governments when determining, as discussed in Chapter 1, which group characteristics implicate social fissure lines. Whereas a state or local entity may find a social fissure line on a local level, Congress may act only on a national level. Indeed, the Supreme Court did just that, albeit implicitly, in determining the scope of sections 1981 and 1982. In enacting a federal bias crime law, Congress would do so explicitly.

## The Prudential Question

One of the main prudential concerns voiced by the federalism problem is that federal criminal civil rights jurisdiction—even assuming a constitutional basis for federal legislation—would broadly encroach upon traditional state matters. The specter of federalizing all state crimes is simply not a serious concern where the federal punishment of bias crimes is concerned. The very requirement of racial motivation for bias crimes provides a workable limit to the imposition of federal criminal jurisdiction upon state law crimes. A federal bias crime statute would bring within federal jurisdiction only those cases in which bias motivation could be proven. Even with our increased awareness of bias crimes, these crimes still constitute only a tiny proportion of the universe of state law crimes.[190]

Another aspect of the prudential question asks whether there is a sufficient federal interest to warrant federal bias crime legislation, again assuming constitutional authority. There are two sources of strong federal interest in support of such legislation. The first arises out of the problem of state default in bias crime prosecution, the prime justification for the original creation of federal criminal civil rights legislation. During the nineteenth and the early twentieth century, state governments, particularly in the South, could not be relied upon to investigate and prosecute bias crimes within their jurisdiction. Even through the middle part of this century, state default has remained a critical factor warranting a federal role in bias crimes. But for federal intervention, criminal charges would never have been brought in such cases as *Screws, Guest,* and *Price.*

This crudest form of state default, present for a full century after the Civil War, is far less common today. Still, a less pernicious form of state default continues to exist is some circumstances, and calls for a federal role in these crimes. The contemporary form of state default arises more from systemic factors than from volitional wrongdoing on the part of state actors. For example, cases involving racially motivated violence are likely to be of great local notoriety and to be politically charged. In most states, these cases would have to be prosecuted by an elected district attorney and decided by a jury from the county in which the event took place. Federal prosecutions would be brought by an appointed United States Attorney who, though not necessarily isolated from the political process, is nonetheless largely immune from politics. It is highly unusual for United States Attorneys to serve more than a single four-year appointed term, whereas local district attorneys are never more than four years (and often less) from the next election. Moreover, federal juries are drawn from federal judicial districts that encompass a far broader cross-section of the population than the community in which a racially charged event took place.

Consider, for example, the tragic events that occurred in Chattanooga, Tennessee, in April 1980. A group of Ku Klux Klansmen fired on five elderly black women after a cross-burning. State criminal charges were brought against three defendants, two of whom were acquitted. The one who was convicted received only a twenty-month sentence and was paroled after four months. In a civil action, however, a federal jury awarded the victims $535,000.[191] It is arguable, therefore, that a federal criminal jury might well have returned a guilty verdict had the defendants been charged with a federal bias crime.[192]

None of this is to say that *all* federal law enforcement authorities will be better than *any* state law enforcement authorities when it comes to dealing with bias crimes. As will be shown, the best arrangement will be one of cooperative investigations through overlapping jurisdiction. Even in an age where, one hopes, a Claude Screws could not be elected to the state senate, there is a strong argument for a federal role in bias crime prosecution on the basis of state default.

The second source of federal interest to support federal bias crime legislation applies even in the absence of state default. Recall that the heart of the federalism problem is the federalization of state law crimes. Although parallel crimes are generally state law crimes, bias crimes are not, or at least not exclusively so. Racial motivation implicates the commitment to equality that is one of the highest values of our national social contract. It is for just this reason that we observed that bias crimes affected not only the immediate individual victims and the target victim community but the general community as well. Racial equality was at the center of the Civil War and the constitutional amendments that marked the end of that war. Needless to say, equality has not always been observed in deed in the United States, and not all would agree on what exactly "the equality ideal" means. But none can deny that the commitment to equality is a core American principal. Bias crimes thus violate the national social contract, and not only that of the local or state community. Even if there were no issue of state default whatsoever, there is a firm prudential basis for a federal role in the investigation and prosecution of bias crimes.

A final aspect of the prudential question concerns the need for new legislation. Existing federal criminal civil rights legislation is inadequate to address bias crimes fully. The federal sentencing-enhancement legislation applies only to federal crimes that are committed with bias motivation. Because the parallel crime must be a federal crime itself, this law misses the most common bias crimes, which have as their parallel crimes the state law offenses of assault or vandalism. In order to obtain a conviction under section 245(b)(2), the closest thing that there is to an actual federal bias crime law today, the prosecution must prove two elements. The first element requires that the perpetrator committed the act with bias motivation. The second requires that the perpetrator intended to interfere with certain of the victim's state rights, for example, use of public highways or public accommodations such as a restaurant or a hotel. This second element is often an insurmountable burden that precludes federal involvement in the prosecution of a serious bias crime. Two cases make the point well.

In California, federal prosecutors decided not to prosecute a racist Skinhead gang under section 245, even though evidence pointed to a conspiracy to bomb a black church and assassinate some of its members. Instead, the gang members were prosecuted under weapons and explosives charges. The United States Attorney, Mark R. Greenberg, explained that "charging a civil rights violation would have made a very difficult case . . . because of the requirement that a specific 'protected right' be the purpose of the planned attacks."[193]

In the Crown Heights section of Brooklyn, New York, calls for federal action intensified after a Brooklyn jury acquitted Lemrick Nelson of murdering Yankel Rosenbaum, a Hasidic scholar who was stabbed during the Crown Heights rioting. United States Attorney General Janet Reno expressed reluctance even to commence a grand jury investigation of the incident owing to a lack of evidence. In particular, Reno stated that using federal civil rights laws would make it more difficult than using state law to prosecute the case successfully.[194] Federal prosecutors would need to prove not only that Nelson committed the crime and that he did so out of religious motivation, but also that the victim was chosen because of his use of public facilities. This last element would be extremely difficult to prove. Indeed, in all likelihood it simply was not true. Despite these evidentiary problems, in August 1994 the federal government indicted Nelson on federal charges that he violated Yankel Rosenbaum's civil rights. Two years later, the government obtained the indictment of Charles Price on similar charges.[195] A federal bias crime law would have permitted the cases against Nelson and Price to go forward on issues of religious motivation. Although both men were convicted, these cases were cluttered with the issue of the use of public facilities.[196] The need for federal intervention in this case and the federal interest in the killing would have been the same had Rosenbaum been killed with religious motivation in a private building, well off a public street. But for the seemingly unimportant fact that this bias-motivated murder took place in a street, under current federal law there would have been no convictions in the Crown Heights case.

### The Pragmatic Question

The best starting point for considering how concurrent federal and state jurisdiction over bias crimes would proceed is to look to the way concurrent federal and state jurisdiction over other civil rights crimes, specifically official crimes such as police brutality, has proceeded. Federal law enforcement has adopted a deferential posture toward state enforcement of civil rights crimes. According to Department of Justice policy, once state or local charges have been filed, federal civil rights investigations are suspended. Although the FBI may conduct an investigation of a civil rights crime at the same time as local authorities, the end-point of this investigation must still be a referral to the Department of Justice, which will defer to any local charges.[197]

The limited federal role is driven by prudential, not constitutional, factors. As a matter of constitutional law, the federal government has the authority to conduct concurrent investigations while state proceedings are underway, and federal prosecutors may proceed even after a full-blown state investigation, trial, and acquittal. This is the scenario that took place in the Rodney King beating case. Ordinarily, dual prosecutions that arise out of the same set of events are barred by the Constitution's double-jeopardy clause.[198] There is an exception, however, for an act that violates both federal and state law. Such an act is deemed to violate the law of two sovereigns and, under the "dual-sovereignty doctrine," is two separate offenses for double-jeopardy purposes.[199] The dual-sovereignty doctrine has been severely criticized over the years; indeed, it is not easy to support a doctrine that allows a defendant to be tried twice for what is in reality the same crime.[200]

There is not space here for a full examination of the merits of the dual-sovereignty doctrine; this has been done well elsewhere.[201] Moreover, the goal here is to devise the best means of facilitating the enforcement of bias crime laws with overlapping federal and state authority. As we shall see shortly, there are good reasons to avoid federal reliance on follow-up prosecutions of racially motivated crimes even aside from questions of double jeopardy. We should note, however, that even though there is federal constitutional *authority* to engage in dual prosecutions, as a matter of *practice* these are very rare. Pursuant to an internal policy known as the "Petite Policy," after a case of the same name, the Department of Justice adopted its own version of a double-jeopardy bar to federal prosecutions following state trials for the same criminal acts, whether those trials resulted in convictions or acquittals. The Petite Policy restricts federal prosecution following a state trial to instances in which compelling reasons exist to prosecute, such as cases in which there remain "substantial federal interests demonstrably unvindicated" by the state procedures.[202] The Rodney King case, where such compelling reasons were deemed to exist, is thus the exceptional case that proves the rule.[203] Interestingly, in the appeal of Stacey Koon's federal sentence for his role in beating King, the Supreme Court ruled that the trial judge had not abused his discretion in making a downward departure from the federal sentencing guidelines because of the burden of successive prosecutions.[204]

The Petite Policy uses some of the right reasons to draw the wrong conclusions. Dual prosecutions are surely to be avoided whenever possible, not only out of concern for the defendant, but also because of resulting problems for the prosecution. Let us assume that the state court prosecution ended in an acquittal. Were there a conviction, the argument for a subsequent federal trial would be weak on its face and would require little further discussion. The testimony of any witness at the state trial would be available for use by the defense in its cross-examination of that witness if called by the prosecution in the subsequent federal trial. Problems in the state case cannot be resolved merely by trying again. Moreover, there is the risk that federal prosecutors in a subsequent action will be seen, even by a federal jury, as officious intermeddlers and outsiders. In the federal Rodney King trial, the judge agreed with a prosecution request that defense counsel not be permitted to refer to Department of Justice lawyers as "Washington lawyers" during the trial, and he issued the following startling ruling: "There will be no reference to 'lawyers from Washington' . . . That's a stigma that cannot be tolerated."[205]

The Petite Policy is thus correct to try to avoid dual prosecutions as often as possible. It is wrong, however, to assume that the single prosecution that is brought must be a state-court prosecution. If, as I have proposed, there were concurrent federal and state criminal jurisdiction over racially motivated crimes, then bias crimes would join numerous other instances of concurrent criminal jurisdiction—narcotics and organized crime, just to mention two. In these areas there is no notion of federal deference to state law enforcement. Indeed, in many instances the presumption is exactly to the contrary. For our purposes, however, the better analogy is to those areas in which federal and state law enforcement work together, particularly at the investigatory stage, and then, when it comes time to determine which criminal charges are to be brought, the merits of each are weighed. At its best, this process produces a careful consideration of whether relevant federal or state law is the best vehicle for law enforcement in order to right the criminal wrong that was committed. Admittedly, at its worst, this process can degenerate into political squabbling about which office will win a "turf battle" and whether the United States Attorney or the district attorney will receive the credit for bringing the case. In determining the best means by which to punish bias crimes, however, we need not assume the worst of law enforcement.

A federal bias crime statute should give federal investigators and prosecutors the authority and incentive to pursue racially motivated violence as vigorously as they might drug cartels or organized crime. Local authorities should do so as well. In cooperation, each may enhance the other's abilities. In states with strong bias crime statutes, and in municipalities with well-organized and well-trained bias investigation units, federal authorities may well decide to defer to state law enforcement. In states that lack these capabilities, federal authorities should, as they historically were charged to do in cases of outright state default, take the lead.

It has long been recognized that the purpose of federal civil rights enforcement is to create both a sword and a shield: a sword for national government action against the perpetrators of serious social wrongs and a shield to protect the victims.[206] This proposed framework provides a means for strengthening the shield and sharpening the sword.

CHAPTER 7

# Why Punish Hate?

Let us dedicate ourselves to what the Greeks wrote so many years ago: to tame the savageness of man and to make gentle the life of this world. Let us dedicate ourselves to that, and say a prayer for our country and for our people.

—Robert F. Kennedy, April 4, 1968

The last several decades have seen a dramatic increase in the awareness of bias crimes—both by the public generally and by the legal culture in particular—and the need for a legal response. We need look no further than the marked rise in the number of bias crime laws.

These developments, however, can obscure the controversy that often surrounds the debate over the enactment of a bias crime law. For example, during the debate over Arizona's bias crime law, enacted in 1997, one legislator objected on the grounds that "I still don't believe that a crime against one person is any more heinous than the same crime against someone else." Another put the matter more bluntly: "a few Jews" in the legislature were making the issue "emotional and divisive."[1] Acrimony has surrounded the debate over many state laws. Is it really worth it?

This question is not entirely rhetorical. Obviously, the entire thrust of the preceding chapters argues that bias crime laws are justifiable and constitutional. But to a large extent, I have assumed the need to punish hate as my starting point. The implicit premise of the task has been to provide justifications for the punishment of racially motivated violence in criminal law doctrine, and to square this punishment with free expression doctrine.

Before concluding, it is wise to step back from this assumption, to ask not merely whether it is justified to punish hate, but whether it is *necessary* to punish hate. A state may do so—but should it? The question is clearer if not conceived as a choice between punishing bias crimes and not doing so. Were the choice truly this stark, the answer would be obvious and compelling. One of the arguments advanced for including sexual orientation in bias crime statutes, for example, is that assaults against gays and lesbians are notoriously under-investigated by the police and under-prosecuted by local district attorneys.[2] (A similar argument is often made concerning laws aimed at domestic violence.) The obvious and compelling response to this situation is that "gay bashing," like domestic violence, should be properly treated by the criminal justice system. The argument based on under-enforcement, however, does not support the conclusion that violence motivated by the victim's sexual orientation should be a bias crime, because it is based on a false choice or, better put, an incomplete choice. The choice between punishing gay bashing as a bias crime or not punishing it at all omits the option of properly handling these crimes as parallel assaults, without regard to the bias motivation. If these cases were investigated as carefully and prosecuted as vigorously as any other assault, then our concerns would be satisfied without the need to include sexual orientation in a bias crime law. One could argue that including sexual orientation is the best way, or perhaps the only way, to improve the manner in which the criminal justice system responds to these crimes. If true, it represents a strong, fairly obvious, justification. But, to be tested properly, the "Is it really worth it?" question must assume that the criminal justice system otherwise works or could be made to work. Is it really worth the acrimony that often accompanies the debates over bias crime laws, to prosecute these crimes *as* bias crimes?

There is one other tempting answer to "Is it really worth it?" that ultimately fails. This answer argues that mere investigation and prosecution of bias crimes are not the only goals. For the reasons discussed in Chapter 3, bias crimes require not only punishment but greater punishment than parallel crimes. One could thus argue that bias crime laws are worth it in order to obtain enhanced punishment of racially motivated violence. There is, however, a softer means of achieving that end, one that would avoid the need to enact bias crime laws per se. Consider, for example, the manner in which the law treats racially motivated violence in Great Britain. Other than the crime of incitement to racial hatred, an offense limited largely to distribution of racist pamphlets, and very difficult to prosecute, there is no specific crime for racially motivated violence in the United Kingdom.[3] In the case of a racially motivated assault, however, British law enforcement officials may take the perpetrator's motivation into account in deciding whether to pursue the case, and the court may similarly take motivation into account in determining the proper sentence. Enhanced punishment of bias crimes therefore exists, at least in theory, without the need for an expressed bias crime law. This brings us back to the question: "Is it worth it?"

The answer is that it is well worthwhile to have laws that expressly punish racially motivated violence. In order to see why, we must return to the general justifications for punishment, and now augment that discussion with a consideration of the expressive value of punishment, or what is sometimes known as the denunciation theory of punishment. The expressive value of punishment allows us to say not only that bias crime laws are warranted, but that they are essential.

### The Expressive Value of Punishment

Criminal punishment carries with it social disapproval, resentment, and indignation. Compare the social stigma involved in a conviction for criminal tax evasion with that triggered by a civil finding of underpayment of taxes. Criminal punishment inherently stigmatizes. One of the strongest modern statements of this view of punishment is found in the report of the British Royal Commission on Capital Punishment:

> Punishment is the way in which society expresses its denunciation of wrong doing: and in order to maintain respect for law, it is essential that punishment inflicted for grave crimes should adequately reflect the revulsion felt by the great majority of citizens for them . . . [T]he ultimate justification for any punishment is, not that it is a deterrent, but that it is the emphatic denunciation by the community of a crime.[4]

Regardless of one's view of capital punishment, this description of punishment is compelling. Henry Hart saw the expressive value of punishment as the key to the distinction between the criminal and the civil: "What distinguishes a criminal from a civil sanction, and all that distinguishes it . . . is the judgment of community condemnation which accompanies and justifies its imposition."[5] This insight allows us to expand the understanding of punishment theory developed in Chapter 3, where we considered both retributive and utilitarian, or consequentialist, theories of punishment. Expressive punishment theory is neither wholly separate from, nor wholly contained by, retributive and consequentialist approaches to punishment.

Emile Durkheim was one of the first to focus upon the role of social denunciation in punishment. Durkheim argued that punishment represents societal condemnation of certain behavior and that social cohesion emerges from the act of punishment.[6] In *The Division of Labor in Society*, Durkheim rejected consequentialist justifications of punishment on practical grounds:

"[Punishment] does not serve, or serves only very incidentally, to correct the guilty person or to scare off any possible imitators. For this dual viewpoint its effectiveness may rightly be questioned; in any case it is mediocre."[7] The real function of punishment, according to Durkheim, "is to maintain inviolate the cohesion of society by sustaining the common consciousness in all its vigor."[8] The criminal law represents the expression of the "common consciousness" of the community. When this shared expression of values is violated, that is, when a crime is committed, the society faces a choice between not responding and responding through criminal punishment. If there is no response, "there would result a relaxation in the bonds of social solidarity." The only appropriate response, punishment of the wrongdoer, "is a sign indicating that the sentiments of the collectivity are still unchanged, and the communion of minds sharing these same beliefs remains absolute." Without punishment, the collective moral consciousness could not be preserved.[9]

Durkheim's denunciation theory of punishment has been subject to two main strands of critique, one based in sociology and the other in punishment theory. The sociological critique questions the linkage, by sheer assertion, between law and moral consensus. There is no room for social conflict in a theory that posits a single collective consciousness that is expressed in the criminal law.[10] If we understand the criminal law to have been produced through social conflict, and not through the expression of a universal societal norm, then, according to this critique, denunciation loses much of its luster as a justification for criminal punishment.

The punishment-theory critique questions the requirement, again by sheer assertion, that denunciation of the violation of social norms should proceed by criminal punishment of the wrongdoer. The denunciatory effect could be achieved by any number of means—for example, public pronouncement by the head of state or a judge, or shooting off a cannon in the public square—so long as the convention is understood by the audience. That punishment is the proper convention requires an independent justification for punishment, a justification that denunciation itself does not provide. Denunciation thus cannot stand on its own as a theory of punishment and ultimately relies upon some other justification for its validity.

Nigel Walker captured this critique well: "denouncers are really either quasi-retributivists or crypto-[consequentialists]."[11] They are quasi-retributivists because the convention of punishment as the means to denounce makes sense only when the defendant deserves to be punished.

Punishment without desert would leave the denunciation vague at best. Alternatively, they are crypto-consequentialists because they justify punishment by the social utility that it produces. Unlike that of classic consequentialists, denouncers' utility comes in the form of social cohesion and not, strictly speaking, crime reduction. But it is a utility calculus nonetheless.[12] Understood this way, Durkheim is seen not as a ground-breaker proposing a third approach to punishment theory, but rather as a utilitarian in the mold of those who advocated the educative theory of punishment, such as Alfred Ewing and Bernard Bosanquet.[13]

Both the sociological- and the punishment-theory critiques of the denunciation theory have merit. Neither calls for an abandonment of that theory, but each calls for its modification. The sociological critique is right to challenge the criminal law as some universal expression of the community's will. Such a wooden view of the law is inconsistent with all we have come to understand about the process by which legislation is created and law is made.[14] But we can relax this extreme view of the criminal law without doing serious violence to the fundamental usefulness of the expressive value of punishment. First, while it is certainly true that criminal laws do not receive unanimous support, there is a considerable social consensus underpinning the criminal law. Most criminal prohibitions, at least at a general level, derive widespread public support.[15] Moreover, we would expect that this level of support would be even higher if we look to find, not those who believe that any particular criminal law or even principal of criminal law represents the moral view of the community, but those who believe that the rule of law generally represents the moral view of the community. Those who believe both that a sufficient weight of the criminal law does reflect the community's sense, and that there is a basic legitimacy to the system that produces criminal law, would thus also believe that there is a moral weight to the criminal law generally, even to those specific laws with which they might happen to disagree. Obedience to the law thus represents a moral value of a broad spectrum of the community.

Even so, there will never be unanimity in the moral sense of the community, and indeed there may be dispute as to whether there is a single "community" that may have a single view. This too may be accommodated by the expressive view of punishment when we exchange the descriptive claim of universal consensus for a normative claim of what the community's values ought to be. Obviously, there will be dispute over the moral value of the criminal law. My argument, however, is twofold. First, the areas of dispute are not as widespread as may first be imagined—all reasonable people will agree that, all things being equal, it is worse to kill than to injure, and that it is worse to cause unjustified harm purposefully than accidentally. Second, as to those areas of dispute, the stakes of the argument are not merely who ought to go to jail, but what the community's moral view of such conduct *should* be.

The punishment-theory critique of Durkheim may also be accommodated in a way that yields a richer expressive theory of punishment. The punishment-theory critique properly contends that expressive theory is not a free-standing independent justification for punishment. As we saw in Chapter 3, however, much of the work in contemporary philosophy of punishment has concerned "mixed theories" of punishment, drawing on aspects of both utilitarian and retributivist thought. So long as expressive theory is not merely redundant with retributive or consequential arguments, it legitimately takes its place among these eclectic approaches. The expressive values of punishment take us beyond classic statements of other punishment theories. To be coherent, expressive punishment does require individual culpability and retributive desert. Whereas deontological notions of desert focus only on the wrongdoer and either the debt that he owes to society or the punishment that society owes him, expressive theory looks to the societal aspects of this punishment. Expressive theory may actually help elucidate some of the murkier aspects of retributive theory.

Consider Kant's famous teaching that, on the last day before an island community disbands "to separate and scatter . . . throughout the world," it should execute its last imprisoned murderers.[16] Typically, this is taken as the paradigmatic expression of Kantian retributivism—this extreme punishment is necessary even after all consequences have become irrelevant. Kant justifies the punishment "in order that every one may realize the desert of [the murderers'] deeds."[17] Joel Feinberg has found expressive aspects in the continuation of Kant's formulation. If the island community members did not execute their murderers, Kant wrote, "they might all be regarded as participators in the murder as a public violation of Justice." Feinberg argues that this punishment, as a means of demonstrating public non-acquiescence with the crime, is more symbolic and expressive than it is retributive.[18]

Expressive theory also has a consequentialist aspect. However, we can distinguish those consequences that seek to reduce crime, whether by incapacitation, deterrence, or rehabilitation, from those consequences that announce values. The ultimate audience for punishment that seeks to reduce crime is composed of criminals and would-be criminals. The ultimate audience for punishment that seeks to announce values is composed of law-abiding citizens.[19] The utilitarian dimension of denunciation, therefore, looks to a greatly expanded set of considerations compared with those traditionally considered by consequentialist approaches to punishment.

Expressive punishment theory, although derivative of retributive and consequentialist theories, builds on these theories and expands our understanding of punishment. In the final analysis, the punishment-theory critique may simply miss the mark—it criticizes denunciation theory for failing to answer adequately a question that denunciation theory does not conceive to be central to its mission. Expressive theory may be concerned less with providing a full justification of punishment than with understanding the full impact of punishment. Indeed, Durkheim may well not have seen his project as one of justifying punishment, which he took to be a sociological fact of all cultures, but rather as one of investigating the role of punishment in advanced societies.[20] Recognizing the expressive value of punishment, by itself, may provide limited help in answering the initial normative question as to whether society may punish its members. Once we answer that question affirmatively, however, societal denunciation must inform our decisions about the nature of that punishment.

### The Expressive Value of Punishing Bias Crimes

We now return to the question raised at the outset of this chapter: Is it really worth it? Is it really worth the acrimony that often accompanies the debates over bias crime laws in order to prosecute these crimes *as* bias crimes?

What happens when proposed bias crime legislation becomes law? This act of law-making constitutes a societal condemnation of racism, religious intolerance, and other forms of bigotry that are covered by that law. Moreover, every act of condemnation is dialectically twinning with an act of expression of values—in Durkheim's terms, social cohesion. Punishment not only signals the border between that which is permitted and that which is proscribed, but also denounces that which is rejected and announces that which is embraced. Because racial harmony and equality are among the highest values held in our society, crimes that violate these values should be punished and must be punished specifically as bias crimes. Similarly, bias crimes must be punished more harshly than crimes that, although otherwise similar, do not violate these values. Moreover, racial harmony and equality are not values that exist only, or even primarily, in an abstract sense. The particular biases that are implicated by bias crimes are connected with a real, extended history of grave injustices to the victim groups, resulting in enormous suffering and loss. In many ways these injustices, and their legacies, persist.

What happens if bias crimes are not expressly punished in a criminal justice system, or, if expressly punished, are not punished more harshly than parallel crimes? Here, too, a message is expressed by the legislation, a message that racial harmony and equality are not among the highest values held by the community. Put differently, it is impossible for the punishment choices made by the society *not* to express societal values. There is no neutral position, no middle ground. The only question is the content of that expression and the resulting statement of those values.

Two cases, one of which involves the debate over a bias crime law, illustrate the point. Consider first the case of the creation of a legal holiday to commemorate the birth of Dr. Martin Luther King, Jr. Once the idea of such a holiday gained widespread attention, the federal government and most states created Martin Luther King Day within a relatively short period of time.[21] It was impossible, however, for a state to take "no position" on the holiday. Several states, including South Carolina, Arizona, New Hampshire, North Carolina, and Texas, did not immediately adopt the holiday. These states were perceived generally as rejecting the holiday. More significantly, they were perceived as rejecting the values associated with Dr. King, which were to be commemorated by the holiday marking his birthday. Civil rights groups brought pressure against these states with economic boycotts and the like.[22] Once ignited, the debate over Martin Luther King Day thus became one in which there was no neutral position. The lack of legislation was a rejection of the holiday and the values with which it was associated.

The second case concerns the debate in 1997 over a bias crime law in Georgia, the site of one of the most acrimonious legislative battles over such legislation. The tension surrounding the debate was heightened by the bombing that year of a lesbian nightclub in Atlanta. Ultimately, the legislation failed to reach the floor of the Georgia legislature for a vote. As with Martin Luther King Day, there was no middle position for Georgia to adopt. Either a bias crime law would be established, with the attending expression of certain values, or it would not, with a rejection of these values and an expression of other, antithetical values. The values expressed by the rejection of the law are aptly caught by the unusually blunt view of one Georgia legislator: "What's the big deal about a few swastikas on a synagogue?" Others derided the legislation as the "Queer Bill."[23]

Thus far we have considered the enactment of a bias crime law to be a simple binary choice: a legislature enacts a bias crime law or it does not. To do so denounces racial hatred, and to fail to do so gives comfort to the racist. We can make a similar observation in the more subtle context of establishing grades of crimes and levels of criminal punishment. In Chapter 3, we discussed the ways in which both retributive and consequentialist theories of punishment embraced a concept of proportionality. Now we can see that expressive punishment theory does as well. Conduct that is more offensive to society should receive relatively greater punishment than that which is less offensive. We would be shocked if a legislature punished shoplifting equally with aggravated assault. We might disagree as to whether one was punished excessively or the other insufficiently, but we would agree that these crimes ought not to be treated identically. Society's most cherished values will be reflected in the criminal law by applying the harshest penalties to those crimes that violate these values. There will certainly be lesser penalties for those crimes that in some respects are similar but do not violate these values. The hierarchy of societal values involved in criminal conduct will thus be reflected by the lesser crime's status as a lesser offense included within the more serious crime.

The enshrinement of racial harmony and equality among our highest values not only calls for independent punishment of racially motivated violence as a bias crime and not merely as a parallel crime; it also calls for enhanced punishment of bias crimes over parallel crimes. If bias crimes are not punished more harshly than parallel crimes, the implicit message expressed by the criminal justice system is that racial harmony and equality are not among the highest values in our society. If a racially motivated assault is punished identically to a parallel assault, the racial motivation of the bias crime is rendered largely irrelevant and thus not part of that which is condemned. The individual victim, the target community, and indeed the society at large thus suffer the twin insults akin to those suffered by the narrator of Ralph Ellison's *Invisible Man*.[24] Not only has the crime itself occurred, but the underlying hatred of the crime is invisible to the eyes of the legal system. The punishment of bias crimes as argued for in this book, therefore, is necessary for the full expression of commitment to American values of equality of treatment and opportunity.

## The Model Bias Crime Law

An exploration of racially motivated violence and the punishment of bias crimes properly concludes with the elements of a model bias crime law. Such models have been proposed, the most influential being that of the Anti-Defamation League.[25] The model proposed here is not so much inconsistent with the ADL's as it is more sharply focused upon animus, rather than mere discriminatory selection. Drawing on the analysis developed over the course of this book, this model statute targets racial animus as the gravamen of bias crimes. In particular, this model draws upon the conclusions derived from the discussion of the hypothetical cases in Chapter 4: the Clever Bias Criminal, the Unconscious Racist (variations I, II, and III), the Unknowingly Offensive Actor (the "Unlucky" variation and the "Negligent" variation, and a new "Reckless" variation introduced below), the Purse Snatcher, and, finally, the Violent Show-Off. For the reasons discussed in Chapter 6, this model is appropriate for either federal or state law. For the reasons discussed in Chapter 5, this model, including the section dealing with the crime of verbal assaults, is consonant with free expression principles. Rooted in fundamental notions of proportionality of punishment, this is a model law that expresses the values of racial equality that are basic to our society.

*Bias Crimes*

A. FIRST-DEGREE BIAS CRIME

1. A person is guilty of a first-degree bias crime if he commits any crime against a person or property in this state's criminal code (the "parallel crime"):

   (a) motivated in substantial part by ill will, hatred, or animus due to the real or perceived race, color, religion [may also include, depending on the jurisdiction, gender, sexual orientation, and/or other group characteristics], of the victim; or

   (b) with the knowledge that it is virtually certain that his conduct will be perceived by the individual victim or victim target group to have been motivated in substantial part by ill will, hatred, or animus due to the real or perceived race, color, religion [may also include, depending on the jurisdiction, gender, or sexual orientation, and/or other group characteristics], of the victim.

2. A first-degree bias crime is a felony and shall be punished by a term of

imprisonment and/or fine that exceeds that of the relevant parallel crime by two levels.

B. SECOND-DEGREE BIAS CRIME (RECKLESS BIAS CRIME)

1. A person is guilty of a second-degree bias crime if he commits any crime against a person or property in this state's criminal code (the "parallel crime") with conscious disregard for the substantial and unjustifiable risk that his conduct will be perceived by the individual victim or victim target group to have been motivated in substantial part by ill will, hatred, or animus due to the real or perceived race, color, religion [may also include, depending on the jurisdiction, gender, sexual orientation, and/or other group characteristics], of the victim.
2. A second-degree bias crime is a felony and shall be punished by a term of imprisonment and/or fine that exceeds that of the relevant parallel crime by one level.

Whereas the absolute level of punishment of first- and second-degree bias crimes will differ among jurisdictions, the relative levels will not: punishment for first-degree bias crimes will be more severe than that for second-degree bias crimes, which in turn will be more severe than that for parallel crimes.

The hypothetical cases and examples analyzed in Chapter 4 provide a helpful means of applying the model statute.

THE CLEVER BIAS CRIMINAL The Clever Bias Criminal articulates a nonbias motivation for an assault that was in fact motivated by his bias. The nonbias motivation that he asserts is a mere pretext for his true motivation, which is his bias. An example of the Clever Bias Criminal is a white bias criminal who seeks to plead guilty to a parallel crime in order to avoid being charged with the bias crime. As we noted earlier, this is the least problematic of the hypothetical cases. The Clever Bias Criminal poses only challenges of proof. Once these problems are solved—possibly through circumstantial evidence—the Clever Bias Criminal will be found guilty of a first-degree bias crime.

THE UNCONSCIOUS RACIST The Unconscious Racist commits an interracial assault that, although unconsciously motivated by bias, is without conscious racial motivation. Here we imagined a situation in which the defendants in the Yousef Hawkins beating in Bensonhurst, New York, asserted that they were not motivated by Hawkins's race but rather by the fact that he did not belong in their neighborhood. Suppose that a jury hearing this case is fully persuaded that

(1) the defendants were consciously motivated by a desire to protect their neighborhood from outsiders;
(2) the defendants' unconscious motivation was to keep African-Americans out of their neighborhood; and
(3) the defendants were honestly unaware of their unconscious motivation.

The jury would then conclude that these defendants lack the requisite purpose or knowledge for a first-degree bias crime and even the *conscious* recklessness necessary for a second-degree bias crime.

Unconscious Racist II allowed us to consider a case in which the jury does not believe the proffered "turn motivation" of the Unconscious Racist. Unconscious Racist II articulates a nonracial motivation—for example, anti-"outsider"—but that is a pretext for racial motivation. Suppose, for example, a prosecutor could show that nonresidents of Bensonhurst walked through the neighborhood the same night that Yousef Hawkins was beaten, unharmed by these defendants, but that these nonresidents happened to be white. Further suppose that the jury were persuaded that, although the assault was motivated by the victim's status as "outsider," to the defendants, "outsider" is identical to blacks, and indeed a pretext for racial bias—that is, they regard all African-Americans, and only African-Americans, as outsiders. Once the pretextual mask is removed from Unconscious Racist II, he will be found guilty of a first-degree bias crime for his racial animus toward the victim.

Unconscious Racist III, having some reason to know of his unconscious racism—for example, he knows that he feels exceedingly uncomfortable around people of races other than his own—spends time at a bar frequented by a violent racist gang, and thus puts himself in a position where his unconscious racism is likely to come to the surface. On one such occasion, a racist assault is committed by the gang. He joins in the attack, claiming afterwards that he shared the gang's purpose to assault, but not their racism. He thus claims to be not guilty of a bias crime. Unconscious Racist III's defense is valid against a charge for first-degree bias crime, but it is not a valid defense if Unconscious Racist III is charged with a second-degree bias crime. He lacks the purposeful animus of the gang, nor, unless we know more, did he act with a virtual certainty that a racially motivated assault would occur. He did consciously disregard this possibility, however, and thus has behaved recklessly with respect to a bias crime. He is guilty of a second-degree bias crime.

THE UNKNOWINGLY OFFENSIVE ACTOR    The Unknowingly Offensive Actor seeks to shock or offend the community generally, but chooses to do so in a manner that is particularly threatening to a certain racial or ethnic group. He defaces public property with a swastika because he knows that this public use of a societal taboo will shock people in general. He neither intends to offend Jews in particular, nor is he even aware of the fact that the swastika has this particularized effect on the Jewish community. We considered two variations on the Unknowingly Offensive Actor: one whose unknowingly offensive behavior is obnoxious but not criminally negligent—Unknowingly Offensive Actor (Unlucky)—and one whose behavior crosses the line of criminal negligence, Unknowingly Offensive Actor (Negligent). Although the latter has clearly behaved worse than the former, neither would violate the model bias crime law. The approach adopted here is consonant with the conclusions developed in Chapter 4, that mere negligence, even criminal negligence, is insufficient for bias crime liability. There is more to a bias crime than the combination of a parallel crime and rank stupidity exhibited by the Unknowingly Offensive Actor, even in the Negligent variation.

Let us now consider a third variation, however, one where there is some consciousness of animus. Suppose that the youthful offender we have been considering defaces a building with swastikas but the building that he chooses is a synagogue. He claims to lack bias motivation per se, and in truth, the prime motivation for his vandalism is the "thrill" of it—he knows that his behavior will shock adults. But why did he choose a synagogue? Suppose that a jury is persuaded that the perpetrator of this crime gave some thought to the impact of his conduct on the local Jewish community, and then decided to proceed with his crime anyway. If the Un*know*ingly Offensive Actor consciously disregards the possibility that his conduct will cause the harm associated with a bias crime, he is not merely ignorant, he is reckless. This Recklessly Offensive Actor would be guilty of a second-degree bias crime.

THE PURSE SNATCHER    The Purse Snatcher is the thief who preys exclusively upon women because he believes that he will better achieve his criminal goals by grabbing purses from women than by trying to pick wallets out of the pockets of men. The Purse Snatcher discriminatorily selects his victims on the basis of gender, but he has no animus toward women as a group, nor are his thefts motivated by any attitudes about women other than the manner in which they carry their valuables. He thus lacks the requisite purpose or knowledge for a first-degree bias crime and even the recklessness necessary for a second-degree bias crime. He is guilty of theft, but not of a bias crime.

THE VIOLENT SHOW-OFF    The last hypothetical is the case of the Violent Show-Off. The Violent Show-Off's sole motivation in selecting his victim is to impress his friends. He is otherwise indifferent as to the choice of his victim. Thus his selection of a victim is racially based, but lacks any racial animus.

We saw, however, that the critical aspect of the Violent Show-Off's state of mind was his knowledge that his friends do bear such animus, and his willingness to proceed with the crime under these circumstances. This knowledge is sufficient to render him guilty of a bias crime either because it permits us to infer that he acted purposely with regard to the racially motivated attack, or because his knowledge alone justifies his guilt. The model statute adopts the latter approach.

The Violent Show-Off's knowledge of the racially charged aspects of his conduct and his willingness to proceed make him like the Assassin we discussed in Chapter 4. The Assassin places a bomb on an airplane with the conscious objective of killing the one person under whose seat the bomb is placed, and with the awareness that the other ninety-nine people on board will die as a result, although this is not his conscious objective. We concluded that the Assassin is guilty of the murder of all one hundred people on the plane because his willingness to proceed in the knowledge that his conduct will cause the death of the other ninety-nine is morally indistinguishable from the actual desire to achieve this result. Similarly, the Violent Show-Off acts with the knowledge of the animus that his conduct furthers and the harm it will cause. He is thus guilty of a first-degree bias crime.

We come finally to a variation on the Violent Show-Off, one whose underlying motivation is less clear than the Violent Show-Off's desire to impress his friends, but who nonetheless acts with the knowledge that it is virtually certain that his conduct will be perceived by the individual victim or victim target group to have been motivated in substantial part by racial animus. Under section A(1)(b) of the model statute, this perpetrator is guilty of a first-degree bias crime. His knowledge is sufficient for his guilt. A person who knowingly throws a match into a pool of gasoline, claiming that he merely wished to get rid of the match, has no defense to the highest degree of arson. Even if we believe that arson was not his purpose, his willingness to act with the practical certainty that an explosion will occur makes him an arsonist of the first degree. Similarly, our perpetrator who burns a cross on the lawn of a black family, knowing with virtual certainly that it will be perceived as a racially motivated act, is guilty of a first-degree bias crime, even if we believe that he lacked the purpose to commit a bias crime.

## Final Considerations

It has been more than forty years since Gordon Allport, in *The Nature of Prejudice,* asked whether America would continue to make progress toward tolerance and stand as a "staunch defender of the right to be the same or different," or whether "a fatal retrogression will set in."[26] Laws that identify racially motivated violence for enhanced punishment are only one means of answering Allport's call, but they do constitute a critical element in the defense of the "right to be the same or different." Racially motivated violence is different from other forms of violence. When bias crimes are compared with parallel crimes, something more may be said: bias crimes are worse. They are worse in a manner that is relevant to setting levels of criminal punishment. The unique harm caused by bias crimes not only justifies their enhanced punishment, but compels it.

Bias crimes ought to single out criminal conduct that is motivated by racial animus. Discriminatory selection of a victim will ordinarily be part of racial animus. Indeed, we would expect that the proof of animus in the prosecution of a bias crime will begin with evidence relating to victim selection. Elements of proof, however, must not be confused with the gravamen of the crime. The gravamen of a bias crime is the animus of the accused.

The punishment of hate will not end bigotry in society. That great goal requires the work not only of the criminal justice system but also of all aspects of civil life, public and private. Criminal punishment is indeed a crude tool and a blunt instrument. Montesquieu foresaw that "as freedom advances, the severity of the penal law decreases."[27] We are not yet, however, in the world that Montesquieu envisioned. We inhabit a time and a culture that continue to suffer from bias in general and bias crimes in particular. But our inability to solve the entire problem should not dissuade us from dealing with parts of the problem. If we are to be "staunch defender[s] of the right to be the same or different," we cannot desist from this task.

APPENDIXES

NOTES

BIBLIOGRAPHICAL ESSAY

ACKNOWLEDGMENTS

INDEX

# Appendix A: State Bias Crime Laws

| State | Statute | Nature of statute | | State-of-mind requirement | | |
|---|---|---|---|---|---|---|
| | | Penalty enhancement | Pure bias crime | Racial animus | Discriminatory selection | "Because of" |
| Alabama | Ala. Code 1975 §13A-5-13 | x | | x | | |
| | Ala. Code 1975 §13A-11-12 | | | | | |
| Alaska | Alaska Stat. §12.55.155 | x | | | | x |
| Arizona | Ariz. Rev. Stat. Ann. §13-702 | x | | x | | |
| | Ariz. Rev. Stat. Ann. §13-1604 | | | | | |
| Arkansas | Ark. Code Ann. 5-71-215 | | | | | |
| | Ark. Code Ann. 5-71-207 | | | | | |
| California | Cal. Penal Code 422.6 | | x | | | x |
| | Cal. Penal Code 422.75 | x | | | | x |
| | Cal. Penal Code 1170.75 | x | | | | x |
| | Cal. Penal Code 11411 | | | | | |
| | Cal. Penal Code 11412 | | | | | |
| | Cal. Penal Code 302 | | | | | |
| | Cal. Penal Code 594.3 | | | | | |
| Colorado | Co. Rev. Stat. 18-9-121 | | x | | | x |
| | Co. Rev. Stat. 18-9-113 | | | | | |
| Connecticut | Conn. Gen. Stat. §53a-181b | | x | x | | |
| | Conn. Gen. Stat. §46a-58 | | | | | |
| | Conn. Gen. Stat. §53a-40a | x | | x | | |
| | Conn. Gen. Stat. §53-37(a) | | | | | |

| Race | Color | Ethnicity | National origin | Religion | Creed | Ancestry | Sexual orientation | Sex/gender | Age | Disability | Political affiliation | Other | Institutional vandalism (includes desecration of religious institutions) | Disturbing/ obstructing religious worship | Cross-burning | Mask-wearing |
|---|---|---|---|---|---|---|---|---|---|---|---|---|---|---|---|---|
| x | x | x | x | x |  |  |  |  |  | x |  |  |  |  |  |  |
|  |  |  |  |  |  |  |  |  |  |  |  |  | x |  |  |  |
| x | x |  | x |  | x | x |  | x |  | x |  |  |  |  |  |  |
| x | x |  | x | x |  |  |  | x | x | x |  |  |  |  |  |  |
|  |  |  |  |  |  |  |  |  |  |  |  |  | x |  |  |  |
|  |  |  |  |  |  |  |  |  |  |  |  |  | x |  |  |  |
|  |  |  |  |  |  |  |  |  |  |  |  |  | x |  |  |  |
| x | x |  | x | x |  | x | x | x |  | x |  |  |  |  |  |  |
| x | x |  | x | x |  | x | x |  |  | x |  |  |  |  |  |  |
| x | x |  | x | x |  | x | x | x |  | x |  |  |  |  |  |  |
|  |  |  |  |  |  |  |  |  |  |  |  |  |  |  | x |  |
|  |  |  |  |  |  |  |  |  |  |  |  |  |  | x |  |  |
|  |  |  |  |  |  |  |  |  |  |  |  |  |  | x |  |  |
|  |  |  |  |  |  |  |  |  |  |  |  |  | x |  |  |  |
| x |  |  | x | x |  |  | x |  |  |  |  |  |  |  |  |  |
|  |  |  |  |  |  |  |  |  |  |  |  |  | x |  |  |  |
| x |  | x | x |  |  |  |  | x |  |  |  |  |  |  |  |  |
|  |  |  |  |  |  |  |  |  |  |  |  |  | x |  | x |  |
|  |  |  |  |  |  |  |  |  |  |  |  |  |  |  |  | x |

| State | Statute | Nature of statute | | State-of-mind requirement | | |
| | | Penalty enhancement | Pure bias crime | Racial animus | Discriminatory selection | "Because of" |
|---|---|---|---|---|---|---|
| Delaware | De. Code Ann. Tit.11 §1304 | | x | | x | |
| | De. Code Ann. Tit.11 §4209 | x | | | | x |
| | De. Code Ann. Tit.11 §1301(1)(g) | | | | | |
| | De. Code Ann. Tit.11 §805 | | | | | |
| District of Columbia | DC Code Ann. §22-4003 | x | | x | | |
| | DC Code Ann. §22-3112.3 | | | | | |
| | DC Code Ann. §22-3112.2 | | | | | |
| Florida | Fla. Stat. Ann. §775.085 | x | | x | | |
| | Fla. Stat. Ann. §775.0845 | | | | | |
| | Fla. Stat. Ann. §876.17 | | | | | |
| | Fla. Stat. Ann. §876.18 | | | | | |
| | Fla. Stat. Ann. §806.13 | | | | | |
| Georgia | Ga. Code Ann. §16-11-38 | | | | | |
| | Ga. Code Ann. §16-11-37(b)(1) | | | | | |
| | Ga. Code Ann. §16-7-26 | | | | | |
| Hawaii | Ha. Rev. Stat. §711-1107 | | | | | |
| Idaho | Id. Code §18-7902 | | x | | | x* |
| Illinois | 720 Il. C.S. 5/12-7.1 | | x | | | x |
| | 730 Il. C.S. 5/5-5-3.2 | | | | | |
| | 720 Il. C.S. 5/21-1.2 | | | | | |
| Indiana | In. Code §35-43-1-2 | | | | | |
| Iowa | Iowa Code §729A.2 | | x | | | x |
| Kansas | Kan. Stat. Ann. §21-4003 | | x | | | x |
| | Kan. Stat. Ann. §21-4716 | x | | | | x |
| | Kan. Stat. Ann. §21-4111 | | | | | |
| Kentucky | Ky. Rev. Stat. Ann. §525.110 | x | | | | |

Categories — columns 1–13. Additional statutes — columns 14–17.

| Race | Color | Ethnicity | National origin | Religion | Creed | Ancestry | Sexual orientation | Sex/gender | Age | Disability | Political affiliation | Other | Institutional vandalism (includes desecration of religious institutions) | Disturbing/ obstructing religious worship | Cross-burning | Mask-wearing |
|---|---|---|---|---|---|---|---|---|---|---|---|---|---|---|---|---|
| X | X |  | X | X |  |  | X |  |  | X |  |  |  |  |  |  |
| X | X |  | X | X |  |  | X |  |  | X |  |  |  |  |  |  |
|  |  |  |  |  |  |  |  |  |  |  |  |  |  |  |  | X |
|  |  |  |  |  |  |  |  |  |  |  |  |  |  | X |  |  |
| X | X | X | X | X | X |  | X | X | X |  | X | X |  |  |  |  |
|  |  |  |  |  |  |  |  |  |  |  |  |  |  |  |  | X |
|  |  |  |  |  |  |  |  |  |  |  |  |  | X |  | X |  |
| X | X | X | X | X |  | X | X |  |  |  |  |  |  |  |  |  |
|  |  |  |  |  |  |  |  |  |  |  |  |  |  |  |  | X |
|  |  |  |  |  |  |  |  |  |  |  |  |  |  |  | X |  |
|  |  |  |  |  |  |  |  |  |  |  |  |  |  |  | X |  |
|  |  |  |  |  |  |  |  |  |  |  |  |  | X |  |  |  |
|  |  |  |  |  |  |  |  |  |  |  |  |  |  |  |  | X |
|  |  |  |  |  |  |  |  |  |  |  |  |  |  |  | X |  |
|  |  |  |  |  |  |  |  |  |  |  |  |  | X |  |  |  |
|  |  |  |  |  |  |  |  |  |  |  |  |  | X |  |  |  |
| X | X |  | X | X |  | X |  |  |  |  |  |  |  |  |  |  |
| X | X |  | X | X | X | X | X | X |  | X |  |  |  |  |  |  |
|  |  |  |  |  |  |  |  |  |  |  |  |  |  | X |  |  |
|  |  |  |  |  |  |  |  |  |  |  |  |  | X |  |  |  |
|  |  |  |  |  |  |  |  |  |  |  |  |  | X |  |  |  |
| X | X |  | X | X |  | X | X | X | X | X | X |  |  |  |  |  |
| X | X |  | X | X |  | X | X | X | X | X | X |  |  |  |  |  |
| X | X |  | X | X |  | X |  |  |  |  |  |  |  |  |  |  |
|  |  |  |  |  |  |  |  |  |  |  |  |  | X |  |  |  |
|  |  |  |  |  |  |  |  |  |  |  |  |  | X |  |  |  |

| State | Statute | Nature of statute | | State-of-mind requirement | | |
| | | Penalty enhancement | Pure bias crime | Racial animus | Discriminatory selection | "Because of" |
| --- | --- | --- | --- | --- | --- | --- |
| Louisiana | La. Rev. Stat. Ann. §14:107.2<br>La. Rev. Stat. Ann. §14:225 | | x | | | x |
| Maine | Me. Rev. Stat. Ann. 17-A §1151<br>Me. Rev. Stat. Ann. 17-A §507<br>Me. Rev. Stat. Ann. 17-A §507A | x | | | | x |
| Maryland | Md. Code Ann. Art. 27§470A | x | | | x | |
| Massachusetts | Ma. Gen. Laws 22c §32<br>Ma. Gen. Laws ch.272, §38<br>Ma. Gen. Laws ch.266, §98<br>Ma. Gen. Laws ch.266, §127A | | x | x | | |
| Michigan | Mich. Comp. Laws Ann. §750.147b<br>Mich. Comp. Laws Ann. §752.525 | | x | | | x* |
| Minnesota | Mn. Stat. Ann. §609.2231<br>Mn. Stat. Ann. §609.749<br>Mn. Stat. Ann. §609.28 | x | x | | | x<br>x |
| Mississippi | Ms. Code Ch.19 §99-19-305<br>Ms. Code Ch.19 §97-35-17<br>Ms. Code Ch.19 §97-17-39 | x | | | | x* |
| Missouri | Mo. Stat. Ann. 574.093<br>Mo. Stat. Ann. 574.090<br>Mo. Stat. Ann. 574.085 | | x<br>x | | | x<br>x |
| Montana | Mt. Code Ann. 45-5-222<br>Mt. Code Ann. 45-5-221 | x | x | | | x<br>x |
| Nebraska | Ne. Rev. Stat. §28-111 | x | | | | x |
| Nevada | Nv. Rev. Stat. 193.1675<br>Nv. Rev. Stat. 207.185<br>Nv. Rev. Stat. 201.270<br>Nv. Rev. Stat. 206.125 | x<br>x | | | | x<br>x |

| Categories | | | | | | | | | | | | | Additional statutes | | | |
|---|---|---|---|---|---|---|---|---|---|---|---|---|---|---|---|---|
| Race | Color | Ethnicity | National origin | Religion | Creed | Ancestry | Sexual orientation | Sex/gender | Age | Disability | Political affiliation | Other | Institutional vandalism (includes desecration of religious institutions) | Disturbing/ obstructing religious worship | Cross-burning | Mask-wearing |
| X | X |  | X | X | X | X | X | X | X | X |  | X |  |  |  |  |
|  |  |  |  |  |  |  |  |  |  |  |  |  | X |  |  |  |
| X | X |  | X | X |  | X | X | X |  | X |  |  |  |  |  |  |
|  |  |  |  |  |  |  |  |  |  |  |  |  | X |  |  |  |
|  |  |  |  |  |  |  |  |  |  |  |  |  | X |  |  |  |
| X | X |  | X | X |  |  |  |  |  |  |  |  | X | X |  |  |
| X |  | X |  | X |  |  | X | X |  | X |  |  |  |  |  |  |
|  |  |  |  |  |  |  |  |  |  |  |  |  |  | X |  |  |
|  |  |  |  |  |  |  |  |  |  |  |  |  | X |  |  |  |
|  |  |  |  |  |  |  |  |  |  |  |  |  | X |  |  |  |
| X | X |  | X | X |  |  |  | X |  |  |  |  |  |  |  |  |
|  |  |  |  |  |  |  |  |  |  |  |  |  |  | X |  |  |
| X | X |  | X | X |  | X |  | X | X | X |  |  |  |  |  |  |
| X | X |  | X | X |  | X |  | X | X | X |  |  |  |  |  |  |
|  |  |  |  |  |  |  |  |  |  |  |  |  |  | X |  |  |
| X | X | X | X | X |  | X |  | X |  |  |  |  |  |  |  |  |
|  |  |  |  |  |  |  |  |  |  |  |  |  |  | X |  |  |
|  |  |  |  |  |  |  |  |  |  |  |  |  | X |  |  |  |
| X | X |  | X | X |  |  |  |  |  |  |  |  |  |  |  |  |
| X | X |  | X | X |  |  |  |  |  |  |  |  |  |  |  |  |
|  |  |  |  |  |  |  |  |  |  |  |  |  | X |  |  |  |
| X | X |  | X | X | X |  |  |  |  |  |  | X | X |  |  |  |
| X | X |  | X | X | X |  |  |  |  |  |  | X | X |  | X |  |
| X | X |  | X | X |  | X | X | X | X | X |  |  |  |  | X |  |
| X | X |  | X | X |  | X | X | X | X | X |  |  |  |  |  |  |
| X | X |  | X | X |  |  |  | X |  | X |  |  |  |  |  |  |
|  |  |  |  |  |  |  |  |  |  |  |  |  |  |  | X |  |
|  |  |  |  |  |  |  |  |  |  |  |  |  | X |  |  |  |

| State | Statute | Nature of statute | | State-of-mind requirement | | |
|---|---|---|---|---|---|---|
| | | Penalty enhancement | Pure bias crime | Racial animus | Discriminatory selection | "Because of" |
| New Hampshire | N.H. Stat. Ann. §651:6 | x | | x | | |
| New Jersey | N.J. Stat. Ann. 2C:44-3 | x | | x | | |
| | N.J. Stat. Ann. 2C:33-4 | | x | | | x |
| | N.J. Stat. Ann. 2C:33-9 | | | | | |
| | N.J. Stat. Ann. 2C:33-11 | | | | | |
| New Mexico | N.M. Stat. Ann. §30-13-1 | | | | | |
| | N.M. Stat. Ann. §30-15-4 | | | | | |
| New York | N.Y. Penal Law §240.31 | | x | | | x |
| | N.Y. Penal Law §240.21 | | | | | |
| North Carolina | N.C. Gen. Stat. §14-3 | x | | | | x |
| | N.C. Gen. Stat. §14-12.14 | | | | | |
| | N.C. Gen. Stat. §14-12.12 | | | | | |
| | N.C. Gen. Stat. §14-199 | | | | | |
| | N.C. Gen. Stat. §14-144 | | | | | |
| | N.C. Gen. Stat. §14-49 | | | | | |
| | N.C. Gen. Stat. §14-62 | | | | | |
| North Dakota | N.D. Crim. Code 12.1-12-04 | | x | | | x |
| Ohio | Oh. Code Rev. §2927.12 | x | | | | x |
| | Oh. Code Rev. §2927.11 | | | | | |
| | Oh. Code Rev. §2909.05 | | | | | |
| Oklahoma | Ok. Stat. Ann. tit.21 §850 | | x | | | x* |
| | Ok. Stat. Ann. tit.21 §915 | | | | | |
| | Ok. Stat. Ann. tit.21 §1765 | | | | | |
| Oregon | Or. Rev. Stat. 166.165 | | x | | | x |
| | Or. Rev. Stat. 166.155 | | x | | | x |
| | Or. Rev. Stat. 166.075 | | | | | |

| | | | | | | Categories | | | | | | | Additional statutes | | | |
|---|---|---|---|---|---|---|---|---|---|---|---|---|---|---|---|---|
| Race | Color | Ethnicity | National origin | Religion | Creed | Ancestry | Sexual orientation | Sex/gender | Age | Disability | Political affiliation | Other | Institutional vandalism (includes desecration of religious institutions) | Disturbing/ obstructing religious worship | Cross-burning | Mask-wearing |
| x |  |  | x | x | x |  | x | x |  |  |  |  |  |  |  |  |
| x | x | x |  | x |  |  | x |  |  | x |  |  |  |  |  |  |
| x | x | x |  | x |  |  | x | x |  | x |  |  |  |  |  |  |
|  |  |  |  |  |  |  |  |  |  |  |  |  | x |  |  |  |
|  |  |  |  |  |  |  |  |  |  |  |  |  | x |  |  |  |
|  |  |  |  |  |  |  |  |  |  |  |  |  |  | x |  |  |
|  |  |  |  |  |  |  |  |  |  |  |  |  | x |  |  |  |
| x | x |  | x | x |  |  |  |  |  |  |  |  |  |  |  |  |
|  |  |  |  |  |  |  |  |  |  |  |  |  |  | x |  |  |
| x | x |  | x | x |  |  |  |  |  |  |  |  |  |  |  |  |
|  |  |  |  |  |  |  |  |  |  |  |  |  |  |  |  | x |
|  |  |  |  |  |  |  |  |  |  |  |  |  |  |  | x |  |
|  |  |  |  |  |  |  |  |  |  |  |  |  |  | x |  |  |
|  |  |  |  |  |  |  |  |  |  |  |  |  | x |  |  |  |
|  |  |  |  |  |  |  |  |  |  |  |  |  | x |  |  |  |
|  |  |  |  |  |  |  |  |  |  |  |  |  | x** |  |  |  |
| x | x |  | x | x |  |  | x |  |  |  |  |  |  |  |  |  |
| x | x |  | x | x |  |  |  |  |  |  |  |  |  |  |  |  |
|  |  |  |  |  |  |  |  |  |  |  |  |  | x |  |  |  |
|  |  |  |  |  |  |  |  |  |  |  |  |  | x |  |  |  |
| x | x |  | x | x |  |  |  |  |  | x |  |  |  |  |  |  |
|  |  |  |  |  |  |  |  |  |  |  |  |  |  | x |  |  |
|  |  |  |  |  |  |  |  |  |  |  |  |  | x |  |  |  |
| x | x |  | x | x |  |  | x |  |  |  |  |  |  |  |  |  |
| x | x |  | x | x |  |  | x |  |  |  |  |  |  |  |  |  |
|  |  |  |  |  |  |  |  |  |  |  |  |  | x |  |  |  |

| State | Statute | Penalty enhancement | Pure bias crime | Racial animus | Discriminatory selection | "Because of" |
|-------|---------|:-------------------:|:---------------:|:-------------:|:------------------------:|:------------:|
| | | Nature of statute | | State-of-mind requirement | | |
| Pennsylvania | Pa. Stat. Ann. tit.18 §2710<br>Pa. Stat. Ann. tit.18 §3307<br>Pa. Stat. Ann. tit.18 §5509 | | x | | | x |
| Rhode Island | R.I. Gen. Laws 11-42-3<br>R.I. Gen. Laws 11-53-2<br>R.I. Gen. Laws 11-11-1<br>R.I. Gen. Laws 11-44-31 | | x | | | x |
| South Carolina | S.C. Code of 1976 §16-5-10<br>S.C. Code of 1976 §16-17-520<br>S.C. Code of 1976 §16-17-600 | | | | | |
| South Dakota | S.D. Cod. Laws Ann. 22-19B-1<br>S.D. Cod. Laws Ann. 22-19B-2<br>S.D. Cod. Laws Ann. 22-27-1 | | x | | | x* |
| Tennessee | Tn. Code Ann. 39-17-309<br>Tn. Code Ann. 39-17-311 | | | | | |
| Texas | Tx. Code Ann. Art. 42.014<br>Tx. Penal Code Ann. §28.03 | | x | | | x |
| Utah | Ut. Stat. Ann. §76-3-203.3 | x | | | x | |
| Vermont | Vt. Stat. Ann. tit.13 §1455<br>Vt. Stat. Ann. tit.13 §1456 | x | | | | x* |
| Virginia | Va. Code Ann. §18.2-57<br>Va. Code Ann. §18.2-422<br>Va. Code Ann. §18.2-423<br>Va. Code Ann. §18.2-127<br>Va. Code Ann. §18.2-138 | x | | | x | |
| Washington | Wa. Rev. Code Ann. 9A.36.080 | | x | | | x* |
| West Virginia | W.Va. Code §61-6-21<br>W.Va. Code §61-6-22<br>W.Va. Code §61-6-13 | | x | | | x* |

|  | Categories | | | | | | | | | | | | | Additional statutes | | | |
| --- | --- | --- | --- | --- | --- | --- | --- | --- | --- | --- | --- | --- | --- | --- | --- | --- | --- |
| | Race | Color | Ethnicity | National origin | Religion | Creed | Ancestry | Sexual orientation | Sex/gender | Age | Disability | Political affiliation | Other | Institutional vandalism (includes desecration of religious institutions) | Disturbing/ obstructing religious worship | Cross-burning | Mask-wearing |
| | X | X |  | X | X |  |  | X |  |  |  |  |  |  |  |  |  |
| | | | | | | | | | | | | | | X | | | |
| | | | | | | | | | | | | | | X | | | |
| | X | | | X | X | | | | | | | | | | | | |
| | | | | | | | | | | | | | | | | X | |
| | | | | | | | | | | | | | | | X | | |
| | | | | | | | | | | | | | | X | | | |
| | | | | | | | | | | | | | | | | | X |
| | | | | | | | | | | | | | | | X | | |
| | | | | | | | | | | | | | | X | | | |
| | X | X | | X | X | | X | | | | | | | | | | |
| | | | | | | | | | | | | | | | | X | |
| | | | | | | | | | | | | | | | X | | |
| | | | | | | | | | | | | | | | | | X |
| | | | | | | | | | | | | | | X | | | |
| | | | | | | | | | | | | | X | | | | |
| | | | | | | | | | | | | | | X | | | |
| | | | | | | | | | | | | | X | | | | |
| | X | X | | X | X | | X | X | X | X | X | | X | X | | | |
| | | | | | | | | | | | | | | | | X | |
| | X | X | | X | X | | | | | | | | | | | | |
| | | | | | | | | | | | | | | | | | X |
| | | | | | | | | | | | | | | | | X | |
| | | | | | | | | | | | | | | X | | | |
| | | | | | | | | | | | | | | X | | | |
| | X | X | | X | X | | X | X | X | | X | | | X | | X | |
| | X | X | | X | X | | X | | X | | | X | | | | | |
| | X | X | | X | X | | X | | X | | | X | | | | | X |
| | | | | | | | | | | | | | | | X | | |

| State | Statute | Nature of statute | | State-of-mind requirement | | |
|-------|---------|---------------------|--|---------------------------|--|--|
|       |         | Penalty enhancement | Pure bias crime | Racial animus | Discriminatory selection | "Because of" |
| Wisconsin | Wis. Stat. Ann. 939.645 | x | | | x | |
|           | Wis. Stat. Ann. 939.641 | x | | | | |
|           | Wis. Stat. Ann. 943.012 | | | | | |
| Wyoming | Wy. Stat. 1997 §6-9-102 | | x | | | x |

*Added requirement of maliciousness
**North Carolina statute prohibits specifically church-burning

*Other categories:*
District of Columbia: personal appearance, family responsibility, matriculation
Louisiana: membership or service in, or employment with, an organization
Montana: involvement in civil rights or human rights activities
Texas: no categories specified
Utah: no categories specified
Vermont: service in the armed forces

| | | | | Categories | | | | | | | | | Additional statutes | | | |
|---|---|---|---|---|---|---|---|---|---|---|---|---|---|---|---|---|
| Race | Color | Ethnicity | National origin | Religion | Creed | Ancestry | Sexual orientation | Sex/gender | Age | Disability | Political affiliation | Other | Institutional vandalism (includes desecration of religious institutions) | Disturbing/ obstructing religious worship | Cross-burning | Mask-wearing |
| x | x | | x | x | | x | x | | | x | | | | | | x |
| | | | | | | | | | | | | | x | | | |
| x | x | | x | | x | | | x | | | | | | | | |

# Appendix B:
# Sample Discriminatory
# Selection Statutes

Del. Code Ann. §1304 (1995): A person is guilty of a hate crime when he "selects the victim because of the victim's race, religion, color, disability, national origin or ancestry."

Code of Virginia §18.2-57 (1997): A mandatory prison term is required "if the person intentionally selects the person against whom [the crime is committed] because of his race, religious conviction, color or national origin."

Wis. Stat. Ann. §939.645 (West 1997): "The penalties for the underlying crime are increased" if the offender "intentionally selects the person against whom the crime . . . is committed or selects the property that is damaged or otherwise affected by the crime . . . in whole or in part because of the actor's belief or perception regarding the race, religion, color, disability, sexual orientation, national origin or ancestry of that person or the owner or occupant of that property, whether or not the actor's belief or perception was correct."

# Appendix C:
# Sample Racial
# Animus Statutes

Fla. Stat. Ann. §775.085 (West 1995): "The penalty for any felony or misdemeanor shall be [enhanced] if the commission of such felony or misdemeanor evidences prejudice based on the race, color, ancestry, ethnicity, religion, sexual orientation, or national origin of the victim."

Mass. Gen. Laws ch. 22c, §32 (1997): A "'Hate Crime' [is] any criminal act coupled with overt actions motivated by bigotry and bias . . ."

N.H. Rev. Stat. Ann. §651:6 (1997): Term of imprisonment may be extended if offender "was substantially motivated to commit the crime became of hostility towards the victim's religion, race, creed, sexual orientation . . . national origin, or sex."

# Appendix D:
# Sample "Because of"
# Statutes

Colo. Rev. Stat. Ann. §18-9-121 (West 1997): "A person commits ethnic intimidation if, with the intent to intimidate or harass another person because of that person's race, color, religion, ancestry, or national origin causes injury, fear, or damage to property."

720 Ill. Comp. Stat. Ann. §5/12-7.1 (1996): A person commits a hate crime where, "by reason of the actual or perceived race, color, creed, religion, ancestry, gender, sexual orientation, physical or mental disability, or national origin of another individual or group of individuals," he commits an enumerated crime.

Iowa Code Ann. §729A.2 (West 1992): A "hate crime" is committed when a crime is "committed against a person or a person's property because of the person's race, color, religion, ancestry, national origin, political affiliation, sex, sexual orientation, age, or disability."

Minn. Stat. Ann. §609.2231 (West 1993): Assault is criminalized if committed "because of the victim's or another's actual or perceived race, color, religion, sex, sexual orientation, disability . . . age, or national origin."

Mont. Code Ann. §45-5-221 (1996): "A person commits the offense of malicious intimidation or harassment when, because of another person's race, creed, religion, color, national origin . . . he purposely or knowingly, with the intent to terrify, intimidate, threaten, harass, annoy, or offend," causes injury or property damage.

# Appendix E:
# Sample "Because of" Statutes
# with Additional Element
# of Maliciousness

Idaho Code §18-7902 (1991): A person commits malicious harassment if "maliciously and with the specific intent to intimidate or harass another person because of that person's race, color, religion, ancestry, or national origin" he causes injury or damage to property.

Mich. Comp. Laws §750.147b (1991): A person is guilty of "ethnic intimidation" if that person "maliciously, and with specific intent to intimidate or harass another person because of that person's race, color, religion, gender, or national origin," causes injury or damage to property.

Okla. Stat. tit. 21, §850 (1996): A person commits "malicious intimidation or harassment because of race" if he "maliciously and with the specific intent to intimidate or harass another person because of that person's race, color, religion, ancestry, national origin, or disability" causes injury or damage to property.

S.D. Cod. Laws Ann. §22-19B-1 (1993): "No person may maliciously and with the specific intent to intimidate or harass another person because of that person's race, color, religion, ancestry, or national origin" cause injury or damage to property.

Wash. Rev. Code Ann. §9A.36.080 (West 1994): "A person is guilty of malicious harassment if he or she maliciously and intentionally commits . . . acts because of his or her perception of the victim's race, color, religion, ancestry, national origin, gender, sexual orientation, or mental, physical, or sensory handicap."

# Appendix F:
# Sample Institutional
# Vandalism Statutes

Ala. Code §13A-11-12 (1975): A person "commits the crime of desecration of vener-
ated objects if he intentionally desecrates any public monument or structure or
place of worship or burial."

D.C. Code 1981 §22-3112.2 (West 1981): "It shall be unlawful for any person to
burn, desecrate, mar, deface, or damage a cross or other religious symbol on . . .
property . . . primarily used for religious, educational, residential, memorial,
charitable, or cemetery purposes."

Haw. Rev. Stat. §711-1107 (1992): A person commits "the offense of desecration if
he intentionally desecrates . . . a place of worship or burial."

In. Code Ann. §35-43-1-2 (West 1998): A person is guilty of criminal mischief "who
recklessly, knowingly, or intentionally damages a structure used for religious
worship [or] a cemetery or facility used for memorializing the dead."

Me. Rev. Stat. Ann. tit. 17-A, §507 (West 1991): A person is "guilty of desecration
and defacement if he intentionally desecrates any . . . place of worship or burial."
Desecrate "means marring, defacing, damaging, or otherwise physically mistreat-
ing, in a way that will outrage the sensibilities of an ordinary person likely to observe or discover the actions."

# Appendix G:
# Other Relevant Statutes

## Disturbing/Obstructing Religious Worship Statutes

Ca. Penal Code §11412 (West 1997): "Any person who, with intent to cause, attempts to cause or causes another to refrain from exercising his or her religion or from engaging in a religious service by means of a threat, directly communicated to such person, to inflict an unlawful injury upon any person or property, and it reasonably appears to the recipient of the threat that such threat could be carried out is guilty of a felony."

730 Ill. Comp. Stat. 5/5-5-3.2 (1998): Sentences may be increased if "the offense took place in a place of worship or on the grounds of a place of worship, immediately prior to, during or immediately following worshipping services . . . 'place of worship' shall mean any church, synagogue or other building, structure or place used primarily for religious worship."

Mich. Stat. §752.525 (1997): "No person shall willfully disturb, interrupt, or disquiet any assembly of people met for religious worship, by profane discourse, by rude and indecent behavior, or by making a noise either within the place of worship, or so near it as to disturb the order and solemnity of the meeting."

Miss. Code 1972 Ann. §97-35-17 (1997): "If any person shall willfully disturb any congregation of persons lawfully assembled for religious worship, he may be immediately arrested by any officer or private person, without warrant, and taken before any justice of the peace of the county, present or convenient, and on conviction thereof by such justice or in the circuit court, shall be fined not more than five hundred dollars or imprisoned not more than six months, or both."

Nev. Rev. Stat. §201.270 (1997): No person "shall willfully disturb, interrupt, or disquiet any assemblage or congregation of people met for religious worship . . ."

## Cross-Burning Statutes

Ga. Code §16-11-37 (1974): "A person commits the offense of a terroristic act when he uses a burning or flaming cross or other burning or flaming symbol or flambeau with the intent to terrorize another's household . . ."

Mt. Code Ann. §45-5-221 (1989): "A person commits the offense of malicious intimidation or harassment when [he] . . . defaces any property of another or any public property. For purposes of this section, 'deface' includes but is not limited to cross burning . . ."

Gen. Stat. N.C. §14-12.12 (1967): "It shall be unlawful for any person or persons to place or cause to be placed on the property of another in this State a burning or flaming cross or any manner of exhibit in which a burning or flaming cross, real or simulated, is a whole or a part, without first obtaining written permission of the owner or occupier of the premises to do so. It shall be unlawful for any person or persons to place or cause to be placed on the property of another in this State or on a public street or highway, a burning or flaming cross or any manner of exhibit in which a burning or flaming cross, real or simulated, is a whole or a part, with the intention of intimidating any person or of preventing them from doing any act which is lawful, or causing them to do any act which is unlawful."

Gen. Laws R.I. Ann. §11-53-2 (1994): "Any person who, with the intent of terrorizing a group of others . . . burns or otherwise desecrates a cross or other religious symbol or who places or displays a sign, mark, symbol, emblem, or other physical impression, including but not limited to, Nazi swastika . . . shall be punished . . ."

S.D. Cod. Laws §22-19B-2 (1997): It is unlawful to deface property. "'Deface' includes cross-burning or the placing of any word or symbol commonly associated with racial, religious or ethnic terrorism on the property of another person without that person's permission."

## Mask-Wearing Statutes

Ct. Gen. Stat. Ann. §53-37a (1982): "Any person who, with the intent to subject, or cause to be subjected, any other person to a deprivation of rights . . . on account of religion, national origin, alienage, color, race, sex, blindness or physical disability . . . while wearing a mask, hood or other device designed to conceal the identity of such person shall be guilty of a class D felony."

Gen. Stat. N.C. §14-12.14 (1967): "It shall be unlawful for any person or persons, while wearing a mask, hood or other device whereby the person, face or voice is disguised so as to conceal the identity of the wearer . . . [to intimidate] any person or persons, or . . . [prevent] them from doing any act which is lawful, or [cause] them to do any act which is unlawful."

Tenn. Code Ann. §39-17-309 (1989): "It is an offense to wear a mask or disguise" to intimidate others from exercising their civil rights.

Code of Va. §18.2-422 (1986): "It shall be unlawful for any person over sixteen years of age while wearing any mask, hood or other device whereby a substantial portion of the face is hidden or covered so as to conceal the identity of the wearer, to be or appear in any public place . . . without first having obtained . . . consent to do so in writing." Exceptions are made for "traditional holiday costumes . . . professions, trades, employment and other activities . . . [where] wearing protective masks [is] deemed necessary . . . bona fide theatrical production or masquerade ball . . . bona fide medical reasons . . ."

# Historical Appendix

## The Civil Rights Act of 1866

The federalism problem preoccupied the congressional debates over the 1866 Civil Rights Act. Senator Garrett Davis, a Democrat from Kentucky, objected that "this short bill repeals all the penal laws of the States . . . The result would be to utterly subvert our Government."[1] There was no monolithic Republican position in defense of the statute. The lack of consensus between moderate and radical Republicans concerning the reordering of federal-state relations gave rise to much ambiguity in the responses to Senator Davis's argument. For example, in explaining the significance of the words "under color of law" in section 2, Senator Lyman Trumbull stated that

> these . . . words were inserted as words of limitation, and not for the purpose of punishing persons who would not have been subject to punishment under the act if they had been omitted. If an offense is committed against a colored person simply because he is colored, in a State where the law affords him the same protection as if he were white, this act neither has nor was intended to have anything to do with his case, because he has adequate remedy in the State court.[2]

Trumbull's position on the scope of the act in light of federalism concerns, however, cannot be ascertained from the text of these remarks alone. Rather, these remarks must be seen in context. It has been suggested that Trumbull may have intended to restrict the reach of the Civil Rights Act to those acts in which the state government is directly complicitous. It is at least as likely, however, that Trumbull was addressing a different aspect of the issue, namely, whether or not the existence of an authorizing state law could provide a defense for conduct that violated a federal right. Moments after the remarks quoted above, Trumbull stated that "[t]he right to punish persons who violated the laws of the United States cannot be questioned, and the fact that in doing so they acted under color

198

of law or usage in any locality affords no protection."[3] Moreover, Trumbull was speaking about President Johnson's objection to exclusive federal jurisdiction over civil rights crimes contained in his veto message. Trumbull, far from restricting the reach of federal jurisdiction, stated that it "is no new thing. The United States courts have always had jurisdiction of crimes and offenses committed against United States laws."[4]

Whichever view is taken of Trumbull's response to the congressional Democrats, the Civil Rights Act of 1866 demonstrates the significant reordering of the federal-state relationship in congressional Reconstruction.

## The Enforcement Act of 1870 and the Ku Klux Klan Act of 1871

During the period of the First Reconstruction, there was wide-scale violence toward both the freedmen and the Southern unionists. This violence was typified by the riots that took place in New Orleans and Memphis in 1866.

The riot in Memphis, Tennessee, in early May 1866 resulted in the death of at least forty-six black men and women; the congressional committee charged with investigating the riots believed that the actual number of fatalities far exceeded this figure. Numerous whites who did business with or were otherwise engaged in helping blacks were also attacked, and the property damage was estimated at $127,000.[5] The committee explicitly considered the need for an outside federal role in prosecuting the perpetrators of the massacre and noted the total absence of response by local law enforcement officials. The committee, however, was unconvinced that the recently enacted criminal sanctions contained in the 1866 act would provide sufficient basis for this federal role. Nothing in the law authorized federal prosecutions of private defendants. Moreover, the committee expressed serious concerns about the enforceability of the law at that time, concluding that the "civil rights bill . . . is treated as a dead letter."[6]

The New Orleans riot in late July 1866 was equally violent and, from a political perspective, perhaps even more damaging to Presidential Reconstruction than the Memphis riots because it arose directly from Reconstruction politics. Louisiana was one of the first states readmitted to the Union under Presidential Reconstruction. Its governor, James Madison Wells, was a Southern unionist who had been a prewar slave-owner and sought to reintegrate Confederate veterans into state government. In mid-1866, Wells supported a radical Republican effort to reconvene the 1864 Constitutional Convention in an effort to ensure black suffrage and to reconstitute the state government. Fighting broke out among armed white police officers and the mostly black group of supporters of the convention. The violence culminated in more than thirty deaths and more than 100 injuries. The vast majority of the victims were black.[7]

In addition to the extraordinary events in Memphis and New Orleans in 1866, a general and persistent level of violence dominated the lives of the newly freed slaves and of Southern unionists in the first years after the war. The predominate antebellum racial and political attitudes of the majority of Southern whites remained largely unchanged in the early years of Reconstruction, despite the ratification of the Fourteenth and Fifteenth Amendments by the Southern states and the establishment of radical governments in many of those states. Perhaps the very expansion of constitutional protections for the freedmen led many Southern whites to turn increasingly to violence as a means of protest and reaction. Far from being aberrations, therefore, Memphis and New Orleans were only the most sensational examples of intimidation, violence, and murder foisted upon ex-slaves by members of the former Southern establishment. Well-known organizations such as the Ku Klux Klan, and lesser known groups such as the Knights of the White Camellia, the White Brotherhood, the Pale Faces, and the '76 Association, were largely unchecked.[8]

The Enforcement Act of 1870 and the Ku Klux Klan Act of 1871 each contained substantial criminal provisions. The Enforcement Act of 1870 was intended primarily to guarantee the rights of due process of law and equal protection of the law guaranteed by the Fourteenth Amendment, and, particularly, the right to vote established by the Fifteenth Amendment. Section 1 explicitly protected the right to vote in all elections "without distinction of race, color or previous condition of servitude," regardless of any state law or custom to the contrary.

Section 2 of the act provided civil and criminal remedies should a state official fail to allow an equal opportunity to vote or to qualify to vote. The criminal sanction for such a violation was a misdemeanor, punishable by more than one month but less than one year in jail. Similar jail terms were established for any voting official who refused to count a vote under these circumstances and for anyone who hindered or prevented any citizen from voting or from doing any act required to vote.

One additional section of the Enforcement Act bears mention because of the light it sheds on the developing federalism problem. The provisions of section 7 federalized all state-law crimes that were committed in the course of any violation of sections 5 or 6 of the Enforcement Act.[9]

The Enforcement Act was ineffective at stemming the violence in the South. In response, Congress enacted the Ku Klux Klan (or sometimes "Antilynching") Act of 1871. The act is best known today for its primary civil-enforcement mechanism, the creation of a common law cause of action for a violation of federal rights under color of law.[10] In 1871, however, the Ku Klux Klan Act was seen primarily as a federal criminal statute designed to create a federal role in suppressing violence in the Southern states.

As originally proposed, the act would have federalized such common law crimes as murder, manslaughter, robbery, assault, or arson.[11] The bill was seen as the most extreme shift of power from the states to the federal government of any of the Reconstruction-era constitutional amendments or statutes. This was a perception shared by the Democrats and white Southerners who opposed the statute[12] as well as by the Republicans who supported it.[13] Moreover, even the Republican party was split over the bill on grounds related to the federalism problem.[14] Among those Republicans who opposed the original Ku Klux Klan bill was Lyman Trumbull, the floor-manager of the Civil Rights Act of 1866.[15] The moderate Republicans' efforts led to the language of the Ku Klux Klan Act as it was ultimately enacted. This language emerged as the compromise in the conflict between the radical Republicans on the one hand and the Democrats and moderate Republicans on the other.[16] As amended, the legislation still provided criminal sanctions for numerous conspiracies, but the grounds for federal criminal prosecution were narrowed to conspiracies to violate an enumerated set of civil rights, each of which implicated an explicitly federal issue.

In proposing the amendment, Representative Shellabarger succinctly stated the distinction between the original section 2 and section 2 as amended:

> The object of the amendment is . . . to confine the authority of this law to the prevention of deprivation which shall attack the equality of rights of American citizens; that any violation of the right, the *animus* and effect of which is to strike down the citizen, to the end that he may not enjoy equality of rights as contrasted with his and other citizens' rights, shall be within the scope of the remedies of this section.[17]

The legislation as amended applied criminal sanctions to the violence in the South without the federalization of all or most crimes of violence in the Southern states.

## The Civil Rights Act of 1875

The final civil rights act of the First Reconstruction period—and the last piece of major federal civil rights legislation for more than eighty years—was the Civil Rights Act of 1875.[18] On its face, the statute was a broad, aggressive tool for enforcing federal civil rights. But by the time the bill was enacted into law, administrative commitment to civil rights enforcement was already virtually nonexistent, and judicial curtailment of civil rights legislation was clear.

The main thrust of the Civil Rights Act of 1875 was the prohibition of discrimination based on race in public accommodations such as inns and theaters. The act, which created both civil and criminal remedies, was the result of protracted legislative consideration. The legislation that became the Civil Rights Act of 1875 was first introduced during the debates over the Ku Klux Klan Act of 1871. During the four years that the bill languished in Congress, support for civil rights legislation continued to erode. It is true that President Grant publicly expressed support for the legislation in his second Inaugural Address in March 1873, and the Republicans continued to hold majorities in both houses of the Forty-third Congress. But the combination of weakening Northern resolve and the economic pall cast by the Panic of 1873 left civil rights legislation without strong congressional or executive support.[19]

Senator Charles Sumner, the tireless Radical Republican from Massachusetts, was instrumental in the passage of the Civil Rights Act of 1875. Sumner introduced the legislation in March 1871 and worked for it throughout the remainder of his life. Indeed, the act was passed largely as a memorial to him. His dying words are said to have been about its enactment.[20] On May 22, 1874, two months after Sumner's death, the Senate passed the civil rights bill. The bill remained mired in the House of Representatives for another year. Debate in the House featured Democratic opposition based upon the doctrine announced by the Supreme Court in *Slaughter-House*. The Republican majority in the House delayed consideration of the bill until after the 1874 elections, in which the Democrats won a majority of the seats in the House of Representatives for the Forty-fourth Congress. The Civil Rights Act was finally passed into law during the "lame-duck" session of the Forty-third Congress in February 1875.[21]

As finally enacted, the Civil Rights Act of 1875 presented the federalism problem in a compelling light. More than any other Reconstruction-era statute, this act expanded the role of federal law enforcement into matters previously left solely to state jurisdiction. By authorizing the use of federal criminal remedies for denial of access to public accommodations, the act encompassed a broad set of rights that would be protected by federal criminal civil rights law. Despite its apparent scope, however, in reality the criminal provisions of the Civil Rights Act of 1875 were more aspirational than substantive. By 1875, federal enforcement of criminal civil rights laws was virtually moribund. The law's contemporary significance, if any, was for its civil provisions, though these civil remedies were scarcely enforced either, because those whom the statute protected were ill-equipped to use the legal system.[22] Ironically, then, it was a mostly symbolic and little enforced statute that the Supreme Court nonetheless struck down as unconstitutional in 1883 when it reviewed the 1875 act in the *Civil Rights Cases*.[23]

## The Federalism Problem as Viewed through Successful Civil Rights Prosecutions

Interference with election-related rights was by far the most prominent source for criminal civil rights cases during the late nineteenth and early twentieth centuries. As discussed in the text, direct interference with federal elections, whether committed by private persons or by state officials, was among the very few areas of federal criminal jurisdiction that satisfied even the Court's view of federalism. The expressed constitutional authorization of congressional power over federal elections was the basis for the decision in *Ex Parte Yarbrough*, which upheld the conviction of nine white men who were indicted under the Enforcement Act of 1870 for beating a black man because he had voted in a federal congressional election.[24] The recognition of voting rights as a solid basis for federal civil rights enforcement culminated in *United States v. Classic*.[25]

*Classic* was the first major case in which the newly established Civil Rights Section of the Department of Justice sought to expand federal criminal civil rights enforcement. Frank Murphy was the first United States Attorney General since Amos Akerman to employ Reconstruction-era civil rights crimes statutes aggressively. As Attorney General, Murphy was responsible in large measure for the establishment of the Civil Liberties Unit and then the Civil Rights Section, the predecessors of the present-day Civil Rights Division of the Department of Justice. By the time the *Classic* investigation resulted in indictments, Murphy had become an Associate Justice of the Supreme Court and Robert Jackson, another future Supreme Court Justice, had succeeded him as Attorney General.[26]

*Classic* arose out of a series of ongoing federal investigations into the manner in which elections were conducted in Louisiana during the political "civil war" within that state's Democratic party following the assassination of Huey Long in 1935. One of the investigations discovered improprieties in ballot counting in the September 1940 primary election. Ironically, the accused were members of a reform movement who were challenging the remnants of the Long machine.

The indictments in *Classic* charged deprivation of the rights of voters to have their votes properly counted.[27] The Supreme Court upheld these indictments in a majority opinion by Justice Harlan Fiske Stone. On the surface, *Classic* can be seen simply as the extension of the right to vote in a federal general election, previously recognized in *Ex Parte Yarbrough*, to primary elections. The most important aspect of Stone's opinion was the justification for this extension. Justice Stone took judicial notice of the "integral role" in Louisiana politics played by that state's Democratic primary. Because the "primary effectively controls the choice [in the general election]," the right to vote in the primary and have one's vote counted is as much a part of the constitutional guarantee as is that right with respect to a general election.[28]

The more complex issues underpinning *Classic*, however, are best viewed through the dissenting opinion of Justice William O. Douglas, joined by Justices Hugo Black and Frank Murphy, by then on the Court. Douglas's dissent was based in part on the federalism problem. Justice Douglas conceded that Congress, pursuant to Article I of the Constitution, possessed the authority to regulate the conduct of primary elections and thus to federalize crimes associated with the right to vote in these elections.[29] Primary elections were nonetheless matters that were essentially of state concern, according to Douglas. Congress had wisely stayed out of this area, and the Court was in "perilous territory" when it allowed the Executive Branch to enter through the prosecutorial function.[30] Stone later said that

> [w]hen the *Classic* case came to us, I made a thorough study of the clauses dealing with federal elections and came to the conclusion that the purpose was to give the Federal Government power over the whole electoral process.[31]

As the Court had concluded years earlier in *Ex Parte Yarbrough*, the explicit constitutional basis for congressional oversight of federal elections warranted federalization of criminal deprivations of voting rights in federal elections. As a practical matter, *Classic* provided the Civil Rights Section of the Department of Justice with a much needed affirmation of federal criminal civil rights jurisdiction. As a doctrinal matter, however, *Classic* avoided the difficult federalism questions facing criminal civil rights enforcement because of its explicit constitutional foundation.

# Notes

## Introduction

1. Church Arson Prevention Act of 1996, 104th Cong., 2d sess. H.R. 3525, amending 18 U.S.C. §247.
2. "Judge Drops City, Roache from Stuart Lawsuit," *Boston Globe,* 32 (Oct. 13, 1995).
3. *Nightline* (ABC television broadcast, Apr. 30, 1992). See, e.g., "Bush Wins Points for Speech on L. A. Riots," *Christian Science Monitor,* 1 (May 4, 1992); "Los Angeles Jury Widens Inquiry in Policy Beating," *New York Times,* sec. 1, p. 23 (Mar. 10, 1991).
4. See "Death Penalty for 3 Weighed/ Dragging Murder Horrifies Nation," *Newsday* (June 11, 1998); Scott Baldauf and Kyle Johnson, "Texas Case Highlights US Problem," *Christian Science Monitor* (June 11, 1998); "Clinton Voices Outrage over Texas Murder," *Boston Globe* (June 11, 1998); Bob Hohler, "Brutal Slaying Tears at a Texas Town," *Boston Globe* (June 12, 1998); James Hill, "Slaying Feeds Fears of Racism in Texas Town; Services Are Held for Black Man Beaten, Dragged to His Death," *Chicago Tribune* (June 14, 1998); Joanna Weiss, "Jasper Gripped by Shame, Fear; America Watches Town as It Mourns," *Times-Picayune* (June 14, 1998); "Dragging Death in Texas," *Los Angeles Times* (June 16, 1998); Bob Hohler, "After Texas Killing, New Hate-Crime Law Urged," *Boston Globe* (July 9, 1998).

## 1. What Is a Bias Crime?

1. See Susan Forrest and Phil Mintz, "Seething Hate Led to Rampage aboard Train," *Buffalo News,* A8 (Dec. 9, 1993); Malcolm Gladwell and Rachel E. Stassen-Berger, "Slaying Blamed on Bias," *Chicago Sun-Times,* 7 (Dec. 9, 1996); Shirley E. Perlman, Craig Gordon, and Michael Alexander, "An Angry Young Man," *Newsday,* 4 (Mar. 6, 1994).
2. Edgar Allan Poe, *The Tell-Tale Heart* (1895).
3. Aviam Soifer, *Law and the Company We Keep,* 13 (1995); Charles Taylor, *Multiculturalism and the Politics of Recognition* (1992).
4. Andrew Hacker, *Two Nations, Black and White, Separate, Hostile, Unequal,* 4–6

(1992); Jennifer L. Hochschild, *Facing Up to the American Dream: Race, Class and the Soul of the Nation* (1996).

5. United Brotherhood of Carpenters and Joiners of America v. Scott, 463 U.S. 825 (1983). The plaintiffs in *Scott* brought suit under a federal civil statute that allows civil recovery in federal court for victims of conspiracies formed "for the purpose of depriving . . . any person or class of persons of the equal protection of the laws, or of equal privileges and immunities under the laws." 42 U.S.C. §1985(3). In prior cases, the Court had interpreted section 1985(3) to require a class-based animus. The Court in *Scott,* by a 5–4 vote, dismissed the suit on the grounds that section 1985(3) did not apply to private conduct except in limited circumstances that were inapplicable here, and also on the grounds that union membership was not deemed to satisfy the class animus. The position advocated in this book as a matter of normative argument is consonant with the statutory interpretation proposed by the four dissenting justices in *Scott.*

6. 463 U.S. at 839–854 (dissenting opinion of Justice Blackmun).

7. For example, Arizona Governor Fife Symington threatened to veto a bias crime bill that included gender and sexual orientation, calling the measure an "exercise in political correctness." Two weeks later, he signed the bill into law, surprising both supporters and opponents of the law. "New Hate Crimes Bill Gains, But Faces Veto," *Arizona Daily Star* (Apr. 17, 1997); "Governor Signs Bill on Hate Crime, Move Catches Both Sides Off Guard," *Arizona Republic* (Apr. 29, 1997).

   In New York, then-Governor Mario Cuomo proposed a hate crime bill, the Bias-Related Violence and Intimidation Act, in 1987. The bill, which includes sexual orientation as a protected category, has been blocked since 1989 in the Republican-controlled Senate. Walter Ruby, "Suffolk Group Presses Albany on Anti-Bias Law," *New York Times* (Mar. 13, 1994).

   In Pennsylvania, Republican state senators, after a closed-door caucus, canceled a plan to vote on bias crime legislation before an upcoming election, out of fear of voter backlash against the inclusion of gays and lesbians in the bill. Adam Bell, "State Senate Delays Gay Rights Vote," *Harrisburg Patriot* (June 5, 1996).

8. See Steven Bennett Weisburd and Brian Levin, "'On the Basis of Sex': Recognizing Gender-Based Bias Crimes," 5 *Stanford Law and Policy Review,* 21 (1994); see also Elizabeth A. Pendo, "Recognizing Violence against Women: Gender and the Hate Crimes Statistics Act," 17 *Harvard Women's Law Journal,* 157, 162 n.28 (1994), listing the fourteen factors contained in the U.S. Department of Justice Crime Reporting Guidelines that may, alone or in combination, be indicative of bias.

9. See, e.g., comments by Rep. Woody Burton of the Indiana House, arguing that gays and lesbians choose homosexuality and thus do not deserve protection under the state's hate crimes bill. "Gay Protection Stays in Hate Crimes Bill," *Chicago Tribune,* 3 (Feb. 2, 1994). See also comments by Sen. John Hilgert of the Nebraska State Legislature arguing that gays and lesbians do not need protection under the state's bias crimes bill because they are an "affluent, power-

ful class." "State Hate Crimes Law Urged, Nebraska Legislators Hear from Police, Civil Rights Officials," *Omaha World-Herald* (Feb. 14, 1997).

10. See Center for Women Policy Studies, *Violence against Women as Bias Motivated Hate Crime: Defining the Issues,* 32 (1991); Weisburd and Levin, "On the Basis of Sex," 36.

11. Weisburd and Levin, "On the Basis of Sex," 38 (discussing the personal relationship dynamic and arguing that the existence of such a relationship should not preclude bias crime classification where there is also evidence of a group component, that is, evidence that victimization is due at least in part to bias against the victim's gender).

12. Joe Cutbirth, "Hate-Crime Bill Slows in Austin as Scope Widens," *Fort Worth Star-Telegram,* 1 (Apr. 1, 1993).

13. "Montreal Gunman Kills 14 Women and Himself," *New York Times,* A23 (Dec. 7, 1989); "Montreal Killer Laid Blame on Women for 'Ruining' Him," *Boston Globe,* 1 (Dec. 8, 1989); "Montreal Women's Slayer Identified; Long Suicide Note Blames 'Feminists' for Troubles," *Washington Post,* A1 (Dec. 8, 1989).

14. Marguerite Angelari, "Hate Crime Statutes: A Promising Tool for Fighting Violence Against Women," 2 *American University Journal of Gender and Law,* 63, 65–66 (1994), citing Elaine Hilberman, "Overview: The 'Wife-Beater's Wife' Reconsidered," 137 *American Medical Journal of Psychiatry,* 1336, 1337 (1980); *Hate Crime Statistics Act of 1988:* Hearing on S.2000 before the Subcommittee on the Constitution of the Senate Comm. on the Judiciary, 100th Cong., 2d sess. 262, 268 (1988). See also Wendy Rae Willis, "The Gun Is Always Pointed: Sexual Violence and Title III of the Violence against Women Act," 80 *Georgetown Law Journal,* 2197 (1992).

15. Weisburd and Levin, "On the Basis of Sex," 36.

16. See landlord-tenant hypothetical on p. 10 of this chapter.

17. Angelari, "Hate Crime Statutes: A Promising Tool for Fighting Violence Against Women," 98–99.

18. See Steve Lipsher, "Hate-Crime Bill Dies in 7–6 Vote," *Denver Post* (Feb. 17, 1995).

19. See Eric Rothschild, "Recognizing Another Face of Hate Crimes: Rape as a Gender-Bias Crime," 4 *Maryland Journal Contemporary Legal Issues,* 231 (1993).

20. Anthony S. Winer, "Hate Crimes, Homosexuals, and the Constitution," 29 *Harvard Civil Rights–Civil Liberties Law Review,* 353 (1994).

21. Gary D. Comstock, *Violence against Lesbians and Gay Men,* 36 (1991).

22. National Institute of Justice, United States Department of Justice, *The Response of the Criminal Justice System to Bias Crime: An Explanatory Review* (1987).

23. See "Hate Crimes May Affect Legislation," *Charleston Daily Mail* (Mar. 13, 1997); "Panel Hears Harassment Bill Testimony," *Portland Oregonian,* D8 (Feb. 10, 1993); Jo-Ann Armao, "Hate-Crime Bill Voted to Aid Gays," *Washington Post,* B1 (Sept. 20, 1989); "Lawyers Tell Legislators: Strengthen, Broaden 'Hate Crimes' Law," *AIDS Weekly* (May 5, 1992).

24. Stuart Eskenazi, "Chisum Casts Blame at Gay Victims," *Austin American-Statesman,* B1 (Feb. 17, 1995).

25. "Hate Crime Bill Faces Fight," *New Orleans Times-Picayune* (June 6, 1997). See also "Gay Protection Stays in Hate Crimes Bill," *Chicago Tribune,* 3 (Feb. 2, 1994).

26. See John Travis, "X Chromosome Again Linked to Homosexuality," *Science News,* 295 (Nov. 4, 1995); Eliot Marshall, "NIH's 'Gay Gene' Study Questioned," *Science,* 1841 (June 30, 1995).

27. Fern Shen, "Hate Crime Bill Rejected in Md. House," *Washington Post,* C1 (Mar. 22, 1991).

28. Terri Ann Schroeder, "Different Version," *Indianapolis Star,* A9 (Mar. 7, 1994); Mary Dieter, "House Rejects Bid to Deny Gays Protection under Hate-Crimes Law," *Courier-Journal,* 3B (Louisville, Ky., Feb. 2, 1994).

29. Romer v. Evans, 517 U.S. 620 (1996).

30. Bowers v. Hardwick, 478 U.S. 186 (1986).

31. Romer v. Evans, 517 U.S. at 632.

32. *Conn. Gen. Stat. Ann.* §46a–58 (West 1991), criminalizing deprivation of rights through the use of a burning cross, enacted 1949; *Fla. Stat. Ann.* §876.20 (West 1991), criminalizing wearing a mask or placing an exhibit for the purpose of intimidation, enacted 1951; *Ga. Code Ann.* §16-11-37(b)(1) (Michie 1990), criminalizing the burning of a cross with the intent to terrorize, enacted 1968; *Ga. Code Ann.* §16-11-38 (Michie 1990), criminalizing the wearing of a hood or a mask that conceals one's identity, enacted 1986; *N.C. Gen. Stat.* §§14-12.7 through 14-12.10 (1991), criminalizing the wearing of hoods or masks, enacted 1953; *N.C. Gen. Stat.* §14-12.12 (1991), criminalizing cross-burning, enacted 1953; *Va. Code Ann.* §18.2-422 (Michie 1991), prohibiting the wearing of masks or hoods under specific circumstances, enacted 1950; *Va. Code Ann.* §18.2-423 (Michie 1991), criminalizing cross-burning, enacted 1950.

33. *Conn. Gen. Stat. Ann.* §53-57 (West 1991), criminalizing the ridiculing of an individual based on race, color, or creed, enacted in 1949.

34. The state bias crime statutes can be found in Appendix A. There are a number of means by which federal law seeks to punish bias crimes, and these are discussed in Chapter 6, pp. 148–150.

35. See, e.g., Lisa S. L. Ho, "Substantive Penal Hate Crime Legislation: Toward Defining Constitutional Guidelines Following the R.A.V. v. City of St. Paul and Wisconsin v. Mitchell Decisions," 34 *Santa Clara Law Review,* 711 (1994). See also "Conference to Focus on Rise in Hate Crime," *Los Angeles Times,* 9 (sec. City Times, Mar. 12, 1995), stating that "every jurisdiction throughout the country that collects monthly statistics reported [in February 1995] either a record high or an increase over the previous month."

36. Craig Peyton Gaumer, "Punishment for Prejudice: A Commentary on the Constitutionality and Utility of State Statutory Responses to the Problem of Hate Crime," 39 *South Dakota Law Review,* 1, 5 (1994).

37. Anti-Defamation League, *Audit of Anti-Semitic Incidents for 1997;* Anti-Defamation League, *Audit of Anti-Semitic Incidents for 1994.*

38. Ibid.; "Attacks on Gays Decline Nationwide," *San Francisco Chronicle* (Mar. 12, 1996).

39. Anti-Defamation League, *Audit of Anti-Semitic Incidents for 1996;* "Rise in Hate Crimes Looms behind Church Burnings," *Christian Science Monitor* (June 28, 1996); "Combating Hate Crimes," *Los Angeles Times,* 1B (May 17, 1994).

40. Charles Lewis Nier III, "Racial Hatred: A Comparative Analysis of the Hate Crime Laws of the United States and Germany," 13 *Dickinson Journal of International Law,* 241, 263 (1995); "The Face of Hatred in America," *Christian Science Monitor,* 8 (Nov. 27, 1991).

41. "Around the South Hate Crimes by Blacks Soar, Anti-Klan Group Says," *Atlanta Constitution,* A3 (Dec. 14, 1993).

42. Ibid.

43. "Group Says Hate-Crime Figures Bogus," *Bangor Daily News,* 1 (Jan. 10, 1995).

44. See James B. Jacobs and Kimberly Potten, *Hate Crimes: Criminal Law and Identity Politics,* 45–64 (1998); James B. Jacobs and Jessica S. Henry, "The Social Construction of a Hate Crime Epidemic," *Journal of Criminal Law and Criminology,* 391 (Winter 1996).

45. 101st Cong., 1st sess., 1989, S. Rept. 21, 158.

46. Joseph M. Fernandez, "Bringing Hate Crime into Focus—The Hate Crime Statistics Act of 1990, Pub. L. No. 101–275," 26 *Harvard Civil Rights–Civil Liberties Law Review,* 261, 263 (1991).

47. "Statement of Steven L. Pomerantz, Assistant Director, Criminal Justice Information Services Division, FBI, on the Hate Crime Statistics Act before the Senate Subcommittee on the Constitution of the Committee on the Judiciary," *Federal Document Clearing House Congressional Testimony,* June 28, 1994, available in LEXIS, Nexis Library, CURNWS File.

48. Ibid.

49. Federal Bureau of Investigation, United States Department of Justice, *Uniform Crime Reports, Hate Crime Statistics 1996; Uniform Crime Reports, Hate Crime Statistics 1995; Uniform Crime Reports, Hate Crime Statistics 1994; Uniform Crime Reports, Hate Crime Statistics 1993; Uniform Crime Reports, Hate Crime Statistics 1992; Uniform Crime Reports, Hate Crime Statistics 1991.*

    In 1994, the only year of a decline in FBI bias crime statistics, Massachusetts, Alabama, and Kansas, states that had previously reported bias crimes to the FBI, did not participate in the annual survey. If Massachusetts alone had participated in the 1994 survey, 808 bias crimes would have added to that year's total, yielding an overall level of 8,306, a 7.5 percent increase over 1993. See Sally J. Greenberg, "The Massachusetts Hate Crime Reporting Act of 1990: Great Expectations Yet Unfulfilled?" 31 *New England Law Review,* 125, n. 107 (1996).

50. "Spielberg Speaks Out against Hate Crimes," *Arizona Republic,* 1A (June, 29, 1994).

51. "Statement of the Anti-Defamation League for Hate Crime Statistics Act Over-

sight Hearings before the Senate Judiciary Subcommittee on the Constitution" [hereinafter ADL's HCSA Oversight Hearings], *Federal Document Clearing House Congressional Testimony,* June 28, 1994, available in LEXIS, Nexis Library, CURNWS file.

52. Ibid. Only twenty of the United States' largest thirty cities reported bias crime data to the FBI in 1992. Of the twenty that did report, eight submitted data that were "obviously incomplete."

53. "Some Question Use of Hate Crime Laws by Victimized Whites," *San Diego Union-Tribune,* 36A (May 5, 1994).

54. "Rise in Hate Crimes Looms behind Church Burnings," *Christian Science Monitor* (June 28, 1996); Abraham Abramovsky, "Bias Crime: A Call for Alternative Responses," 19 *Fordham Urban Law Journal,* 875, 885 (1992).

55. Fernandez, "Bringing Hate Crime into Focus," 291; "Police Beat: Fear, Intimidation Cloud True Statistics on Hate-Bias Crimes," *Nashville Banner* (Jan. 9, 1996).

56. ADL's HCSA Oversight Hearings.

57. "Hate Crime Reports Rise in Boston," *Boston Globe,* 1 (June 20, 1994). The Boston Police Department actually recorded its highest rate of bias crimes during 1978, its first year implementing the recording practice. In that year, the department recorded 607 bias crimes, a figure that fell steadily to 152 in 1988, but has since risen to 276 in 1993.

58. Fernandez, "Bringing Hate into Focus," 267. See *Maryland Annotated Code* art. 88B, §§9(b), 10 (1985).

59. See 1987 *Conn. Legis. Serv.* 279 (West); *Fla. Stat. Ann.* §877.19 (West 1990); *Idaho Code* §67-2905; *Ill. Rev. Stat.* ch. 127, para. 55a (1988); *Minn. Stat.* §626.5531 (1990); *N.J. Exec. Directive No. 3* (1987); *Okla. Stat. Ann.* tit. 21, §850 (West Supp. 1988); *Or. Rev. Stat.* §181.550 (1989); 71 *Pa. Cons. Stat. Ann.* §250 (Purdon Supp. 1987); *R. I. Gen. Laws* §42-28-46 (1988); *Va. Code Ann.* §52-8.5 (1988).

60. *Klanwatch Intelligence Report* (Winter 1998).

61. "Hate Crime Reports Rise in Boston," 1A (quoting Jack McDevitt, the associate director for Applied Social Research at Northeastern University, as saying, "[This] is the most racist and sexist generation of high school kids I've ever seen."); "The Face of Hatred in America," 8; "Conference to Focus on Rise in Hate Crime," 9; "Youth Linked to Hate Crimes," *Pittsburgh Post-Gazette* (July 16, 1997).

62. "Students Say Racial Slurs Go beyond Hatred," *New York Times,* B2 (June 26, 1995).

63. Ibid.

64. The classic source for the correlation between bias-motivated violence and harsh economic conditions is C. J. Hovland and R. R. Sears, "Minor Studies in Aggression: VI. Correlation of Lynchings with Economic Indices," 9 *Journal of Psychology,* 301–310 (1940). The magnitude of Hovland and Sears's conclusions has been challenged, but not the underlying correlation. See, e.g., Joseph T.

Hepworth and Stephen G. West, "Lynchings and the Economy: A Time-Series Reanalysis of Hovland and Sears," 55 *Journal of Personality of Social Psychology,* 239–246 (1988). See also Valerie Jenness and Ryken Grattet, "The Criminalization of Hate: A Comparison of Structural and Polity Influences on the Passage of 'Bias-Crime' Legislation in the United States," 39 *Sociological Perspectives,* 129, 136 (1996).

65. "The Face of Hatred in America," 8; David H. Bennett, *The Party of Fear: From Nativist Movements to the New Right in American History,* 85–92 (1988).

66. Stewart E. Tolnay and E. M. Beck, *A Festival of Violence,* 55–85 (1992); Seymour Martin Lipset and Earl Rabb, *The Politics of Unreason,* 110–145 (1978, 2nd ed.); Bennett, *The Party of Fear,* 199–231.

67. David Chalmers, *Hooded Americanism,* 308–310 (1965); Steven A. Blum, "Public Executions: Understanding the 'Cruel and Unusual Punishments' Clause," 19 *Hastings Constitutional Law Quarterly,* 413, 419 (1992); Richard H. McAdams, "Cooperation and Conflict: The Economics of Group Status Production and Race Discrimination," 108 *Harvard Law Review,* 1003, 1054–1055 (1995).

68. Stephen B. Bright, "The Politics of Crime and the Death Penalty: Not 'Soft on Crime,' But Hard on the Bill of Rights," 39 *St. Louis University Law Journal,* 479, 482 (1995).

69. "As Bias Crime Seems to Rise, Scientists Study Roots of Racism," *New York Times,* C1 (May 29, 1990).

70. "Conference to Focus on Rise in Hate Crime," 9.

71. "As Bias Crime Seems to Rise, Scientists Study Roots of Racism," C1.

72. William J. Wilson, "The Political Economy and Urban Racial Tensions," 39 *American Economist,* 3–14 (1995). See Thomas B. Edsall and Mary D. Edsall, *Chain Reaction: The Impact of Race, Rights, and Taxes on American Politics,* 196–197, 284–285 (1991).

73. "Gay Men Become No. 1 Hate Crime Targets," *Los Angeles Times,* 1B (May 10, 1994).

74. Rita Kirk Whillock, "The Use of Hate as a Stratagem for Achieving Political and Social Goals," in *Hate Speech,* 29–31 (1995). See Thomas B. Edsall and Mary D. Edsall, "When the Official Subject Is Presidential Politics, Taxes, Welfare, Crime, Rights, or Values . . . The Real Subject Is Race," 267 *The Atlantic,* 53–86 (1991). See also Timur Kuran, "Seeds of Racial Explosion," *Society,* 55–67 (Sept.–Oct. 1993).

75. See Levin and McDevitt, *Hate Crimes,* 57–58.

76. "Asians Latest Victims of Hate Crimes," *Charleston Gazette and Daily Mail* (Aug. 4, 1996); Connie Kang, "Hate Crimes against Asians in Southland Rose Last Year," *Los Angeles Times* (Aug. 2, 1996).

77. Elinor Langer, "The American Neo-Nazi Movement Today," *The Nation,* 85 (July 16, 1990).

78. "The Face of Hatred in America," 8; "Klan Leader Fights On, Low Membership Hurts KKK's Influence," *Greensboro News and Record* (Apr. 1, 1997).

79. Anti-Defamation League, *Audit of Anti-Semitic Incidents for 1996.*

80. Ibid.

81. Ibid.

82. Ibid.

83. "Text of the ADL Report: 'Beyond the Bombing: The Militia Menace Grows,'" *U.S. Newswire* (June 19, 1995), available in LEXIS, Nexis Library, WIRE File [hereinafter "Beyond the Bombing"].

84. Ibid.

85. Kenneth Stern, *A Force upon the Plain: The American Movement and the Politics of Hate* (1996); Morris Dees, *Gathering Storm: America's Militia Threat* (1996); "Citizen Militias and Support Groups in the United States," *Klanwatch Intelligence Report,* 8–9 (June, 1995); "Excerpts from the ADL Report on Militias," *U.S. Newswire,* (Apr. 21, 1995), available in LEXIS, Nexis Library, WIRE File. In this report, the ADL states that some Northwestern militia leaders have backgrounds in the Aryan Nations, while some members are former neo-Nazis and Ku Klux Klan members. (See also "Beyond the Bombing.") The ADL outlines specific ties between militias and hate groups. These ties range from the distribution of known racist and anti-Semitic propaganda at militia meetings (as documented in Florida, Georgia, Idaho, Nebraska, New Mexico, and Texas) to militia members' personal ties with racist organizations (e.g., Montana Militia founder John Trochman spoke at a major conclave of the white supremacist Aryan Nations; leaders of the Missouri Militia are also members of the White Knights of the Ku Klux Klan).

86. "Terror on the Right: Swelling Ranks of Militia Heighten Violence Threat," *Houston Chronicle* (Apr. 20, 1997); "Facing the Fear of an Enemy from Within," *Los Angeles Times,* 1A (Apr. 22, 1995).

87. "Oklahoma Bombing: The Aftermath," *Atlanta Journal and Constitution,* 12A (Apr. 28, 1995).

88. "Hate Speech," *Plain Dealer,* 1A (June 11, 1995).

89. "Militias' Presence Being Felt in Pennsylvania," *Morning Call,* A7 (Allentown, Pa., Apr. 28, 1995).

90. Ibid. See also Mack Tanner, "Extreme Prejudice: How the Media Misrepresent the Militia Movement," 27 *Reason,* 42–50 (1995). In this article, Tanner asserts that the militias' "motivations, members, attitudes and tactics have been grossly mischaracterized by culturally ignorant reporters more concerned with telling sensational stories than telling the more-complicated truth" (p. 43). He further asserts that militia members actually identify with the Jews who suffered under a fascist German government, and cites the militias' success in recruiting blacks and Jews (p. 46).

91. Transcript from "Sonya Live," Cable News Network, 4 (Sept. 8, 1993). See also *Gathering Storm,* 200.

## 2. How Are Bias Crimes Different?

1. Wisconsin v. Mitchell, 113 S. Ct. 2194 (1993).

2. In Beauharnais v. Illinois, 343 U.S. 250, 266 (1952), the Supreme Court up-

held a group libel law that punished the dissemination of racially slanderous or inflammatory statements. *Beauharnais* was premised on the idea that, just as interpersonal libel fell outside the protection of the First Amendment, group libel was similarly unprotected. Ibid., 266–267. *Beauharnais,* however, was significantly undercut by New York Times v. Sullivan, 376 U.S. 254, 283 (1964), which held that "defamatory" statements made against public officials will receive First Amendment protection unless such statements were made with malice or a reckless disregard for the truth. Moreover, the kind of harm recognized in *Beauharnais* is far more attenuated than the incitement of "imminent lawless action" standard created in Brandenburg v. Ohio, 395 U.S. 444, 448 (1969). Nevertheless, it may be more accurate to say that Wisconsin v. Mitchell is the first time that the *modern* court has explicitly upheld a bias crime statute.

3. *Wis. Stat. Ann.* §§939.05, 939.50(3)(e), 940.19(1m) (West 1991); sentence for complicity in aggravated battery is two years.

4. *Wis. Stat. Ann.* §939.645 (West 1991) provides:

(1) If a person does all of the following, the penalties for the underlying crimes are increased as provided in sub. (2):
(a) Commits a crime under chs. 939 to 948.
(b) Intentionally selects the person against whom the crime under par. (a) is committed or selects the property which is damaged or otherwise affected by the crime under par. (a) because of the race, religion, color, disability, sexual orientation, national origin or ancestry of that person or the owner or occupant of that property.

(2) (a) If the crime cimmitted under sub. (1) is a misdemeanor other than a Class A misdemeanor, the revised maximum fine is $10,000 and the revised maximum period of imprisonment is one year in the county jail.
(b) If the crime committed under sub. (1) is ordinarily a Class A misdemeanor, the penalty increase under this section changes the status of the crime to a felony and the revised maximum fine is $10,000 and the revised maximum period of imprisonment is 2 years.
(c) If the crime committed under sub. (1) is ordinarily a felony, the maximum fine prescribed by law may be increased by not more than $5,000 and the maximum period of imprisonment prescribed by law for the crime may be increased by not more than 5 years.

(3) This section provides for the enhancement of the penalties applicable for the underlying crime. The court shall direct that the trier of fact find a special verdict as to all of the issues specified in sub. (1).

(4) This section does not apply to any crime if proof of race, religion, color, disability, sexual orientation, national origin or ancestry is required for a conviction for that crime.

5. Wisconsin v. Mitchell, 485 N.W. 2d 807 (Wisc. 1992).
6. *Wis. Stat. Ann.* §939.645 (West 1991).

7. State v. Mitchell, 163 Wis. 2d 652, 473 N.W. 2d 1 (Ct. App. 1991), reversed, 485 N.W. 2d 807 (1992).

8. R.A.V. v. City of St. Paul, 505 U.S. 377 (1992).

9. See Katia Hetter, "Enforcers of Hate-Crime Laws Wary after High Court Ruling," *Wall Street Journal*, B1 (Aug. 13, 1992). *Mitchell* was seen as resolving those doubts. See, e.g., Brian Levin, "U.S. Supreme Court Upholds Stiffer Sentences for Hate Crimes," *Intelligence Report*, 4–5 (Sept. 1993).

10. The *St. Paul Bias-Motivated Crime Ordinance* provides:

   Whoever places on public or private property a symbol, object, appellation, characterization or graffiti, including, but not limited to, a burning cross or Nazi swastika, which one knows or has reasonable grounds to know arouses anger, alarm or resentment in others on the basis of race, color, creed, religion or gender commits disorderly conduct and shall be guilty of a misdemeanor. (*St. Paul Minn. Legis. Code* §292.02 [1990])

   The defendant in *R.A.V.* had been charged under the ordinance for burning a cross on the lawn of an African-American family who had recently moved into his neighborhood.

11. R.A.V. v. St. Paul, 378–396.

12. See Chapter 5,

13. Ohio v. Wyant, 597 N.E. 2d 450 (Ohio 1992), vacated and remanded, 508 U.S. 969 (1993), aff'd and reinstated in part, rev'd and remanded in part, 624 N.E. 2d 722 (Ohio 1994).

14. Wisconsin v. Mitchell, 485 N.W. 2d 807–10. The reasoning of the Court in *R.A.V.* formed the basis of two state court decisions, striking down state bias crime statutes. See Washington v. Talley, 858 P. 2d 192 (Wash. 1993) and Maryland v. Sheldon, 629 A. 2d 753 (Md. 1993). In addition, *R.A.V.* was central to the New Jersey Supreme Court oral argument in State v. Vawter, 627 A.2d 1123 (N.J. 1993) and State v. Mortimer, 627 A.2d. 1124 (N.J. 1993), challenging the constitutionality of the New Jersey bias crime laws. See Tony Hagen, "Bias Laws Face Constitutional Probe at Court," 2 *New Jersey Lawyer*, 1619 (Oct. 18, 1993).

   Not every state court, however, read *R.A.V.* as requiring the invalidation of its bias crime law. In Oregon v. Plowman, 838 P. 2d. 558 (Ore. 1992), the Supreme Court of Oregon upheld the Oregon racial intimidation law. This law makes it a crime for two or more persons to intentionally, knowingly, or recklessly cause physical injury to another because of their perception of that person's race, color, religion, national origin, or sexual orientation. *Ore. Rev. Stat.* §166.165(1)(a)(A). The court concluded that the Oregon statute could be distinguished from the St. Paul ordinance struck down in *R.A.V.* because the St. Paul ordinance "was directed against the substance of speech," whereas the Oregon statute "was directed at conduct." Oregon v. Plowman, 838 P.2d at 565. See also Dobbins v. Florida, 605 So. 2d 922 (Fla. Dist. Ct. App. 1992), upholding a sentence imposed under Florida's bias crimes statute.

15. See, e.g., Steven M. Freeman, "Hate Crimes: They're Still against the Law,"

*Anti-Defamation League Frontline,* 1 (Sept. 1992). In Massachusetts, the state attorney general convened a task force, of which the author was a member, to re-examine the constitutionality of the Massachusetts Civil Rights Crimes statutes in light of *R.A.V.* See "Constitutionality of Massachusetts Civil and Criminal Civil Rights Laws," *Massachusetts Attorney General Report* (1993).

16. *Wis. Stat. Ann.* §939.645(1)(b) (West 1991).

17. In Chapter 5 I strongly criticize the purported dichotomy between speech and conduct as a distinction that is inherently flawed and thus without analytic value as a tool in constitutional analysis. Nevertheless, the distinction continues to play a substantial role in First Amendment jurisprudence. This is particularly true in the debate over the constitutionality of bias crime laws as seen in *R.A.V.* and *Mitchell.*

   In *R.A.V.,* Justice Scalia observed that "a particular content-based subcategory of a proscribable class of speech can be swept up incidentally within the reach of a statute directed at conduct rather than speech." 505 U.S. 389. The Supreme Court in *Mitchell* distinguished *R.A.V.,* utilizing a speech-conduct distinction. Wisconsin v. Mitchell, 113 U.S. 2200–2201 ("whereas the ordinance struck down in *R.A.V.* was explicitly directed at expression . . . the statute in this case is aimed at conduct unprotected by the First Amendment.").

18. Wisconsin v. Mitchell, 485 N.W.2d at 812. The Ohio Supreme Court reached essentially the same conclusion in Ohio v. Wyant, 597 N.E.2d at 812–814.

19. Petitioner's Brief at 136–37, Wisconsin v. Mitchell, 508 U.S. 476 (1993).

20. Ibid., 36. During his argument to the Supreme Court in support of the Wisconsin statute, State Attorney General James Doyle stated that the statute would have applied to Todd Mitchell if his sole motivation in selecting a white victim had been to impress his friends and if Mitchell himself was otherwise indifferent as to the choice of his victim. Transcript of Oral Argument at 9–10, Wisconsin v. Mitchell, 508 U.S. 476 (1993).

21. Wisconsin v. Mitchell, 479.

22. Ibid., 485 (emphasis added).

23. Ibid., 485–486 (rejecting the argument that the statute impermissibly punishes motive because the "defendant's motive for committing the offense is one important fact" in the sentencing, and because "motive plays the same role under the Wisconsin statute as it does under federal and state anti-discrimination laws, which we have previously upheld against constitutional challenge").

24. *N.J. Stat. Ann.* §2C:44-3(e) (1992).

25. See, e.g., Jack Levin and Jack McDevitt, *Hate Crimes,* 33–44 (1993); Abraham Abramovsky, "Bias Crime: A Call for Alternative Responses," 19 *Fordham Urban Law Journal,* 875, 878 (1992); Brian Levin, "Bias Crimes: A Theoretical and Practical Overview," *Stanford Law & Policy Review,* 165, 166 (Winter 1992–1993); Jeffrie G. Murphy, "Bias Crimes: What Do Haters Deserve?" 11 *Criminal Justice Ethics,* 20, 22 (Summer–Fall 1992).

26. See, e.g., *Federal Bureau of Investigation, U.S. Department of Justice, Hate Crimes Data Collection Guidelines,* 4 (1990) [hereinafter *FBI, Hate Crimes Data*].

27. The classic definition of "prejudice" remains that proposed forty years ago by Gordon Allport. He argued that "ethnic prejudice is an antipathy based upon a faulty and inflexible generalization. It may be felt or expressed. It may be directed toward a group as a whole, or toward an individual because he is a member of that group." Gordon Allport, *The Nature of Prejudice*, 10 (1954).

28. *FBI, Hate Crimes Data*, 4. See also *Hate Crimes Statistics Act*, 28 U.S.C. 534 (Supp. V 1993). States have implemented the mandate of the Hate Crime Statistics Act through legislation and regulations. See, e.g., *Mass. Gen. Law* ch. 22C §§32–35 (1992); *Mass. Regs. Code* tit. 520 §§13.00-.08 (1992).

    The FBI refers to bias crimes as "hate crimes." For the reasons discussed above, the term "bias crimes" is used here. It is illustrative of the reasons for preferring the nomenclature "bias crime" that the FBI defines a "hate crime" as a "criminal act to which a *bias* motive is evident as a contributing factor." See *FBI, Hate Crimes Data*, 2; *Mass. Regs. Code* tit. 520 §§13.02.

29. *FBI, Hate Crimes Data*, 4. The essential role of animosity in the racial animus model is seen even more strongly in the Massachusetts regulations promulgated under the state "Hate Crimes Reporting Act." Under the Massachusetts regulations, a bias crime is defined as conduct in which "[h]atred, hostility, or negative attitudes towards or prejudice against, any group or individual on account of race, religion, ethnicity, handicap, or sexual orientation . . . is a contributing factor, in whole or in part, in the commission of a criminal act." *Mass. Regs. Code* tit. 520 §§13.02.

30. The list of bias indicators in the Massachusetts regulations provides, in part, as follows:

    (b) Bias-related oral comments, written statements, or gestures were made by the offender which indicate his/her bias. For example, the offender shouted a racial or anti-gay epithet at the victim.

    (c) Bias-related drawings, markings, symbols, or graffiti were left at the crime scene. For example, a swastika was painted on the door of a synagogue.

    (d) Certain objects, items, or things which indicate bias were used (e.g., the offenders wore white sheets and white hoods) or left behind by the offenders(s) [sic] (e.g., a burning cross was left in front of the victim's residence).
    . . .
    (h) Victims or witnesses perceive that the incident was motivated by bias ["bias" is defined as "hatred, hostility, or negative attitudes towards or prejudice towards" the target group].

    (i) The victim was engaged in activities promoting a racial, religious, ethnic/national origin, handicap, or sexual orientation group. For example, the victim is a member of the NAACP, participated in gay rights demonstrations, etc.
    . . .
    (l) There were indications that a hate group [defined in animus-based terms as a group that promotes "animosity, hostility, or malice" against a target group] was involved. For example, a hate group claimed responsibility for the crime or was active in the neighborhood.

(m) A historically established animosity exists between the victim's group and the offender's group.

(n) The victim, although not a member of the targeted racial, religious, ethnic/national origin, handicap, or sexual orientation group, is a member of an advocacy group supporting the precepts of the victim group, or is friendly with members of a victim group. (*FBI, Hate Crimes Data*, 2–3)

31. For example:

(a) The offender and the victim were of different racial, religious, ethnic/national origin, handicap, or sexual orientation groups. For example, the victim was black and the offenders were white.

. . .

(e) The victim is a member of a racial, religious, ethnic/national origin, handicap, or sexual orientation group which is overwhelmingly outnumbered by members of another group in the area where the victim lives and the incident took place.

. . .

(g) Several incidents have occurred in the same locality at or about the same time, and the victims are all of the same racial, religious, ethnic/national origin, handicap, or sexual orientation group. (*FBI, Hate Crimes Data*, 2–3)

32. For example:

(f) The victim was visiting a location where previous hate crimes had been committed against other members of his/her racial, religious, ethnic/national origin, handicap, or sexual orientation group and where tensions remain high against his/her group.

. . .

(j) The incident coincided with a holiday relating to or a date of particular significance to, a racial, religious, ethnic/national origin, handicap, or sexual orientation group (e.g., Martin Luther King Day, Rosh Hashanah, Gay/Lesbian Pride Day, etc.).

(k) The offender was previously involved in a similar hate crime or is a member of, or associates with, a hate group. (*FBI, Hate Crimes Data*, 2–3)

33. *Cal. Penal Code* §422.6 (West Supp. 1994), emphasis added; *Cal. Penal Code* §422.7 (West 1991).

34. See Oregon v. Plowman, 838 P. 2d. 563.

35. 42 U.S.C. §2000e–2 (1988), emphasis added. See, e.g., Texas Dept. of Community Affairs v. Burdine, 450 U.S. 248, 253 (1981); Albemarle Paper Co. v. Moody, 422 U.S. 405, 405–406 (1975); McDonnell Douglas v. Green, 411 U.S. 792, 796 (1973); Griggs v. Duke Power Co., 401 U.S. 424, 425–435 (1971).

36. See David A. Strauss, "Discriminatory Intent and the Taming of *Brown*," 56 *University of Chicago Law Review* 935, 956–959 (1989).

37. See, e.g., *Okla. Stat. Ann.* tit. 21, §1760 (West 1992). In Hummel v. State, 99 P.2d 913 (1940), the court stated that this statute requires proof of actual or implied malice toward the owner of the defaced property. See also 18 *Pa. Cons. Stat.* §5506 (1992). In Commonwealth v. Williams, 137 A.2d 903 (1958), the

court held that the term "malicious" in this statute meant an intent to do a wrongful act without legal justification or excuse.

38. Washington v. Talley, 858 P. 2d 217 (Wash. 1993). The Washington bias crime statute under review in *Talley* may be found at *Wash. Rev. Code Ann.* §9A.36.080 (West 1991).

39. See, e.g., Ohio v. Wyant, 597 N.E.2d 453.

40. The only state bias crime laws which utilize a *because of* formulation that have been definitively construed by the highest court of that state are those of Ohio, Oregon, and Washington, which were interpreted in *Wyant, Plowman,* and *Talley,* respectively.

41. *Violent Crime Control and Law Enforcement Act of 1994,* 42 U.S.C. §13701 et. seq. (1994); *Congressional Record* 139: S13176, Oct. 6, 1993 (statement of Sen. Feinstein).

42. The only exception to this general rule is the law in Virginia. The Virginia institutional vandalism statute requires not only that the offender know the nature of the institution that he attacks, but that he act with racial animus as well. *Va. Code Ann.* §8.01-42.1 (Michie 1993).

43. See Levin and McDevitt, *Hate Crimes,* 11.

44. Ibid., 11–12.

45. Ibid., 12–15 (whereas approximately 60 percent of all crimes are committed upon strangers, more than 85 percent of the victims of bias crimes are strangers to their perpetrators). See, e.g., Laurie Goodstein, "Black Youth Acquitted in Hasidic Jew's Slaying in Crown Heights Riot," *Washington Post,* A3 (Oct. 30, 1992); "The Effects of Hate: A Partial List of Hate Crimes Reported across the Country in Recent Months," *Detroit Free Press,* 8A (Jan. 18, 1993). Even the cross-burning in *R.A.V.* was directed not at the victim family *qua* individuals, but rather at *an* African-American family who had moved into a previously all-white neighborhood. See R.A.V. v. City of St. Paul, 112 S. Ct at 2538.

46. In one California case, for example, the court relied on the defendant's indifference to the personal selection of the victim as persuasive evidence of bias motivation. See People v. Baker, 5 Cal. Rptr. 2d 372, 378–379, opinion superseded by 28 Cal. Rptr. 2d 794 (Cal. 1994).

47. Levin and McDevitt, *Hate Crimes,* 16 (whereas approximately 25 percent of all crimes are committed by more than one perpetrator, more than 60 percent of bias crimes are committed by more than one perpetrator).

48. Joan Weiss, "Ethnoviolence: Impact upon the Response of Victims and the Community," in *Bias Crime: American Law Enforcement and Legal Response,* 174, 182 (1993).

49. See, e.g., Weiss, *Bias Crime,* 182–183; Melinda Henneberger, "For Bias Crimes, a Double Trauma," *Newsday,* 113 (Jan. 9, 1992); N. R. Kleinfield, "Bias Crimes Hold Steady, But Leave Many Scars," *New York Times,* A1 (Jan. 27, 1992).

50. Joan C. Weiss, Howard J. Ehrlich, Barbara E. K. Larcom, "Ethnoviolence at Work," 18 *Journal of Intergroup Relations,* 28–29 (Winter 1991–92).

51. Ibid. The data collected for the study of bias-motivated violence at work were

analyzed by ethnicity. There was no statistically significant difference among whites, blacks, and Hispanics in the average number of psychological symptoms experienced as a result of being the victim of bias-motivated violence. Ibid., 29. Moreover, the rates of "ethnoviolent victimization" among whites and blacks in the study were approximately the same. Ibid., 23.

52. Ibid., 29. The defensive behavior changes included staying home at night more often, watching children more closely, trying to be "less visible," or moving to another neighborhood. Ibid., 27–28.

53. See Charles R. Lawrence III, "If He Hollers Let Him Go: Regulating Racist Speech on Campus," 1990 *Duke Law Journal*, 461 (1990).

54. Abram Kardiner and Lionel Ovesey, *The Mark of Oppression: Explorations in the Personality of the American Negro*, 301–305, 384 (1951); James L. Robinson, *Racism or Attitude?: The Ongoing Struggle for Black Liberation and Self-Esteem*, 208–214 (1995); Stephen C. Ainlay, Gaylene Becker, and Lerita M. Coleman, eds., *The Dilemma of Difference: A Multi-Disciplinary View of Stigma*, 6–9, 48–51, 132–139 (1986). See Richard Delgado, "Words That Wound: A Tort Action for Racial Insults, Epithets, and Name Calling," 17 *Harvard Civil Rights–Civil Liberties Law Review*, 136–137 (1982).

55. See, e.g., Allport, *Nature of Prejudice*, 148–149; Erving Goffman, *Stigma: Notes on the Management of Spoiled Identity*, 7–17, 130–135 (1963); Robert M. Page, *Stigma*, 1 (1984); Harold W. Stevenson and Edward C. Stewart, "A Developmental Study of Racial Awareness in Young Children," 29 *Child Development*, 399 (1958).

56. See, e.g., Harburg, Erfurt, Havenstein, Chape, Schull, and Schork, "Socio-Ecological Stress, Suppressed Hostility, Skin Color, and Black-White Male Blood Pressure: Detroit," 35 *Psychosomatic Medicine*, 276, 292–294 (1973).

57. See, e.g., Kenneth Clark, *Dark Ghetto: Dilemmas of Social Power*, 82–90 (1965).

58. See, e.g., Irwin Katz, *Stigma: A Social Psychological Analysis* (1981); Harry H. L. Kitano, *Race Relations*, 125–126 (1974); Ari Kiev, "Psychiatric Disorders in Minority Groups," *Psychology and Race*, 416, 420–424 (P. Watson, ed., 1973).

59. Allport, *Nature of Prejudice*, 56–59.

60. See, e.g., Martha Minow, *Making All the Difference: Inclusion, Exclusion, and American Law*, 221 (1990).

61. See, e.g., Robert Elias, *The Politics of Victimization*, 116 (1986); A. Karmen, *Crime Victims: An Introduction to Victimology*, 262–263 (2d ed., 1990); Levin and McDevitt, *Hate Crimes;* Mari J. Matsuda, "Public Response to Racist Speech: Considering the Victim's Story," 87 *Michigan Law Review*, 2330–2331 (1989).

62. See Robert Kelly, Jess Maghan, and Woodrow Tennant, "Hate Crimes: Victimizing the Stigmatized," in *Bias Crime: American Law Enforcement Responses*, 26 (Robert Kelly, ed., 1993). The Crown Heights Riots exemplify how the mere perception of a bias crime can lead to violence between racial groups. See, e.g., Lynne Duke, "Racial Violence Flares for 3rd Day in Brooklyn," *Washington Post*, A04 (Aug. 22, 1991); "Crown Heights: The Voices of Hate Must Not Prevail," *Detroit Free Press*, 2F (Aug. 25, 1991).

63. See, e.g., Delgado, "Words That Wound," 140–141. See generally Paul Brest, "The Supreme Court, 1975 Term Forward: In Defense of the Antidiscrimination Principle," 90 *Harvard Law Review,* 1 (1976).

64. See Kitano, *Race Relations,* 100–101.

## 3. Why Are Bias Crimes Worse?

1. H. L. A. Hart, *Punishment and Responsibility,* 26–27 (1968).

2. Jeffrie Murphy provides the following terse and insightful definition of the retributive theory of punishment: "[S]peaking very generally, [retribution] is a theory that seeks to justify punishment, not in terms of social utility, but in terms of *this* cluster of moral concepts: rights, desert, merit, moral responsibility, justice, and respect for moral autonomy." Jeffrie Murphy, "Retributivism, Moral Education and the Liberal State," 4 *Criminal Justice Ethics,* 3–11 (1985), quoted in Jeffrie Murphy, *Retribution Reconsidered,* 21 (1992).

3. George Fletcher, *Rethinking Criminal Law,* §6.3.2, 417 (1978).

4. See, e.g., G. W. F. Hegel, *Hegel's Philosophy of Right,* trans. T. M. Knox, 70–71 (1952); Joshua Dressler, "Substantive Criminal Law through the Looking Glass of *Rummel v. Estelle:* Proportionality and Justice as Endangered Doctrines," 34 *Southwestern Law Journal,* 1063 (1981); Margaret Radin, "Cruel Punishment and Respect for Persons: Super Due Process for Death," 53 *Southern California Law Review,* 1143, 1164–1170 (1980).

5. See Immanuel Kant, *The Metaphysical Elements of Justice,* trans. John Ladd, 99–110 (1965). For contemporary expositions of this strand of retributive punishment theory, see, e.g., Fletcher, *Rethinking Criminal Law,* 417–418; Herbert Morris, "Persons and Punishment," 52 *Monist,* 475–501 (1968), reprinted in Herbert Morris, *On Guilt and Innocence,* 31–57 (1976); Murphy, "Retributivism, Moral Education and the Liberal State," 5–23. See also John Rawls, "Legal Obligation and the Duty of Fair Play," *Law & Philosophy,* 3–18 (S. Hook, ed., 1964).

6. See Radin, "Cruel Punishment and Respect for Persons," 1164–1169. Radin terms personhood-based retribution "protective retribution" for its foundation in protecting the integrity and autonomy of the individual.

7. See Fletcher, *Rethinking Criminal Law,* 416–417; Kant, *Metaphysical Elements of Justice,* 332; J. D. Mabbot, "Punishment," 48 *Mind,* 152, 162 (1939), reprinted in H. Acton, *Philosophy of Punishment,* 22–25 (R. Baird and S. Rosenbaum, eds., 1988); George Schedler, "Retributive Punishment and the Fall of Satan," 30 *American Journal of Jurisprudence,* 137 (1985).

8. See Hart, *Punishment and Responsibility,* 161; Murphy, *Retribution Reconsidered,* 58–59.

9. See, e.g., Michael Davis, "How to Make the Punishment Fit the Crime," vol 17, *Nomos: Criminal Justice,* 131–138 (1985); Mabbot, "Punishment," 23–25; Murphy, *Retribution Reconsidered,* 58–59.

10. See, e.g., Jeremy Bentham, *An Introduction to the Principles of Morals and Legislation* (1st ed. 1789, J. H. Burns and H. L. A. Hart, eds., 1996).

11. Herbert L. Packer, *The Limits of the Criminal Sanction*, 140 (1968). See also Igor Primoratz, *Justifying Legal Punishment*, 37–38 (1989).

12. Alfred C. Ewing, *The Morality of Punishment*, 45 (1929). It was a critical object of Ewing's enterprise to achieve by utilitarian means those notions of desert and proportionality previously associated only with retribution. Unlike other utilitarian punishment theorists of the period, such as Hastings Rashdall, John McTaggart, T. H. Green, and Bernard Bosanquet, Ewing saw utilitarianism as requiring an account of the deeply held intuitive notion of desert and of "'justice' as a good-in-itself," and he expressly set out to provide such an account. See Alan W. Norrie, *Law, Ideology and Punishment*, 121–125 (1991).

13. See Primoratz, *Justifying Legal Punishment*, 115–117.

14. Ewing, *The Morality of Punishment*, 100.

15. Ibid., 104.

16. Ibid., 106.

17. See Norrie, *Law, Ideology and Punishment*, 123–125; Mabbot, "Punishment," 162.

18. This is the response mounted by Ewing himself. See Ewing, *The Morality of Punishment*, 91. For a contemporary statement of this argument, see Jean Hampton, "The Moral Education Theory of Punishment," 13 *Philosophy and Public Affairs*, 208 (1984).

19. Mabbot, "Punishment," 162.

20. See Norrie, *Law, Ideology and Punishment*, 123–125.

21. Paul Robinson and John Darley have proposed another version of an eclectic approach to punishment theory, arguing that retributive punishment serves the utilitarian goal of providing a criminal justice system that has moral social credibility. A morally credible criminal justice system, they argue, is more likely to produce compliance with the law and thus a safe society. See Paul Robinson and John Darley, "Utility of Desert," 91 *Northwestern University Law Review*, 453 (1997).

22. See Hart, *Punishment and Responsibility*, 8–24.

23. Ibid., 24–25.

24. Ibid., 25.

25. Ibid.

26. Packer, *The Limits of the Criminal Sanction*, 62–72, 139–140.

27. Ibid., 143–144. Why an offense might be taken more seriously can be a matter of a retributive assessment of wrongdoing or a utilitarian measure of potential social damage. To Packer, "[t]he point is that different offenses are perceived differentially" regardless of the reason they are perceived in this way. Ibid.

28. See, e.g., Andrew von Hirsch, *Past or Future Crimes*, 64–65 (1986).

29. See *Model Penal Code* §2.02(2) (1962).

30. See Fletcher, *Rethinking Criminal Law*, 398–401.

31. See, e.g., *Model Penal Code* §210.

32. Ibid., §5.05(1). See Joshua Dressler, *Understanding Criminal Law*, 331, 363 (1987). See also Andrew Ashworth, "Criminal Attempts and the Role of Resulting Harm under the Code, and the Common Law," 19 *Rutgers Law Journal*,

725 (1988); Hart, *Punishment and Responsibility*, 1–27; Packer, *The Limits of the Criminal Sanction*, 100–102.

33. See Kant, *Metaphysical Elements of Justice*, 100.

34. See Morris, *On Guilt and Innocence*, 34–36. See also Fletcher, *Rethinking Criminal Law*, 472–483.

35. This is to be distinguished from strict liability crimes, which do not require culpability. A defendant is not *guilty* of a strict liability crime. Rather, the defendant has violated the strictures of such a crime. Similarly, there is no "punishment" for strict liability crimes in the same sense that there is punishment for other crimes, owing to the absence of criminal culpability. See, e.g., *Model Penal Code* §§1.04(5), 2.05.

36. See, e.g., *Model Penal Code* §§2.02(2) and 210.

37. See, e.g., Fletcher, *Rethinking Criminal Law*, §6.6.2, 461–463; Martin Wasik, "Excuses at the Sentencing Stage," 1983 *Criminal Law Review*, 450 (1983).

38. The Model Penal Code defines "criminal homicide" as purposely, knowingly, recklessly, or negligently causing the death of another. *Model Penal Code* §210.1(1). Criminal homicide that is committed recklessly constitutes manslaughter. Ibid., §210.3(1)(a).

39. See *Model Penal Code* §211.2 (reckless risk of death is a misdemeanor). Several states have adopted this approach to the punishment of reckless endangerment. Compare, e.g., *Alaska Stat.* §11.41.250 (b)(1989) (making reckless endangerment a class A misdemeanor) with *Alaska Stat.* §11.41.120 (1993) (making manslaughter a class A felony); *Arizona Rev. Stat. Ann.* §13-1201 (1989) (making reckless endangerment a class 1 misdemeanor or, if there was a substantial risk of imminent death, a class 6 felony) with *Arizona Rev. Stat. Ann.* §13-1103 (West Supp. 1993) (making manslaughter a class 2 felony); *Conn. Gen. Stat.* §53a-63 (West 1985) (making reckless endangerment class A misdemeanor) with *Conn. Gen. Stat.* §53a-55 (1993) (making first-degree manslaughter a class B felony).

  Some states grade reckless endangerment as a felony, but in no jurisdiction is it graded as seriously as manslaughter. Compare, e.g., *N.Y. Penal Law* §120.25 (McKinney 1987) (making first-degree reckless endangerment a class D felony) with *N.Y. Penal Law* §125.20 (McKinney 1994) (making first-degree manslaughter a class B felony); *Wis. Stat.* §941.30 (1991–92) (making first-degree reckless endangerment a class D felony) with *Wis. Stat.* §940.06 (1991–92) (making manslaughter a class C felony).

40. This approach to evaluating the relative harms caused by various crimes was proposed by Mabbot, "Punishment," 162. For a more recent exposition of the *ex ante* evaluation of relative harms, see Davis, "How to Make the Punishment Fit the Crime," 134–136. Davis has been criticized for failing to provide a method to determine the amount of punishment that any particular crime deserves. See David Dolinko, "Three Mistakes of Retributivism," 39 *U. C. L. A. Law Review*, 1623, 1639–1640 (1992). This critique does not raise a serious problem for the present project. The purpose here is not to determine what

precise level of punishment would be appropriate for a parallel crime or a bias crime, but rather to formulate a methodology for evaluating the harm caused by each, in order to demonstrate that the punishment for the bias crime should exceed that for the parallel crime.

41. Davis describes this analysis with the following formula: The least crime is the one a rational person would prefer to risk (all else being equal) given a choice between risking it and risking any other of that type; the next least is the one a rational person would prefer to risk given a choice between it and any other of that type except the least; and so on. Davis, "How to Make the Punishment Fit the Crime," 134–135.

42. See *Model Penal Code* §§1.04, 6.01.

43. Andrew von Hirsch and Nils Jareborg, "Gauging Criminal Harm: A Living-Standard Analysis," 11 *Oxford Journal of Legal Studies*, 1 (1991).

44. See, e.g., William Cochrane and Carolyn Shaw Bell, *The Economics of Consumption*, 17 (1956); Carle C. Zimmerman, *Consumption and Standards of Living*, 3 (1936).

45. See Amartya Sen, "The Standard of Living: Lecture II, Lives and Capabilities," in Sen, *The Standard of Living*, 20–38 (1987).

46. Joel Feinberg has proposed measuring the resulting harm from a crime by the impact of the crime on the ability of the victim to make choices as to the manner in which he will conduct his life. Joel Feinberg, *Harm to Others*, 37–61, 188–217 (1984).

47. See Sen, *The Standard of Living*, 1; Von Hirsch and Jareborg, "Gauging Criminal Harm," 13–14.

48. Von Hirsch and Jareborg, "Gauging Criminal Harm," 14, 20.

49. Von Hirsch and Jareborg cite the "extreme example" of the harm caused by rape in Bangladesh as opposed to rape in Western countries. Surely rape causes an excruciating level of harm in our society. The harm that results from a rape in Bangladesh, however, transcends even this level, because in addition to the physical assault and personal trauma caused by rape, there is the additional harm to the rape victim of total social ostracism. See ibid., 14.

50. See Sen, *The Standard of Living*, viii (introductory essay by Geoffrey Hawthorn).

51. Von Hirsch and Jareborg propose a living standard scale of four levels, including the end points: (1) subsistence; (2) minimal well-being; (3) adequate well-being; and (4) enhanced well-being. See von Hirsch and Jareborg, "Gauging Criminal Harm," 17–19.

52. See Sen, *The Standard of Living*, 26–29. In their discussion of a living standard analysis, von Hirsch and Jareborg suggest four interests, although they acknowledge that their compilation is less the result of supporting theory than of "impressions" of the kinds of interests normally involved in crimes committed. They propose physical integrity, material support and amenity, freedom from humiliation, and privacy/autonomy. See von Hirsch and Jareborg, "Gauging Criminal Harm," 19–21.

53. See Robert Elias, *The Politics of Victimization: Victims, Victimology, Human Rights,*

116 (1986); Arthur J. Lurigio and Patricia A. Resick, "Healing the Psychological Wounds of Criminal Victimization: Predicting Postcrime Distress and Recovery," in *Victims of Crime: Problems, Policies, and Programs,* 57 (Arthur J. Lurigio, Wesley G. Skogan, and Robert C. Davis, eds., 1990).

54. See von Hirsch and Jareborg, "Gauging Criminal Harm," 23–35.

55. I have argued elsewhere at length that the most compelling basis for the distinction between parallel crimes and civil rights crimes generally, including bias crimes, is the mental state of the actor. See Frederick M. Lawrence, "Civil Rights and Criminal Wrongs: The Mens Rea of Federal Civil Rights Crimes," 67 *Tulane Law Review,* 2200–2207, 2209–2210 (1993). This argument is further developed in Chapter 4 in order to demonstrate that the guilt of the bias crime offender turns on his possessing a bias motivation.

56. *Model Penal Code* §2.02(2)(b).

57. *Model Penal Code* §2.02(2)(c).

58. See, e.g., *Md. Code Ann. Crim. Law* §470A (Supp. 1993); *Mo. Rev. Stat.* §574.085 (Supp. 1993); *Ohio Rev. Code Ann.* §2909.11(4) (Baldwin 1988). See also Lawrence, "Civil Rights and Criminal Wrongs," 2205–2206.

59. See Lawrence, "Civil Rights and Criminal Wrongs," 2209; Tanya K. Hernandez, Note, "Bias Crimes: Unconscious Racism in the Prosecution of 'Racially Motivated Violence,'" 99 *Yale Law Journal,* 845, 848–850 (1990); James Morsch, Comment, "The Problem of Motive in Hate Crimes: The Argument against Presumptions of Racial Motivation," 82 *Journal Criminal Law and Criminology,* 659, 664–667 (1991).

60. See Lawrence, "Civil Rights and Criminal Wrongs," 2209–2210.

61. See, e.g., Kenneth W. Simons, "Rethinking Mental States," 72 *Boston University Law Review,* 503–508 (1992).

62. See, e.g., ibid., 495–496.

63. See, e.g., Clifford Krauss, "Senate Approves Longer Sentences for Hate Crimes," *New York Times,* A20 (Nov. 5, 1993).

64. See Doreen Iudica Vigue, "Marlborough Eyes Halt to Services as Hate Crime Penalty," *Boston Globe,* 1 (Jan. 26, 1994). The proposed ordinance was later vetoed by the city's mayor, who raised concerns about both the ordinance's enforceability and its constitutionality. See Doreen Iudica Vigue, "Marlborough Mayor Vetoes Hate Crime Law," *Boston Globe,* 22 (Feb. 3, 1994).

65. See Matthew Brelis, "Synagogue Fire Is Traced to Faulty Circuit Breaker," *Boston Globe,* 38 (Jan. 14, 1994).

66. See, e.g., Melinda Henneberger, "For Bias Crimes, a Double Trauma," *Newsday,* 113 (Jan. 9, 1992); N. R. Kleinfield, "Bias Crimes Hold Steady, But Leave Many Scars,"*New York Times,* A-1 (Jan. 27, 1992); Brian Levin, "U.S. Supreme Court Upholds Stiffer Sentences for Hate Crimes," *Intelligence Report,* 166 (Sept. 1993); Joan Weiss, "Ethnoviolence: Impact upon the Response of Victims and the Community," in *Bias Crime: American Law Enforcement and Legal Response,* 182–183 (1993). See also Joan C. Weiss, Howard J. Ehrlich, Barbara E. K. Larcom, "Ethnoviolence at Work," 18 *Journal of Intergroup Relations,* 18 (Winter 1991–92).

67. See A. Karmen, *Crime Victims: An Introduction to Victimology,* 262–263 (2d ed., 1990); Jack Levin and Jack McDevitt, *Hate Crimes* (1993); Robert Kelly et al., "Hate Crimes: Victimizing the Stigmatized," in *Bias Crime: American Law Enforcement Responses,* 26 (Robert Kelly, ed., 1993); Mari J. Matsuda, "Public Response to Racist Speech: Considering the Victim's Story," 87 *Michigan Law Review,* 2330–2331 (1989).

## 4. Who Is Guilty of a Bias Crime?

1. See Bernard Williams, *Moral Luck,* 20–39 (1981); George Fletcher, *Rethinking Criminal Law,* 479 (1978); Kenneth Simons, "Mistake and Impossibility, Law and Fact, and Culpability: A Speculative Essay," 81 *Journal of Criminal Law and Criminology,* 450, 504–506 (1991); Frederick M. Lawrence, "Civil Rights and Criminal Wrongs: The Mens Rea of Federal Civil Rights Crimes," 67 *Tulane Law Review,* 2203–2204 (1993).
2. See, e.g., Richard Delgado, "Words That Wound: A Tort Action for Racial Insults, Epithets, and Name Calling," 17 *Harvard Civil Rights–Civil Liberties Law Review,* 133 (1982).
3. Interviews by the author with Richard W. Cole, chief, Civil Rights Division of the Office of the Attorney General of Massachusetts.
4. See, e.g., *Model Penal Code* §210.6(3)(g).
5. Wisconsin v. Mitchell, 50 U.S. 476, 480 (1993).
6. See, e.g., Alfred C. Ewing, *The Morality of Punishment,* 45 (1929); Herbert L. Packer, *The Limits of the Criminal Sanction,* 140 (1968).
7. See, e.g., Jeffrie Murphy, "Retributivism, Moral Education and the Liberal State," 4 *Criminal Justice Ethics,* 3–11 (1985), in Murphy, *Retribution Reconsidered,* 21 (1992); Margaret Radin, "Cruel Punishment and Respect for Persons: Super Due Process for Death," 53 *Southern California Law Review,* 1164–1169 (1980).
8. There has been a growing recognition of the role of unconscious racism in our understanding of our society in general and our legal system in particular. See, e.g., Sheri Lynn Johnson, "Unconscious Racism and the Criminal Law," 73 *Cornell Law Review,* 1016 (1988); Charles R. Lawrence III, "The Id, the Ego, and Equal Protection: Reckoning with Unconscious Racism," 39 *Stanford Law Review,* 317 (1987). Unconscious racism has not been brought directly to bear on the *mens rea* of civil rights crimes. See Tanya Kateri Hernandez, Note, "Bias Crimes: Unconscious Racism in the Prosecution of 'Racially Motivated Violence,'" 99 *Yale Law Journal,* 845, 852–855 (1990); Note, "Combating Racial Violence: A Legislative Proposal," 101 *Harvard Law Review,* 1270, 1272–1275 (1988).
9. See John DeSantis, *For the Color of His Skin: The Murder of Yusuf Hawkins and the Trial of Bensonhurst* (1991).
10. See Andrew Sullivan, "The Two Faces of Bensonhurst," *New Republic,* 13–16 (July 2, 1990).
11. See *Model Penal Code* §2.01(1); Joshua Dressler, *Understanding Criminal Law,* 65 (1987); Fletcher, *Rethinking Criminal Law,* 802–807; H. L. A. Hart, *Punishment*

*and Responsibility,* 22–24, 140–145 (1968); Packer, *The Limits of the Criminal Sanction,* 73–76.

12. See Michael S. Moore, "Responsibility and the Unconscious," 53 *Southern California Law Review,* 1563, 1621–1627 (1980).

13. See Norval Morris, "Somnambulistic Homicide: Ghosts, Spiders, and North Koreans," 5 *Res Judicatae,* 29–32 (1951). See also James William Cecil Turner, "The Mental Element in Crimes at Common Law," in *The Modern Approach to Criminal Law,* 195, 204 (L. Radzinowicz and J. W. C. Turner, eds., 1945).

14. See Glanville Williams, *Criminal Law: The General Part,* §17 (2d ed., 1961).

15. Desantis, *For the Color of His Skin,* 58–76.

16. Anthony Flint, "Swastikas Often a Tool of Shock, Not Hate," *Boston Globe,* 13 (Jan. 31, 1994). See also Donald Green and Robert P. Abelson, "Understanding Hate Crime: A Case Study of North Carolina, 7 (unpublished manuscript on file with author).

17. Oliver Wendell Holmes, *The Common Law,* 6 (1st ed. 1881, Mark D. Howe, ed., 1963).

18. See Anne Cronin, "America's Grade on 20th Century European Wars: F," *New York Times,* section 4, p. 5 (Dec. 3, 1995).

19. See *Model Penal Code* §§2.02(2)(c) and (d).

20. I have argued elsewhere that the *mens rea* requirement for bias crimes ought to be the requisite *mens rea* for the parallel crime and the purpose to commit a bias crime, that is, conscious racial motivation. See Lawrence, "Civil Rights and Criminal Wrongs," 2209–2210.

21. See Chapter 2, pp. 34–35.

22. See Chapter 2, pp. 30–34.

23. Wisconsin v. Mitchell, United States Supreme Court Oral Argument Transcript, pp. 9–10.

24. Green and Abelson, *Understanding Hate Crime,* 22.

25. See *Model Penal Code* §2.06(3)(a)(ii). A similar, federal law, 18 U.S.C. §22, provides:

    (a) Whoever commits an offense against the United States or aids, abets, counsels, commands, induces, or procures its commissions, is punishable as a principal.

    (b) Whoever willfully causes an act to be done which if directly performed by him or another would be an offense against the United States, is punishable as a principal.

26. United States v. Peoni, 100 F. 2d 401 (2d Cir. 1938).

27. See, e.g., People v. Beeman, 199 Cal. Rptr. 60, 67 (1984): "An act which has the effect of giving aid and encouragement, and which is done with knowledge of the criminal purpose of the person aided, may indicate that the actor intended to assist in fulfillment of the known criminal purpose. However . . . the act may be done with some other purpose which precludes criminal liability."

28. See Ira Robbins, "The Ostrich Instruction: Deliberate Ignorance as Criminal Mens Rea," 81 *Journal of Criminal Law and Criminology,* 191 (1990); Jonathan L.

Marcus, Note, "Model Penal Code Section 2.02(7) and Willful Blindness, 102 *Yale Law Journal*, 2231 (1993).

29. See *Model Penal Code* §§2.06, 5.02. See generally Herbert Wechsler, "The Treatment of Inchoate Crimes in the Model Penal Code of the American Law Institute: Attempt, Solicitation, and Conspiracy (Pt. I)," 61 *Columbia Law Review*, 571 (1961).

30. See Dressler, *Understanding Criminal Law*, 384–385, 422–423.

31. A further alternative would be allowing discriminatory selection in the absence of racial animus to give rise to civil but not criminal liability. This approach is similar to the civil liability in other civil rights contexts that is predicated upon nonintentional conduct with discriminatory results. See, e.g., David Strauss, "Discriminatory Intent and the Taming of Brown," 56 *University of Chicago Law Review*, 956–959 (1989).

## 5. Are Bias Crime Laws Constitutional?

1. The two "Skokie cases" arose out of an attempt by the Neo-Nazi Party of America to hold a march in the predominantly Jewish Chicago suburb of Skokie, Illinois, in 1977 and 1978. The first case involved a state court injunction prohibiting the Nazi Party from holding the march or exhibiting Nazi symbols or other materials that would promote hatred of Jews. An Illinois appellate court refused to stay the injunction, and the United States Supreme Court, per curiam, by a 5–4 vote, reversed the denial of the stay and remanded the case to the Illinois state courts for further proceedings. National Socialist Party v. Village of Skokie, 432 U.S. 43 (1977). On remand, the injunction was modified by an appellate court, 366 N.E. 2d 347 (Ill. 1977), and ultimately fully vacated by the Illinois Supreme Court. 373 N.E. 2d 21 (Ill. 1978).

   The second Skokie case involved three ordinances enacted by the Village of Skokie in May 1977. The ordinances, which established a permit system for assemblies of more than fifty persons, required applicants to obtain insurance in the amount of $350,000, and barred permits for assemblies that would, *inter alia*, incite hatred of an ethnic, religious, or racial group. Each of the ordinances was struck down as unconstitutional. Colin v. Smith, 447 F. Supp. 676 (N.D. Ill.), affirmed 578 F. 2d 1197 (7th Cir.), cert. denied 439 U.S. 916 (1978). See Donald A. Downs, *Nazis in Skokie: Freedom, Community, and the First Amendment* (1985); James L. Gibson and Richard D. Bingham, *Civil Liberties and Nazis: The Skokie Free Speech Controversy* (1985); David Hamlin, *The Nazi Skokie Conflict: A Civil Liberties Battle* (1981).

2. See, e.g., Lee C. Bolinger, *The Tolerant Society: Freedom of Speech and Extremist Speech in Society* (1986); Robert P. Wolff et al., *A Critique of Pure Tolerance* (1969).

3. R.A.V. v. City of St. Paul, 505 U.S. 377 (1992).

4. Ibid., 396.

5. Ohio v. Wyant, 597 N. E. 2d 450, 452 (Ohio 1992).

6. See, e.g., "Symposium, Campus Hate Speech and the Constitution in the After-

math of Doe v. University of Michigan," 37 *Wayne Law Review,* 1309 (1991); "Symposium, Critical Race Theory: Essays on Hate Speech," 82 *California Law Review,* 847 (1994); "Symposium, Free Speech & Religious, Racial & Sexual Harassment," 32 *William & Mary Law Review,* 207 (1991); "Symposium, Hate Speech after R.A.V.: More Conflict between Free Speech and Equality?" 18 *William Mitchell Law Review,* 889 (1992); Richard Delgado, "Campus Antiracism Rules: Constitutional Narratives in Collision," 85 *Northwestern University Law Review,* 343 (1991); Kent Greenawalt, "Insults and Epithets: Are They Protected Speech?" 42 *Rutgers Law Review,* 287 (1990); David Kretzmer, "Freedom of Speech and Racism," 8 *Cardozo Law Review,* 445 (1987); Mari J. Matsuda, "Public Response to Racist Speech: Considering the Victim's Story," 87 *Michigan Law Review,* 2320 (1989); Burt Neuborne, "Ghosts in the Attic: Idealized Pluralism, Community and Hate Speech," 27 *Harvard Civil Rights–Civil Liberties Law Review,* 371 (1992); Rodney A. Smolla, "Rethinking First Amendment Assumptions about Racist and Sexist Speech," 47 *Washington & Lee Law Review,* 171 (1990); Nadine Strossen, "Regulating Racist Speech on Campus: A Modest Proposal?" 1990 *Duke Law Journal,* 484 (1990). A comprehensive list of articles and books on hate speech can be found in the bibliographical essay.

7. Wisconsin v. Mitchell, 508 U.S. 476 (1993).
8. Ronald Dworkin, "The Coming Battles over Free Speech," *New York Review of Books,* 58 (June 11, 1992).
9. See, e.g., Susan Gellman, "Sticks and Stones Can Put You in Jail, but Can Words Increase Your Sentence? Constitutional and Policy Dilemmas of Ethnic Intimidation Laws," 39 *U.C.L.A. Law Review,* 333 (1991).
10. See, e.g., Matsuda, "Public Response to Racist Speech"; Charles R. Lawrence III, "If He Hollers Let Him Go: Regulating Racist Speech on Campus," 1990 *Duke Law Journal,* 431 (1990); Richard Delgado, "Words That Wound: A Tort Action for Racial Insults, Epithets, and Name-Calling," 17 *Harvard Civil Rights–Civil Liberties Law Review,* 133 (1982).
11. See, e.g., Toni M. Massaro, "Equality and Freedom of Expression: The Hate Speech Dilemma," 32 *William & Mary Law Review,* 221 (1991).
12. For a passionate polemic that presents the classic liberal position with respect to protecting the speech rights of the racist, see Nat Hentoff, *Free Speech for Me—But Not for Thee: How the American Left and Right Relentlessly Censor Each Other* (1992). For a nuanced argument that considers the case for limiting the protections of racist speech, but nonetheless concludes that the interests of public discourse will almost always outweigh this case, see Robert Post, *Constitutional Domains: Democracy, Community, Management* (1995).
13. I share the conclusion of those who assert that racist speech may not be regulated. See, e.g., Smolla, "Rethinking First Amendment Assumptions," 156–169; Massaro, "Equality and Freedom of Expression," 218–219. But see Lawrence, "If He Hollers Let Him Go," 449–457; Matsuda, "Public Response to Racist Speech," 2320–2381. As I have argued elsewhere, any theory that limits the protection of expression depending upon the *results* of that expression will

be seriously flawed. See Frederick M. Lawrence, "The Collision of Rights in Violence-Conducive Speech," 19 *Cardozo Law Review,* 1333 (1998). Briefly, my concern is that the resulting harm perceived to be caused by expression can never be measured objectively. Such harm will inevitably turn on a kind of subjective assessment that is particularly dangerous where free expression is concerned. Judge Learned Hand put it well:

> Once you admit that the matter is one of degree, while you may put it where it genuinely belongs you so obviously make it a matter of administration, i.e., you give to Tomdickandharry, D. J. [District Judge], so much latitude that the jig is at once up. Besides even their Ineffabilities, the Nine Elder Statesmen . . . have not shown themselves wholly immune from the "herd instinct" and what seems "immediate and direct" to-day may seem very removed next year even though the circumstances surrounding the utterance be unchanged.

Letter from Learned Hand to Zechariah Chafee, Jr., January 2, 1921, reprinted in Gerald Gunther, "Learned Hand and the Origins of Modern First Amendment Doctrine: Some Fragments of History," 27 *Stanford Law Review,* 719 (1975), Appendix document no. 15, 770.

Not that a purely nonconsequentialist approach to this problem is possible. Any definitive attempt to distinguish a purely consequentialist approach to free expression from a purely nonconsequentialist theory is doomed to failure. The dialectic between the message conveyed by the speaker and the message(s) received by the audience renders it impossible to separate surgically the intent of the speaker from the effect on the listener. Moreover, no First Amendment theory can afford to ignore altogether the consequences of the expression concerned. It is precisely because of the likely consequences that our intuition tells us that a meeting to advocate the decriminalization of narcotics should be protected speech, whereas a meeting to organize a sale of drugs may be prosecuted as a criminal conspiracy.

To acknowledge the futility of a pure nonconsequentialist First Amendment theory, however, is not to be dissuaded from the need to shift the focus, to the extent possible, away from the results of the expression and toward the speaker himself. We may consider the punishment of anarchists in the 1910s, of communists in the 1950s, of neo-Nazis in the 1970s, or of racists in the 1990s. So long as expression may be suppressed on the basis of its anticipated harm, and so long as the gravity of that harm will be in the eye of its legislative and perhaps even its judicial beholder, First Amendment freedoms will expand and contract as a function of the relative heat of public sentiment and the public's tolerance of views that are contrary to those held by the majority. In short, free expression will be restricted the most when the expression concerns the most controversial issues, that is, just when free expression is needed the most.

In any event, for the purposes of this book, I will assume that First Amendment doctrine ought not to permit punishment of racist speech and thought. Put somewhat differently, I intend to show that this assumption does not require the conclusion that bias crime laws are thus similarly unconstitutional. Indeed, the enhanced punishment of bias crimes is fully consonant with the First Amendment views that I have outlined above.

14. Chaplinsky v. State of New Hampshire, 315 U.S. 568 (1942).
15. American Communications Association v. Douds, 339 U.S. 382, 408 (1950).
16. Dennis v. United States, 341 U.S. 495 (1951) (Vinson, C. J., plurality opinion).
17. Thomas I. Emerson, *The System of Freedom of Expression,* 114 (1970).
18. Texas v. Johnson, 491 U.S. 397, 414 (1989).
19. United States v. Schwimmer, 279 U.S. 644, 654–655 (1929) (Holmes, J., dissenting), overruled, Girouard v. United States, 328 U.S. 61 (1946).
20. Emerson, *The System of Freedom of Expression,* 21.
21. Compare Lawrence, "If He Hollers Let Him Go"; Matsuda, "Public Response to Racist Speech"; and Delgado, "Campus Anti-Racism Rules," with Neuborne, "Ghosts in the Attic," and Nadine Strossen, "Regulating Racist Speech on Campus."
22. See Doe. v. University of Michigan, 721 F. Supp. 852 (E. D. Mich. 1989); UWM Post, Inc. v. Board of Regents of the University of Wisconsin, 774 F. Supp. 1163 (E.D. Wis. 1991).
23. *R.A.V.,* 397–415 (White, J., concurring in the judgment); ibid., 415 (Blackmun, J., concurring in the judgment); ibid., 416 (Stevens, J., concurring in the judgment).
24. Ibid., 377–396.
25. *St. Paul Minn. Legis. Code* §292.02 (1990).
26. See *In re* Welfare of R.A.V., 464 N.W. 2d 507, 510 (Minn. 1991).
27. See *R.A.V.,* 397–415 (White, J., concurring).
28. See, e.g., Frederick Schauer, "Categories and the First Amendment: A Play in Three Acts," 34 *Vanderbilt Law Review,* 265, 307 (1981); Cass R. Sunstein, "Pornography and the First Amendment," 1986 *Duke Law Journal,* 589, 601–608 (1986). See also Kenneth L. Karst, "Equality as a Central Principle in the First Amendment," 43 *University of Chicago Law Review,* 20 (1975); Martin H. Redish, "The Value of Free Speech," 130 *University of Pennsylvania Law Review,* 591, 594–595 (1982); Pierre J. Schlag, "An Attack on Categorical Approaches to Freedom of Speech," 30 *U.C.L.A. Law Review,* 671 (1983); Geoffrey R. Stone, "Restrictions of Speech Because of its Content: The Peculiar Case of Subject-Matter Restriction," 46 *University of Chicago Law Review,* 81 (1978).
29. *R.A.V.,* 383.
30. Ibid., 386 (Frankfurter, J., concurring in the result).
31. Ibid., 382.
32. See pp. 102–106 of this chapter.
33. Sable Communications of Cal., Inc. v. F.C.C., 492 U.S. 115 (1989).
34. See ibid., 124–126 (cited in *R.A.V.,* 388).
35. *R.A.V.,* 388.
36. Ibid.
37. Ibid., 392.

38. Wisconsin v. Mitchell, 485 N.W. 2d 807 (Wis. 1992).

39. *Wyant*, 597 N.E. 2d 450.

40. *Wis. Stat. Ann.* §§939.05, 939.50(3)(e), 940.19 (1m) (West 1991).

41. *Wis. Stat. Ann.* §939.645 (West 1991). See Chapter 2, n. 4.

42. *Mitchell*, 485 N.W. 2d, 807.

43. *Ohio Rev. Code Ann.* §2927.12 (Baldwin 1992) provides:
    (a) No person shall violate section 2903.21, 2903.22, 2909.06, or 2909.07, or
    division (A)(3), (4), or (5) of section 2917.21 of the Revised Code by reason of
    the race, color, religion, or national origin of another person or group of per-
    sons.
    (b) Whoever violates this section is guilty of ethnic intimidation. Ethnic intimi-
    dation is an offense of the next higher degree than the offense the commission
    of which is a necessary element of ethnic intimidation.

44. *Mitchell*, 485 N.W. 2d, 812.

45. Ibid., 814.

46. Ibid., 815–816.

47. *Wyant*, 597 N. E. 2d, 454.

48. See Emerson, *The System of Freedom of Expression*, 80–90.

49. See, e.g., John Hart Ely, "Flag Desecration: A Case Study in the Roles of Cate-
    gorization and Balancing in First Amendment Analysis," 88 *Harvard Law Re-
    view*, 1482, 1494–1496 (1975); Frederick M. Lawrence, "Resolving the Hate
    Crimes/Hate Speech Paradox: Punishing Bias Crimes and Protecting Racist
    Speech," 68 *Notre Dame Law Review*, 673 (1993); Melville B. Nimmer, "The
    Meaning of Symbolic Speech under the First Amendment," 21 *U.C.L.A. Law Re-
    view*, 29 (1973).

50. *R.A.V.*, 389.

51. See Oregon v. Plowman, 838 P. 2d. 558 (Or. 1992). The court upheld the Ore-
    gon racial intimidation law that makes it a crime for two or more persons to
    "intentionally, knowingly, or recklessly cause physical injury to another be-
    cause of their perception of that person's race, color, religion, national origin or
    sexual orientation." *Ore. Rev. Stat.* §166.165(1)(a)(A).

52. *Mitchell*, 487.

53. Emerson, *The System of Freedom of Expression*, 80.

54. United States v. O'Brien, 391 U.S. 367, 376 (1968). See also Cox. v. Louisiana,
    379 U.S. 536, 555 (1965); Cohen v. California, 403 U.S. 15, 27 (1971)
    (Blackmun, J., dissenting).

55. Emerson, *The System of Freedom of Expression*, 80.

56. See *O'Brien*, 367 (upholding conviction for burning of a draft card); Watts v.
    United States, 394 U.S. 705 (1969) (upholding validity of law that criminalizes
    threats of violence against the President).

57. Emerson, *The System of Freedom of Expression*, 84.

58. Ibid., 80.

59. See Finis L. Bates, *The Escape and Suicide of John Wilkes Booth*, 157–163 (1907);
    Charles S. Olcott, *The Life of William McKinley* (1916); James F. Kirkham,

Sheldon G. Levy, and William J. Crotty, *Assassination and Political Violence: A Report to the National Commission on the Causes and Prevention of Violence* (1969).

60. Ely, "Flag Desecration," 1495.

61. H.R. 4797, 102d Cong., 2d sess. (1992). The bill was reintroduced on March 1, 1993, as the *Hate Crimes Sentencing Enhancement Act of 1993*, H.R. 1152, 103rd Cong., 1st sess. (1993) and ultimately enacted into law as part of the *Violent Crime Control and Law Enforcement Act of 1994*, Pub. L. No. 103–322, §280003, 108 Stat. 1796, 2096.

62. *The Violent Crime Control and Law Enforcement Act of 1994* directs the U.S. Sentencing Commission to promulgate guidelines enhancing the penalties for federal crimes in which there is racial motivation. Pub. L. No. 103–322 §280003, 108 Stat. 1796, 2096.

63. *Hate Crimes Sentencing Enforcement Act of 1992:* Hearings on H.R. 4797 before the Subcommittee on Crime and Criminal Justice of the House Committee on the Judiciary, 102nd Congress, 2nd Session, 7–30 (1992) [hereinafter Hearings].

64. See, e.g., *Wis. Stat. Ann.* §939.645 (West 1991); *Mo. Rev. Stat.* §574.090 (1989); *N. H. Rev. Stat. Ann.* §651:6(I)(g) (1991).

65. See, e.g., *Ohio Rev. Code Ann.* §2927.12 (Baldwin 1992); *Fla. Stat. Ann.* §775.085 (West 1990); *Vt. Stat. Ann.* Title 13 §1455 (1991).

66. See, e.g., *Fla. Stat. Ann.* §775.085 (West 1990); *N.H. Rev. Stat. Ann.* §651:6(I)(g) (1991).

67. Hearings, 11–12.

68. In burning a cross on the Jones's lawn, Viktora violated Minnesota criminal law proscribing acts of trespass, vandalism, and threats. See *Minn. Stat.* §609.713(1) (1987); *Minn. Stat.* §609.563 (1987); *Minn. Stat.* §609.595 (Supp. 1992).

69. Hearings, p. 22. See also Floyd Abrams, Letter to the Editor, *N.Y. Times*, A24 (July 3, 1992).

70. The parallel crimes of most bias crimes are against the person or property, such as vandalism or assault. To be guilty of these parallel crimes, the accused must have possessed a specific intent with respect to the elements of the crime or at least have acted recklessly.

    The *Model Penal Code* has broadened the traditional concept of specific intent to include not only purposefulness but also knowledge. Under the Code, "[a] person acts knowingly with respect to a material element of an offense when: (i) if the element involves the nature of his conduct or the attendant circumstances, he is aware that his conduct is of that nature or that such circumstances exist; and (ii) if the element involves a result of his conduct he is aware that it is practically certain that his conduct will cause such results." (*Model Penal Code* §2.02[2][b])

    There will also be instances in which the culpability for the parallel crime is less than specific intent, and in which recklessness will suffice for criminal liability. The *Model Penal Code* defines recklessness as follows:

    A person acts recklessly with respect to a material element of an offense when he consciously disregards a substantial and unjustifiable risk that the material element exists or will result from his conduct. The risk must be of such a nature and degree that, considering the nature and purpose of the actor's conduct and the circumstances known to him, its disregard involves a gross deviation from the standard of conduct that a law-abiding person would observe in the actor's situation. (*Model Penal Code* 2.02[c])

Consider, for example, an accused who throws rocks at a place of worship. Although specifically motivated by the religious affiliation of the institution, he does not intend to cause any actual property damage. Culpability with respect to bias is certainly purposeful, but culpability with respect to the parallel crime of vandalism is only recklessness. In several states he would be guilty of the bias crime of religiously motivated vandalism. See, e.g., *Md. Crim. Law Code Ann.* §470A (1989); *Mo. Rev. Stat.* §574.085 (1988); *Ohio Rev. Code Ann.* §2909.07 (Anderson 1987).

71. Gitlow v. New York, 268 U.S. 652, 673 (1925) (Holmes, J., dissenting).
72. *Mitchell*, 485 N.W. 2d, 809.
73. Miller's state plea was vacated following the Supreme Court's decision striking down the ordinance. Subsequently, Miller was indicted under federal housing law, 42 U.S.C. §3631, for conspiring to interfere with the Jones family's right of access to housing by intimidation and the threat of force. "A 2nd Hate-Crime Charge for Man after High Court Voided the First," *New York Times*, B16 (Oct. 23, 1992).
74. *Wyant*, 450.
75. See, e.g., *Model Penal Code* (Official Draft 1985) §§211.1(1)(c), §211.3, §250.4(2). See also, e.g., *Iowa Code* §708.1(2) (West 1989); *Fla. Stat.* §784.011 (West 1992).
76. See generally Kent Greenawalt, *Speech, Crime, and the Uses of Language*, 90–104 (1989); Rodney A. Smolla, *Free Speech in an Open Society*, 48–50 (1992); Greenawalt, "Insults," 298.
77. The *Montana Intimidation Statute*, for example, provides as follows:

(1) A person commits the offense of intimidation when, with the purpose to cause another to perform or to omit the performance of any act, he communicates to another, under circumstances which reasonably tend to produce a fear that it will be carried out, a threat to perform without lawful authority any of the following acts:
(a) inflict physical harm on the person threatened or any other person;
(b) subject any person to physical confinement or restraint; or
(c) commit any felony.

(2) A person commits the offense of intimidation if he knowingly communicates a threat or false report of a pending fire, explosion, or disaster which would endanger life or property. (*Mont. Code Ann.* 45–5–203 [1991])

An earlier version of this statute required only a threat without any requirement that there be a reasonable tendency that the threat would produce fear. This earlier version was held to violate the First Amendment in a federal habeas corpus proceeding. See Wurtz v. Risley, 719 F. 2d 1438 (10th Cir. 1983). The statute was amended to conform with the court's decision and has not been challenged since. See also State v. Lance, 721 P. 2d 1258 (Mont. 1986).

78. The *Colorado Menacing Statute,* for example, provides that "[a] person commits the crime of menacing if, by any threat or physical action, he knowingly places or attempts to place another person in fear of imminent serious bodily injury" (*Co. Rev. Stat.* §18–3–106). See, e.g., Colorado v. McPherson, 619 P. 2d 38 (Col. 1980); State v. Garcias, 679 P. 2d 1354 (Or. 1984).

79. The *Alaska Terroristic Threatening Statute,* for example, provides that a person commits the crime of terroristic threatening if that person:

(1) knowingly makes a false report that a circumstance dangerous to human life exists or is about to exist and
(a) places a person in fear of physical injury to any person;
(b) causes evacuation of a building; or
(c) causes serious public inconvenience; or

(2) with the intent to place another person in fear of death or serious physical injury to the person or the person's immediate family, makes repeated threats to cause death or serious physical injury to another person. (*Alaska Stat.* 11.56.810 [1991])

See, e.g., Allen v. State, 759 P. 2d 451 (Alaska Ct. App. 1988); Thomas v. Commonwealth, 574 S.W. 2d 903 (Ky. 1978).

80. *Chaplinsky,* 568.

81. See, e.g., Stephen W. Gard, "Fighting Words as Free Speech," 58 *Washington University Law Quarterly,* 531 (1983); Thomas F. Shea, "'Don't Bother to Smile When You Call Me That'—Fighting Words and the First Amendment," 631 *Kentucky Law Journal,* 1, 12 (1975).

82. *N.H. Rev. Stat. Ann.* §570:2 (1986); *N.H. Rev. Stat. Ann.* §644:2 (1986).

83. *Chaplinsky,* 569–570; State v. Chaplinsky, 18 A. 2d 754, 758 (N.H. 1941).

84. Zechariah Chafee, *Free Speech in the United States* (1941).

85. *Chaplinsky,* 571–572.

86. Ibid., 572.

87. State v. Chaplinsky, 18 A. 2d, 758, quoting State v. Brown, 68 N.H. 200, 38 A. 731, 732 (1895).

88. *Chaplinsky,* 573.

89. Cohen v. California, 403 U.S. 15 (1971).

90. Ibid., 17, quoting People v. Cohen, 81 Cal. Rptr. 503, 506 (1969).

91. Ibid., 20.

92. See Ely, "Flag Desecration," 1492–1493.

93. Lewis v. New Orleans, 415 U.S. 130 (1974).

94. Ibid., 135.

95. See Gard, "Fighting Words," 550–557.

96. See Feiner v. New York, 340 U.S. 1315 (1951); Niemotko v. Maryland, 340 U.S. 286 (1951) (Frankfurter, J., concurring).

97. See Gregory v. Chicago, 394 U.S 111 (1969); Garner v. Louisiana, 368 U.S. 157 (1961); Terminello v. Chicago, 337 U.S. 1 (1949).

98. See, e.g., Greenawalt, "Insults," 295–298.

99. *R.A.V.*, 381 (citing *In re* Welfare of R.A.V., 464 N.W. 2d at 510–511).

100. Ibid., 391.

101. Ibid., 383.

102. *Ala. Code* §13–6–20 (1992); *Alaska Stat.* §11.41.200 (1992); *Ariz. Rev. Stat. Ann.* §13–1204 (1992); *Cal. Penal Code* §245 (West 1992); *Fla. Stat.* ch. 784.021 (1991); *Ga. Code Ann.* §16–5–21 (Michie 1992); *Idaho Code* §18–905 (1992); *Ill. Rev. Stat.* ch. 38, para. 12–2 (1992).

103. *O'Brien*, 367.

104. Ibid., 377.

105. See Ely, "Flag Desecration," 1496.

106. See 18 U.S.C. §871.

107. *R.A.V.*, 388.

108. Ibid., 389.

109. Ibid.

110. Ibid.

111. *Mitchell*, 485 N.W. 2d at 812. See *Wyant*, 597 N.E. 2d at 812–814.

112. See, e.g., *Model Penal Code* §210.6(3)(g) (Official Draft 1985); *Conn. Gen. Stat. Ann.* ch. 952, §53a–46a (1958); *Del. Code Ann.* ch. 42, §4209 (1974 and Supp. 1992); *N.H. Rev. Stat. Ann.* ch. 630, §5 (1986 and Supp. 1992).

113. Barclay v. Florida, 463 U.S. 939, 940 (1983).

114. Dawson v. Delaware, 503 U.S. 159 (1992).

115. Ibid., 163.

116. See 18 U.S.C. §245(b)(2); 18 U.S.C. §242; 42 U.S.C. §3631. See also Church Arson Prevention Act of 1996, 104th Cong., 2d sess. H.R. 3525, amending 18 U.S.C. §247.

117. See, e.g., *Civil Rights Act of 1964*, Title VII, 42 U.S.C. §2000e (1988 and Supp. III 1992). See also Wards Cove Packing Co. v. Atonio, 490 U.S. 642 (1989); Texas Department of Community Affairs v. Burdine, 450 U.S. 248 (1981).

118. See *Fair Housing Act of 1968*, Title VIII, §804, 42 U.S.C. §3604 (1988).

119. Joshua Dressler, *Understanding Criminal Law*, 96–97 (1987). See also *Model Penal Code* §2.02(2)(a)(i) (Official Draft 1985).

120. See Wayne R. LaFave and Austin W. Scott, *Criminal Law* §3.6, 227–228 (2d ed., 1986).

121. *Mitchell*, 485 N.W. 2d at 820; *Wyant*, 597 N.E. 2d at 456–4578. See also Gellman, "Sticks and Stones," 362–379.

## 6. What Is the Federal Role in Prosecuting Bias Crimes?

1. For a summary of the events surrounding the Jordan assassination attempt, and the arrest, trial, and acquittal of Joseph Paul Franklin, see "Defense Complete in Jordan Assault," *New York Times*, A25 (Aug. 17, 1982), and "Federal

Jury Return Verdict of Not Guilty in Jordan Shooting," *New York Times,* A18 (Aug. 18, 1982). Franklin was subsequently convicted of the deaths of two black teenagers.

2. 18 U.S.C. §1751. See also 18 U.S.C. §871.
3. 18 U.S.C. §1114.
4. 18 U.S.C. §1116.
5. See, e.g., "The Other Jury," *New York Times,* A34 (May 1, 1992). See also, Neil A Lewis, "Police Brutality under Wide Review by Justice Dept.," *New York Times,* A1 (Mar. 15, 1991).
6. 325 U.S. 91 (1945).
7. 26 *American Law Institute Proceedings,* 27, 33 (1959).
8. *The Life and Writings of Frederick Douglass,* 199 (vol. 4, Phillip Foner, ed., 1955).
9. See, e.g., Sara Sun Beale, "Too Many and yet Too Few: New Principles to Define the Proper Limits for Federal Criminal Jurisdiction," 46 *Hastings Law Journal,* 979–1018 (1995); Rory K. Little, "Myths and Principles of Federalization," 46 *Hastings Law Journal,* 1029–1085 (1995); Kathleen F. Brickey, "Criminal Mischief: The Federalization of American Criminal Law," 46 *Hastings Law Journal,* 1135–1174 (1995); Stephen Chippendale, Note, "More Harm Than Good: Assessing Federalization of Criminal Law," 79 *Minnesota Law Review,* 455–483 (1994).
10. *United States Constitution,* Article I, section 8, clause 6.
11. Ibid., Article I, section 8, clause 10.
12. Ibid., Article I, section 8, clause 17.
13. Ibid., Article III, section 3.
14. Ibid., Amendment X.
15. John S. Baker, Jr., "Nationalizing Criminal Law: Does Organized Crime Make It Necessary or Proper?" 16 *Rutgers Law Journal,* 495, 502 (1985); Scott Wallace, "The Drive to Federalize Is a Road to Ruin," 8 *Criminal Justice,* 8 (1993).
16. See Sara Sun Beale, "Federal Criminal Jurisdiction," in *Encyclopedia of Crime and Justice,* 776 (vol. 2, 1985).
17. *United States Constitution,* Article I, section 8, clauses 3 (commerce clause) and 18 (necessary and proper clause).
18. Brickey, "Criminal Mischief," 1135–1174.
19. Lawrence Friedman, *Crime and Punishment in American History,* 116–121, 209 (1994).
20. See act of June 25, 1910, chapter 395, 36 Stat. 825 (interstate transportation of a woman for "illicit purposes"); act of Oct. 29, 1919, chapter 89, 41 Stat. 324 (interstate transportation of stolen motor vehicles); act of Feb. 8, 1897, chapter 172, 29 Stat. 512 (interstate transportation of obscene literature); act of Mar. 3, 1895, chapter 191, 28 Stat. 963 (interstate transportation of lottery tickets ).
21. Brooks v. United States, 267 U.S. 432 (1925).
22. Wickard v. Filburn, 317 U.S. 111 (1942).
23. Perez v. United States, 402 U.S. 146 (1971).

24. 18 U.S.C. §844(j) (1988).
25. 18 U.S.C. §43 (Supp. V 1993).
26. 18 U.S.C. §2710 (1988).
27. 18 U.S.C. §10 (1988).
28. 18 U.S.C. §2119 (Supp. V 1993).
29. Tep Gup, "A Savage Story," *Time Magazine*, 55 (Sept. 21, 1992).
30. *Violent Crime Control and Law Enforcement Act of 1994*, Pub L. No. 103–322, Section 60003(a)(14), 108 Stat. 1796. See 138 *Congressional Record*, S17959–60 (Oct. 8, 1992).
31. United States v. Lopez, 514 U.S. 549 (1995).
32. 18 U.S.C. §922(g)(1)(A) (Supp V 1988).
33. *Lopez*, 514 U.S. at 567–568 (citations omitted).
34. Brzonkala v. Virginia Polytechnic and State University, Virginia Polytechnic and State University, 935 F. Supp. 779 (W.D.Va. 1996). The decision of the district court in this case was reversed by a panel of the Court of Appeals for the Fourth Circuit, which upheld the Violence against Women Act, 132 F. 3d 949 (4th Cir. 1997). This opinion in turn was vacated by the full Fourth Circuit and ordered for rehearing *en banc*. (Feb. 5, 1998). As of the time of publication, no decision has yet been issued on the rehearing of *Brzonkala*.
35. United States v. Mussari, 95 F. 3d 787 (9th Cir. 1996), cert. denied, 117 S. Ct. 1567 (1997); United States v. Oliver, 60 F. 3rd 547 (9th Cir. 1995); Cheffer v. Reno, 55 F. 3rd 1517 (11th Cir. 1995); United States v. Bramble, 894 F. Supp. 1384, 1995 Lexis 10745 (D. Hawaii 1995).
36. *Lopez*, 514 U.S. at 615–618, 630–631 (Breyer, dissenting).
37. See *Civil Rights Act of 1875*, ch. 114, 18 Stat. 335 (1875); *Ku Klux Klan (Antilynching) Act*, ch. 22, 17 Stat. 13 (1871); *Enforcement Act of 1870* (act of May 31, 1870), ch. 114, 16 Stat. 140, amended by act of Feb. 28, 1871, ch. 99, 16 Stat. 433; *Peonage Abolition Act*, ch. 187, 14 Stat. 546, codified at 18 U.S.C. §444 (1940); *Slave Kidnapping Act*, ch. 86, 14 Stat. 50 (1866); Civil Rights Act (Enforcement Act) of 1866, ch. 31, 14 Stat. 27. The discussion both in the text and in the Historical Appendix analyzes the four most important First Reconstruction–era statutes, those that continue to set the landscape of civil rights legislation today and whose interpretation by the courts represented the primary judicial confrontation with the Reconstruction-era civil rights statutes: (1) the Civil Rights Act of 1866; (2) the Enforcement Act of 1870; (3) the Ku Klux Klan Act of 1871; and (4) the Civil Rights Act of 1875.
38. See, e.g., Bruce Ackerman, *We the People: Foundations*, 81–98 (1991); Harold Hyman and William W. Wiecek, *Equal Justice under Law: Constitutional Development, 1835–1875*, 386–438 (1982); Herman Belz, *A New Birth of Freedom*, 65 (1976).
39. James McPherson, *Battle Cry of Freedom*, 699–700 (1988).
40. Ibid., 700–713.
41. See James McPherson, *Abraham Lincoln and the Second American Revolution*, viii (1991); Gary Wills, *Lincoln at Gettysburg*, 121–133 (1992).

42. See Aviam Soifer, "Status, Contract, and Promises Unkept," 96 *Yale Law Journal,* 1916, 1938 (1987); Jacobus tenBroek, "Thirteenth Amendment to the Constitution of the United States—Consummation to Abolition and Key to the Fourteenth Amendment," 39 *California Law Review,* 171, 174 (1951). Charles Fairman, who has taken a relatively restricted view of the scope of the Thirteenth Amendment, agrees that the amendment nonetheless did extend federal power into the states by operation of section 2 of the amendment. See Charles Fairman, *History of the Supreme Court of the United States: Reconstruction and Reunion,* 1136, 1156–1157 (vol. 7, 1971).

43. See, e.g., Eric Foner, *Reconstruction: America's Unfinished Revolution,* 67 (1988); Kenneth Stampp, *The Era of Reconstruction: 1865–1877,* 14–15, 46 (1965); tenBroek, "Thirteenth Amendment to the Constitution of the United States" 174, 181–189.

44. Foner, *Reconstruction: America's Unfinished Revolution,* 171–227; Robert J. Kaczorowski, *The Politics of Judicial Interpretation: The Federal Courts, Department of Justice and Civil Rights, 1866–1876,* 27–44 (1985); Stampp, *The Era of Reconstruction,* 61–82; Hans Trefousse, *Impeachment of a President: Andrew Johnson, the Blacks, and Reconstruction,* 4–16, 22–25 (1975).

45. Foner, *Reconstruction,* 239.

46. See Trefousse, *Impeachment of a President,* 26; Foner, *Reconstruction,* 243–246. See generally Michael L. Benedict, "Preserving the Constitution: The Conservative Basis of Radical Reconstruction," 61 *Journal of American History,* 65–90 (1974).

47. *Congressional Globe,* 211, 599 (39th Cong., 1st sess., 1866).

48. See ibid., at 247, 1755; Trefousse, *Impeachment of a President,* 26; Foner, *Reconstruction,* 243–246; Hyman and Wiecek, *Equal Justice under Law,* 406–407.

49. For the House vote, see *Congressional Globe,* 1861 (39th Cong., 1st sess., 1866); for the Senate vote, see ibid., 1809.

50. Ibid., 1675 (Mar. 27, 1866). See Foner, *Reconstruction,* 250–251.

51. Trefousse, *Impeachment of a President,* 20–23.

52. Ibid., 26; Foner, *Reconstruction,* 250–251.

53. Trefousse, *Impeachment of a President,* 34–35; Stampp, *The Era of Reconstruction,* 199–201. See generally Leon Litwack, *Been in the Storm So Long* (1979). The Memphis and New Orleans riots are discussed in the Historical Appendix at pages 199–200.

54. Foner, *Reconstruction,* 454–455; Alfred Avins, "The Ku Klux Klan Act of 1871: Some Reflected Light on State Action and the Fourteenth Amendment," 11 *St. Louis University Law Journal,* 331–332 (1967); Eugene Gressman, "The Unhappy History of Civil Rights Legislation," 30 *Michigan Law Review,* 1323, 1334 (1952); *Congressional Globe,* 154–166 (42d Cong., 1st sess., 1871); *Congressional Globe,* 244, 236 (42d Cong., 1st sess., 1871). See William S. McFeely, *Grant: A Biography,* 368–369 (1981).

55. H.R. 320, 42d Cong., 1st sess., reprinted in *Congressional Globe,* 42d Cong., 1st sess. app., 138 (1871).

56. Kaczorowski, *The Politics of Judicial Interpretation,* 79–92.

57. The Civil Rights Cases, 109 U.S. 3 (1883).

58. Rejection of the Republican party in the congressional elections of 1874, although probably due more to voter reaction to the Panic of 1873 and the ensuing depression than to rejection of Reconstruction policies per se, was of monumental proportions. The outgoing Forty-third Congress had a Republican majority of 110; the newly elected Forty-fourth Congress would have a Democratic majority of 60. Foner, *Reconstruction*, 512–524.

59. Slaughter-House Cases, 83 U.S. (16 Wall.) 36 (1873).

60. For a detailed discussion of the history and opinions in *Slaughter-House*, see Michael Conant, "Antimonopoly Tradition under the Ninth and Fourteenth Amendments: *Slaughter-House Cases* Re-Examined," 31 *Emory Law Journal*, 785 (1982); Robert C. Palmer, "The Parameters of Constitutional Reconstruction: *Slaughter-House, Cruikshank*, and the Fourteenth Amendment," 1984 *University of Illinois Law Review*, 739 (1984); John Anthony Scott, "Justice Bradley's Evolving Concept of the Fourteenth Amendment from the *Slaughterhouse Cases* to the *Civil Rights Cases*," 25 *Rutgers Law Review*, 552 (1971).

61. Slaughter-House Cases, 83 U.S. at 69; ibid., at 89–90 (Field, J., dissenting).

62. 83 U.S. at 49–51, 53–54.

63. Ibid., 72. See Palmer, "Parameters of Constitutional Construction," 743 n.22.

64. 83 U.S., at 80–82.

65. Ibid., 95–96.

66. Kaczorowski, *The Politics of Judicial Interpretation*, 102–112; Stampp, *The Era of Reconstruction*, 199–201.

67. Foner, *Reconstruction*, 593–594; Kaczorowski, *The Politics of Judicial Interpretation*, 113; McFeely, *Grant*, 370.

68. United States v. Cruikshank, 25 Fed. Cases 707 (1874), affirmed, 92 U.S. 542 (1876).

69. For a detailed description of the setting of the Colfax riot, see H. Cummings and C. McFarland, *Federal Justice*, 241–246 (1937); Manie White Johnson, "The Colfax Riot of April, 1873," 13 *Louisiana Historical Quarterly*, 391 (1930). Typical of most historical work of its period, Johnson's article was premised on the view that Reconstruction represented an unwarranted interference, by Northerners in particular and the federal government in general, in the domestic affairs of the Southern states. "The Colfax Riot of April, 1873" is quite bold in this regard. Johnson writes, for example, that "[b]y 1869, carpet-bag government in Louisiana was in full power and the story of its rule there 'is a sickening tale of extravagant waste, corruption, and fraud'" (ibid., 394). The article is nonetheless evocative in its description of the events surrounding the Colfax massacre.

70. Johnson, "The Colfax Riot of April, 1873," 394, 398.

71. Lestage, "The White League in Louisiana and Its Participation in Reconstruction Riots," 628–635; Ted Tunnell, *Crucible of Reconstruction: War Radicalism and Race in Louisiana, 1862–1877*, 189–193 (1984); Joe Gray Taylor, *Louisiana Reconstructed, 1863–1877*, 268–270 (1974); Johnson, "The Colfax Riot of April, 1873," 414–419.

72. Kaczorowski, *The Politics of Judicial Interpretation*, 176; Lestage, "The White

League in Louisiana and Its Participation in Reconstruction Riots," 635; Tunnell, *Crucible of Reconstruction,* 192–193; Taylor, *Louisiana Reconstructed,* 271–272.

73. Kaczorowski, *The Politics of Judicial Interpretation,* 176–177.
74. 25 Fed. Cases 707, 708 (C.C.D. La. 1874) (no. 14,879). See also 92 U.S. 542, 546, 548, 561 (1876).
75. 25 Fed. Cases at 711.
76. Bradley found some authority for federal civil rights enforcement in the Fifteenth Amendment as well, concluding that the amendment conferred a right "not to be excluded from voting by reason of race, color or previous condition of servitude that is all the right that congress can enforce." All other regulations pertaining to voting rights, however, were exclusively a matter of state jurisdiction. Ibid., 712.
77. 80 U.S. 581 (1872). *Blyew* arose out of the murder of a black woman named Lucy Armstrong by a group of whites. The federal prosecution was brought under the Civil Rights Act of 1866, charging the defendants with depriving Armstrong and two other blacks, solely on account of their race, of the right to testify in a state court murder trial. Under the law of Kentucky at the time, blacks could not testify against white persons. A majority of the Supreme Court rejected the legal basis for the indictment, holding that the Civil Rights Act did not intend to federalize the state crime of murder and that the indictment's reliance on the "right to testify" was an attempt to do just that. Justice Bradley's dissent argued that when the state denies to black crime victims the right to testify in court, it "brand[s] them with a badge of slavery." Accordingly, Congress has power under the Thirteenth Amendment to provide a federal criminal remedy for this wrong (ibid., 581–583, 591–593, 599–601). For a thorough discussion of the *Blyew* case and a persuasive argument that it represents an early and major judicial abandonment of Reconstruction goals, see Robert D. Goldstein, "*Blyew:* Variations on a Jurisdictional Theme," 41 *Stanford Law Review,* 469 (1989).
78. *Cruikshank,* 25 Fed. Cases at 712.
79. Ibid., 708, 715.
80. Kaczorowski, *The Politics of Judicial Interpretation,* 188–193; Foner, *Reconstruction,* 560–561.
81. 92 U.S. 542 (1876). Justice Clifford wrote a separate opinion styled as a "dissent" in which he in fact concurred in the judgment that the indictments should be dismissed. Ibid., 562–569.
82. Ibid., 551–559, quotation from p. 556.
83. Ibid., 549–551, 555, quotation from p. 555.
84. 92 U.S. 214 (1876).
85. Ibid., 215. For a discussion of the context and background of *Reese,* see William Gillette, "Anatomy of a Failure: Federal Enforcement of the Right to Vote in the Border States during Reconstruction," in R. O. Curry, ed., *Radicalism, Racism, and Party Realignment: The Border States during Reconstruction,* 272–277, 286–287 (1969).

86. *Reese*, 92 U.S. at 215–218.
87. Kaczorowski, *The Politics of Judicial Interpretation*, 221.
88. 109 U.S. 3 (1883).
89. Ch. 114, 18 Stat. 335 (Mar. 1, 1875). The Civil Rights Act of 1875 is discussed in detail in the Historical Appendix at pages 201–203.
90. Ibid., 24.
91. Ibid.
92. The Court explored an approach similar to that adopted in the *Civil Rights Cases* in its brief opinion in *U.S. v. Harris*. In *Harris*, the Court struck down sect. 2 of the Ku Klux Klan Act of 1871, the provision that made it a federal crime for two or more persons to conspire to deprive another of "equal protection of the laws" or "equal privileges or immunities under the laws," holding that Congress was without authority over this conduct. 106 U.S. 629, 637–643 (1883).
93. See Baldwin v. Franks, 120 U.S. 678 (1887); James v. Bowman, 190 U.S. 127 (1903); Hodges v. United States, 203 U.S. 1 (1906).

    *Baldwin v. Franks* involved another prosecution under section 2 of the Ku Klux Klan Act, the same provision struck down in *United States v. Harris*. In the *Baldwin* prosecution, however, the indictment was based on violence that, although committed by a private individual, violated federal rights, viz. the right of a Chinese alien, under a treaty between the United States and China, to work in an American town on terms equal with American citizens. The Court nonetheless held section 2 unconstitutional in this context.

    The prosecution in *James v. Bowman* was brought under section 5 of the Enforcement Act of 1870, alleging a conspiracy among private persons to interfere with voting by certain black citizens in a congressional election in Kentucky. The Court held that the statute exceeded Congress's constitutional authority because it applied to private citizens (and thus was not authorized by the Fifteenth Amendment) and to state elections (and thus was not authorized by congressional power over federal elections, under Article I, section 4 of the Constitution).

    *Hodges* was brought under section 16 of the Enforcement Act, which had re-enacted section 1 of the Civil Rights Act of 1866. *Hodges* arose out of violence used by a group of whites to keep black citizens from working in a lumber camp in Arkansas. The indictment in *Hodges* charged the defendants with conspiring to deprive the black victims of the right to make contracts. The Court held that indictment was without authority under the Fourteenth Amendment, because there was no state action involved, and the Thirteenth Amendment, because the violation of the right to make a contract was not an incident of slavery. The latter holding was overruled sixty years later in Jones v. Alfred Mayer, Inc., 392 U.S. 409, 441 (1968).
94. United States v. Mosley, 238 U.S. 383 (1915). See also United States v. Stone, 188 F. 836 (D. Md. 1911); United States v. Munford, 16 F. 223, (E.D. Va. 1883).
95. Ex Parte Yarbrough, 110 U.S. 651 (1884). See also Motes v. United States, 178 U.S. 458 (1900); United States v. Crosby, 25 F. Cas. 701, 1 Hughes 448 (District of South Carolina, 1871).

96. See, e.g., Smith v. United States, 157 Fed. 721 (8th Cir. 1907), cert. denied, 208 U.S. 618 (1908); Motes v. United States, 178 U.S. 458 (1900); *In re* Quarles and Butler, 158 U.S. 532 (1895); Logan v. United States, 144 U.S. 263 (1892); United States v. Waddell, 112 U.S. 76 (1884).

97. 313 U.S. 299 (1941). *Classic* is discussed in detail in the Historical Appendix at pages 203–204.

98. Mary Frances Berry, *Black Resistance, White Law: A History of Constitutional Racism in America* (1971); Robert L. Zangrando, *The NAACP Crusade against Lynching, 1909–1950* (1980); George C. Wright, *Racial Violence in Kentucky, 1865–1940: Lynchings, Mob Rule and "Legal Lynchings"* (1990); Arthur Franklin Raper, *The Tragedy of Lynching* (1970); Jacquelyn Dowd Hall, *Revolt against Chivalry: Jessie Daniel Ames and the Women's Campaign against Lynching* (1979).

99. 76th Cong., 2d sess., 1940, S. Rept. 1380, pp. 1–2; 75th Cong., 1st sess., 1937, S. Rept. 793, pp. 4–5.

100. 75th Cong., 1st sess., 1937, H. Rep. 563, pp. 4–6, quotation from p. 6.

101. Ibid., 6.

102. 76th Cong., 2d sess., 1940, S. Rept. 1380, pp. 1–6, quotations from p. 1.

103. 74th Cong., 1st sess., 1935, S. Rept. 340, 4–11, quotations from p. 4.

104. 75th Cong., 1st sess., 1937, H. Rep. 563, 3.

105. Ibid.

106. 74th Cong., 1st sess., 1935, S. Rept. 340, 4.

107. Mary Frances Berry, *Black Resistance, White Law,* 163.

108. Carr, *Federal Protection of Civil Rights,* 163–164. As no formal executive order exists to this effect, the directive must have been informal.

109. See, e.g., Michael R. Belknap, *Federal Law and Southern Order: Racial Violence and Constitutional Conflict in the Post-Brown South,* 19 (1987); Geoffrey Perrett, *Days of Sadness, Years of Triumph: The American People, 1939–1945,* 143–154 (1973).

110. Screws v. United States, 325 U.S. 91, 92 (1945).

111. Ibid., 93; Loren Miller, *The Petitioners: The Story of the Supreme Court of the United States and the Negro,* 283–284 (1966); *Transcript of Record,* Screws v. United States, 325 U.S. 91 (1945) (hereafter *Transcript of Record*), 64, 177.

112. *Transcript of Record,* 37, 40–44, 46, 176, 194–195.

113. Screws v. United States, 140 F. 2d. at 666 (Sibley, J., dissenting), Screws v. United States, 325 U.S. 91, 92–93.

114. Carr, *Federal Protection of Civil Rights,* 105–106; *Transcript of Record,* Petition for Writ of Certiorari, 7.

115. Carr, *Federal Protection of Civil Rights,* 106–107.

116. *Transcript of Record,* 42.

117. Miller, *The Petitioners: The Story of the Supreme Court of the United States and the Negro,* 286.

118. 18 U.S.C. §§241, 242 (1988). At the time of *Screws,* section 242 was section 20 of the Criminal Code and codified as 18 U.S.C. §52. For the sake of simplicity, I always refer to this statute as section 242 in the text. Similarly, section 241 was previously section 19 of the Criminal Code and codified as 18 U.S.C. §51. That statute is consistently referred to as section 241.

119. *Transcript of Record,* 2–9.
120. Ibid., 3, 5, 7.
121. Address by Victor Rotnem to National Bar Association, Chicago, Illinois, Dec. 1, 1944, quoted in Carr, *Federal Protection of Civil Rights,* 109 n. 42.
122. *Transcript of Record,* 197, 198, 205–206. Screws v. United States, 140 F. 2d 662, 663 (5th Cir. 1944).
123. Each defendant was actually charged with three counts in the indictment:

   (1) "conspir[ing] to injure and oppress Robert Hall . . . in the free exercise and enjoyment of rights, privileges and immunities secured to [Hall] by the Constitution," in violation of 18 U.S.C. §241, *Transcript of Record,* 2–4;

   (2) "under color of the laws . . . of the State of Georgia . . . subject[ing] and cause[ing] to be subjected Robert Hall . . . to the deprivation of rights, privileges and immunities secured and protected . . . by the Constitution," in violation of 18 U.S.C. §242, *Transcript of Record,* 4–6; and

   (3) conspiring to commit the offense charged in the second count, in violation of the federal conspiracy statute, 18 U.S.C. §371, *Transcript of Record,* 6–9
   The case proceeded to trial by a jury on the second and third of these counts.

   The trial judge dismissed the section 241 count and the government did not appeal this dismissal. Accordingly, this count was out of the case before *Screws* reached the Supreme Court and, for that matter, before the case went to trial.
124. *Transcript of Record,* 10–15, 208.
125. Screws v. United States, 140 F. 2d 662 (5th Cir. 1944).
126. The configuration of opinions in *Screws* is unusually complicated and takes some straightening out. The plurality opinion was written by Justice Douglas and joined by Chief Justice Stone and Justices Black and Reed. There were two different dissenting opinions written in *Screws,* and they attacked the plurality opinion and the Court's judgment from two diametrically opposed directions.

   In an uncommon practice, the author of the main dissenting opinion was not given in the opinion. Rather, the opinion merely indicates that "Mr. Justice Roberts, Mr. Justice Frankfurter and Mr. Justice Jackson, dissenting." By Court custom, the justices were listed in order of seniority, beginning with Justice Roberts. There is strong evidence that the opinion was written by Justice Frankfurter. First, the dissenting opinion was based largely on a memorandum by Justice Frankfurter and, to a lesser extent, on a memorandum by Justice Jackson. See Howard, *Mr. Justice Murphy,* 361–363. Second, the argument in the dissent, particularly with respect to the federalism problem, clearly shows the earmarks of the position that Justice Frankfurter would take in future cases. See, e.g., Monroe v. Pape, 365 U.S. 167, 239 (Frankfurter, J., dissenting). I thus shall presume that the dissenting opinion was primarily the work of Justice Frankfurter. See also Carr, *Federal Protection of Civil Rights,* 111 n. 46; Jaffe, "The Judicial Universe of Mr. Justice Frankfurter," 62 *Harvard Law Review,* 357, 384 (1949).

   Justice Murphy wrote a dissent arguing that the convictions should be affirmed. Finally, Justice Rutledge wrote an opinion that, although called a concurrence in the result, was a dissenting analysis with a vote to concur. He believed that the convictions should be affirmed, but added his vote to those of the plurality in order to provide a clear judgment of the Court to remand the case for a new trial. Having set forth his reasons for affirming the convictions, Justice Rutledge wrote that "[w]ere it possible for me to adhere to them in my vote, and for the Court at the same time to dispose of the case, I would act accordingly." Because of the Court's divisions in deciding the *Screws* case, however, Rutledge concluded that "[i]f each member accords his vote to his belief, the case cannot have disposition. Stalemate should not prevail for any reasons, however compelling, in a criminal case or, if avoidable, in any other." 325 U.S. at 134. Justice Rutledge thus cast his vote for the disposition of the case along the lines of the plurality.

127. See Frederick M. Lawrence, "Civil Rights and Criminal Wrongs: The Mens Rea of Federal Civil Rights Crimes," 67 *Tulane Law Review,* 2119–2120 (1993).

128. Screws v. United States, 325 U.S. 104 (emphasis added).

129. United States v. Lanier, 515 U.S. 259, 264–272 (1997).

130. Lawrence, "Civil Rights and Criminal Wrongs: The Mens Rea of Federal Civil Rights Crimes," 2179–2193.

131. Carr, *Federal Protection of Civil Rights,* 113–115; Howard, *Mr. Justice Murphy,* 364–366; Robert K. Carr, "Screws v. United States: The Georgia Police Brutality Case," 31 *Cornell Law Quarterly,* 48, 65 (1945). See generally Julius Cohen, "The Screws Case: Federal Protection of Negro Rights," 46 *Columbia Law Review,* 94 (1946).

132. Carr, *Federal Protection of Civil Rights,* 114.

133. Ibid., 115.

134. *Brief for the Petitioners* in Screws v. United States, 2, 6–16. *Brief for the United States* in Screws v. United States, 3, 52–54.

135. Even the most restrictive judicial interpretations of the federal civil rights statutes always assumed federal constitutional authority to prosecute officially sanctioned violations of federal rights. See *Civil Rights Cases,* 109 U.S. 3, 13 (1883); Home Telephone and Telegraph Co. v. Los Angeles, 227 U.S. 278, 288 (1913).

136. 325 U.S. at 144–145 (citation omitted).

137. Ibid., 142–148.

138. Ibid., 139, 144–145, quotation from 139.

139. Howard, *Mr. Justice Murphy,* 357.

140. Screws v. United States, 325 U.S. 111.

141. Screws v. United States, 325 U.S. 108–109 .

142. Ibid., 107–108.

143. See, e.g., Home Telephone and Telegraph Co. v. Los Angeles, 227 U.S. 278 (1913).

144. Screws v. United States, 325 U.S. 111.

145. Ibid.

146. Ibid.

147. Ibid. (emphasis added).

148. Manning Marable, *Race Reform and Rebellion: The Second Reconstruction in Black America, 1945–1982,* 74 (1984). See also Earl Ofari Hutchinson, *Betrayed: A History of Presidential Failure to Protect Black Lives,* 47 (1996).

149. Michael R. Belknap, "The Vindication of Burke Marshall: The Southern Legal System and the Anti-Civil-Rights Violence of the 1960s," 33 *Emory Law Journal,* 94, 102 (1984).

150. Wiley A. Branton, "Little Rock Revisited: Desegregation to Resegregation," 52 *Journal of Negro Education,* 250, 252, 258 (1983).

151. Boynton v. Virginia, 364 U.S. 454 (1960).

152. Victor S. Navasky, *Kennedy Justice,* 20 (1970).

153. Manning Marable, *Race Reform and Rebellion,* 69; Navasky, *Kennedy Justice,* 20.

154. Taylor Branch, *Parting the Waters: America in the King Years, 1954–63,* 451–482 (1988); Navasky, *Kennedy Justice,* 20, 21; Marable, *Race Reform and Rebellion,* 70.

155. Navasky, *Kennedy Justice,* 21.

156. Burke Marshall, *Federalism and Civil Rights* (1964).

157. Ibid., ix (foreword by Robert F. Kennedy).

158. Hutchinson, *Betrayed,* 57, 105; Richard Gid Powers, *Secrecy and Power: The Life of J. Edgar Hoover,* 323–325 (1987).

159. Hutchinson, *Betrayed,* 104–106; Powers, *Secrecy and Power,* 325–326.

160. Hutchinson, *Betrayed,* 118–120.

161. 18 U.S.C., section 245.

162. United States v. Price, 383 U.S. 787 (1966).

163. Ibid., 793.

164. Ibid., 794.

165. United States v. Guest, 383 U.S. 745 (1966).

166. Ibid., 753.

167. Ibid., 761–762.

168. Ibid., 774–786.

169. *United States Code Congressional and Administrative News,* 1939 (1968).

170. Ibid., 1840.

171. Belknap, "The Vindication of Burke Marshall," 108.

172. 18 U.S.C. §242. See p. 137.

173. 18 U.S.C. §245(b). Section 245(b)(1) punishes pure federal rights interference crimes. Section 245(b)(2) punishes racially motivated state rights interference crimes.

174. *The Violent Crime Control and Law Enforcement Act of 1994,* Pub. L. No. 103–322 §280003, 108 Stat. 1796, 2096, amending 28 U.S.C. §994.

175. Heart of Atlanta Motel v. United States, 379 U.S. 241 (1964).

176. Katzenbach v. McClung, 379 U.S. 294 (1964).

177. 379 U.S. 279–291 (Douglas, J., concurring in both cases); ibid., 291–293

(Goldberg, J., concurring in both cases). *Heart of Atlanta Motel* and *McClung* were argued to the Supreme Court together. The Court summarized the arguments presented by the federal government in *Heart of Atlanta Motel,* 379 U.S. 244–245.

178. "'Civil Rights' Unit Set up by Murphy," *New York Times,* A2 (Feb. 4, 1939).

179. *United States Code Congressional and Administrative News,* 1842–1843 (vol. 2, 1968).

180. United States v. Cruikshank, 25 Fed. Cases 707, 712 (C.C.D. La. 1874) (No. 14,879), affirmed, 92 U.S. 542 (1876).

181. *United States Constitution,* Amendment XIII, sections 1, 2.

182. Hodges v. United States, 203 U.S. 1 (1906). See also discussion in the text (at pp. 124–125 and 127–128) of the Thirteenth Amendment and the judicial interpretation of the Amendment in the *Slaughter-House Cases* and the *Civil Rights Cases.*

183. Jones v. Alfred H. Mayer Co., 392 U.S. 409 (1968).

184. 42 U.S.C. §1982.

185. Runyon v. McCrary, 427 U.S. 160 (1976).

186. 42 U.S.C. §1981.

187. *Slaughter-House Cases,* 83 U.S. 72.

188. St. Francis College v. Al-Khazriji, 481 U.S. 604 (1987); Shaare Tefila Congregation v. Cobb, 481 U.S. 615 (1987).

189. See Charles H. Jones, Jr., "An Argument for Federal Protection against Racially Motivated Crimes: 18 U.S.C. §241 and the Thirteenth Amendment," 21 *Harvard Civil Rights–Civil Liberties Law Review,* 728–733 (1986); Arthur Kinoy, "The Constitutional Right of Negro Freedom," 21 *Rutgers Law Review,* 388–389 (1967).

190. Compare "Few Significant Criminal Victimization Rate Changes 1990–1991," *U.S. Newswire* (Oct. 26, 1992), with "Wisconsin Hate Crimes Reports Low," *States News Service* (Jan. 6, 1993), and Anti-Defamation League, *1992 Audit of Anti-Semitic Incidents,* 41.

191. U.S. House of Representatives Committee on the Judiciary, *Increasing Violence against Minorities: Hearing before the Subcommittee on Crime,* 96th Cong., 2d sess., 1980, 26; Seltzer, "Survey Finds Extensive Klan Sympathy," *Poverty Law Reporter,* 7 (May–June 1982).

192. See Geoffrey Padgett, Comment, "Racially-Motivated Violence and Intimidation: Inadequate State Enforcement and Federal Civil Rights Remedies," 75 *Journal of Criminal Law and Criminology,* 114–118 (1984).

193. Brian Levin, "A Matter of National Concern: The Federal Law's Failure to Protect Individuals from Discriminatory Violence," 3 *Journal of Intergroup Relations,* 4 (1994).

194. "Reno's Doubt on Heights Persists," *Newsday,* 28 (Jan. 27, 1994).

195. Jim Carnes, *Us and Them: A History of Intolerance in America,* 127 (1995); *New York Times,* p. B1, col. 5 (Aug. 22, 1996).

196. See Joseph P Fried, "A New Verdict in Crown Heights," *New York Times,* sec. 4, p. 2, col. 1 (Feb. 16, 1997); Joseph P. Fried, "19 1/2-Year Term Set in Fatal Stabbing in Crown Heights," *New York Times,* sec. A, p. 1, col. 6 (Apr. 1, 1998);

John Sullivan, "21-Year Term for a Death in Crown Hts.," *New York Times,* sec. B, p. 1, col. 5 (July 10, 1998).

197. Laurie L. Levenson, "The Future of State and Federal Civil Rights Prosecutions: The Lessons of the Rodney King Trial," 41 *U.C.L.A. Law Review,* 539–540 (1994); *United States Attorney's Manual,* 8–3.340 (vol. 8, July 1, 1992); Ronald Kessler, *The FBI,* 209 (1993).

198. *United States Constitution,* Amendment V. The double-jeopardy clause states: ". . . nor shall any person be subject for the same offense to be twice put in jeopardy of life, or limb."

199. Heath v. Alabama, 474 U.S. 82 (1985); Bartkus v. Illinois, 359 U.S. 121 (1959); United States v. Lanza, 260 U.S. 377 (1922).

200. See, e.g., Walter T. Fisher, "Double Jeopardy, Two Sovereignties and the Intruding Constitution," 28 *University of Chicago Law Review,* 591 (1961); Lawrence Newman, "Double Jeopardy and the Problem of Successive Prosecutions," *Southern California Law Review,* 252 (1961); Harlan R. Harrison, "Federalism and Double Jeopardy: A Study in the Frustration of Human Rights," 17 *University of Miami Law Review,* 306 (1963); Dominic T. Holzhaus, "Double Jeopardy and Incremental Culpability: A Unitary Alternative to the Dual Sovereignty Doctrine," 86 *Columbia Law Review,* 1697 (1986); Susan Herman, "Double Jeopardy All Over Again: Dual Sovereignty, Rodney King, and the A.C.L.U.," 41 *U.C.L.A. Law Review,* 609 (1994).

201. There are, roughly speaking, three positions on the dual-sovereignty doctrine: (1) opposition to the doctrine in all cases because it violates the defendant's constitutional rights; (2) support of the doctrine as a recognition of the duality of governmental power in a federal system; and (3) opposition to the doctrine in most cases, but supporting the doctrine in certain exceptional cases, particularly the enforcement of criminal civil rights laws, as was at issue in the Rodney King case. Those interested in the doctrine should see three articles in a symposium issue following the Rodney King cases: Herman, "Double Jeopardy All over Again"; Paul Hoffman, "Double Jeopardy Wars: The Case for a Civil Rights 'Exception,'" 41 *U.C.L.A. Law Review,* 649 (1994); and Paul G. Cassell, "The Rodney King Trials and the Double Jeopardy Clause: Some Observations on Original Meaning and the ACLU's Schizophrenic Views of the Dual Sovereign Doctrine," 41 *U.C.L.A. Law Review,* 693 (1994).

202. Executive Office for United States Attorneys, United States Department of Justice, *United States Attorney's Manual,* 21–25 (vol. 9, 1985).

203. See United States Commission on Civil Rights, *Who Is Guarding the Guardians?* 112, 116 (Oct. 1981); United States v. Davis, 906 F. 2d 829, 832 (2nd Cir. 1990).

204. Koon v. United States, 518 U.S. 81, 64 U.S.L.W. 4512, 4521 (1996).

205. Levenson, "Civil Rights Prosecutions," 41 *U.C.L.A. Law Review,* 560 (1994); Jim Newton, "Judge Rejects Talk of New Riots, Refuses to Delay Trial of Officers," *Los Angeles Times,* B4 (Feb. 3, 1993).

206. Carr, *Federal Protection of Civil Rights,* 1–5, quoting Pollock v. Williams, 322 U.S. 4, 8 (1944).

## 7. Why Punish Hate?

1. "Governor Signs Bill on Hate Crime, Move Catches Both Sides Off-Guard," *Arizona Republic* (Apr. 29, 1997); George Roche, "Activists Beating the Hate Drums for More Power," *Tulsa World* (Apr. 12, 1990).

2. See, e.g., Hate Crimes Statistics Act of 1988: Hearings on S. 702, S. 797, S. 2000 before the Subcommittee on the Constitution of the Senate Committee on the Judiciary, 100th Congress, 2nd Session, 242 (1988) (statement of Leonard D. Goodstein, executive vice-president and chief executive officer of the American Psychological Association).

3. Public Order Act of 1986, 1986 Chapter 64, pp. 2691–2730 Eliz. II 1986 (especially Part III, sections 17–29, Racial Hatred). This omission of a bias crime law is not due to oversight. As recently as 1994, a bill was introduced in Parliament. See [1994] Crim. L. Rev. at 313–314. The bill failed for lack of government support. The government preferred to treat bias crimes generally, using the provisions of the existing law that proscribes assaults. In 1997, the labor government announced its intention to submit racial violence legislation.

4. Royal Commission on Capital Punishment, Minutes of Evidence, Ninth Day, December 1, 1949, Memorandum submitted by the Rt. Hon. Lord Justice Denning (1950).

5. Henry M. Hart, Jr., "The Aims of the Criminal Law," 23 *Journal of Law and Contemporary Problems*, 404 (1958).

6. Emile Durkheim, *The Division of Labor in Society*, 62–63 (W. D. Hall, trans., 1984). See also *Durkheim and the Law*, 61–63 (Steven Lukes and A. Scull, eds., 1983); Steven Lukes, *Emile Durkheim: His Life and Work*, 160–163 (2d ed., 1985); Robert Reiner, "Crime, Law and Deviance: The Durkheim Legacy," in Steve Fenton, *Durkheim and Modern Sociology*, 176–182 (1984).

7. Durkheim, *The Division of Labor in Society*, 62–63.

8. Ibid., 63.

9. Ibid.

10. See, e.g., Reiner, "Crime, Law and Deviance: The Durkheim Legacy," 177–178.

11. Nigel Walker, *Punishment, Danger and Stigma*, vii (1983).

12. Ibid., 22–45. See also H. L. A. Hart, *Punishment and Responsibility*, 170–173 (1968).

13. See, e.g., Alfred Ewing, *The Morality of Punishment* (1929); Bernard Bosanquet, *Some Suggestions in Ethics* (1918). Ewing's attempt to produce a utilitarian theory based in part on the educative effect of punishment is discussed in Chapter 3.

14. See, e.g., Allan J. Cigler and Burdett A. Loomis, eds., *Interest Group Politics* (1983); Dennis C. Mueller, *Public Choice II* (1989); Mancur Olsen, *The Logic of Collective Action: Public Goods and the Theory of Groups* (1971).

15. See Paul H. Robinson and John M. Darley, *Justice, Liability, and Blame* (1995). Robinson and Darley's study of community attitudes on various issues of criminal law doctrine is the most comprehensive recent study of its kind. Their work

illustrates areas of confluence and divergence of public opinion and doctrine. For their conclusions regarding the significant level of confluence where central issues of criminal law doctrine are concerned, see pp. 203–204.

16. Immanuel Kant, *The Philosophy of Law,* 198 (trans. William Hastie, 1887).

17. Ibid.

18. Joel Feinberg, "The Expressive Function of Punishment," in Joel Feinberg, *Doing and Deserving,* 103–104 (1970).

19. Ibid., 102–104, 114–116; Ronald J. Rychlak, "Society's Moral Right to Punish: A Further Exploration of the Denunciation Theory of Punishment," 65 *Tulane Law Review,* 299, 332–335 (1990). See generally David Garland, *Punishment and Modern Society* (1990).

20. Durkheim, *The Division of Labor in Society,* 44–52, 62–64. Durkheim reviewed the role of punishment in primitive cultures as an emotional and mechanical process; he then traced the development of punishment in advanced cultures with its function to maintain societal cohesion.

21. The federal statute creating a legal holiday to commemorate the birth of Dr. King, codified at 36 U.S.C. §169(j), was enacted in 1983. By 1989, two-thirds of the states had passed similar legislation. By 1991, roughly forty states had such holidays.

22. For example, the National Football League refused to grant the 1993 and 1995 Super Bowls to Phoenix and Houston, respectively, in part because Arizona and Texas had failed to establish a Martin Luther King, Jr., holiday. Rose Mofford, then the governor of Arizona, said that "we lost $256 million last year because of the lack of a Martin Luther King holiday." "Mofford Wants King Day on Special Session Agenda," *Phoenix Gazette* (Sept. 15, 1989); "MLK Holiday as Political Football," *Houston Chronicle* (May 25, 1991).

23. "Hate Crime Bills Die Quietly," *Fulton County Daily Report* (Mar. 24, 1997).

24. Ralph Ellison, *Invisible Man* (1953).

25. Anti-Defamation League Model Hate Crimes Legislation, reprinted in, for example, Anti-Defamation League, *Hate Crimes Laws* (1997); *Bias Crime: American Law Enforcement Responses,* 210–213 (Robert Kelly, ed., 1993).

26. Gordon Allport, *The Nature of Prejudice,* 518 (1954).

27. Quoted in Charles L. Chute and Marjorie Bell, *Crime, Courts, and Probation,* 8 (1956).

## Historical Appendix

1. *Congressional Globe,* 598 (39th Cong., 1st sess., 1866).

2. Ibid., 1758.

3. Ibid., 1759.

4. Ibid.

5. The committee, consisting of Elihu B. Washburne of Illinois, John M. Broomall of Pennsylvania, and George S. Shanklin of Kentucky, reached Memphis on May 22 and filed its report two months later. 39th Cong., 1st sess., House Re-

port 101 ("Memphis Riots and Massacres," July 25, 1866; hereinafter "Memphis Riot Report"), pp. 1, 10–21, 35.

6. Ibid., 27–29, 33–34.

7. Eric Foner, *Reconstruction: America's Unfinished Revolution,* 182–183, 262–263 (1988); Gilles Vandal, *The New Orleans Riot of 1866: Anatomy of a Tragedy* (1983). For a critical view of Reconstruction that attributes to the New Orleans Riot much of the success of pro-Reconstruction forces in obtaining control of Congress in the 1866 elections, see H. Oscar Lestage, Jr., "The White League in Louisiana and Its Participation in Reconstruction Riots," 18 *Louisiana Historical Quarterly,* 617, 619–628 (1935).

8. Foner, *Reconstruction,* 442–444; Kenneth Stampp, *The Era of Reconstrcution: 1865–1877,* 199–201 (1965); Trefousse, *The Radical Republicans,* 432; H. Oscar Lestage, Jr., "The White League in Louisiana and Its Participation in Reconstruction Riots," 18 *Louisiana Historical Quarterly,* 628–630 (1935).

9. Section 7 of the Enforcement Act of 1870 provides that if
    > in the act of violating any provision in either [section 5 or section 6] any other felony, crime, or misdeameanor [sic] shall be committed, the offender . . . shall be punished for the same with such punishments as are attached to the said felonies, crimes and misdemeanors by the laws of the State in which the offense may be committed. (16 Stat. 140, 141, c. 114, sec. 7)

    Section 7 of the Enforcement Act was declared unconstitutional by the Supreme Court in United States v. Cruikshank, 92 U.S. 542 (1876).

10. Section 1 of the Ku Klux Klan Act is today codified as 42 U.S.C. §1983.

11. H.R. 320, 42d Cong., 1st sess., reprinted in *Congressional Globe,* 42d Cong., 1st sess. app., 138 (1871).

12. See, e.g., *Congressional Globe,* 42d Cong., 1st sess. app., 219–220 (1871) (remarks of Sen. Thurman); ibid., 455 (remarks of Rep. Rice); ibid., at 259–260.

13. Ibid., 68–70 (remarks of Rep. Shellabarger); ibid., 81–83 (remarks of Rep. Bingham).

14. Ibid., 514 (remarks of Rep. Poland); ibid., 113–116 (remarks of Rep. Farnsworth).

15. Senator Trumbull opposed the bill as originally proposed because it would "undertake to enter the States for the purpose of punishing individual offenses against their authority committed by one citizen against another." He supported the amended version, understanding it not to "furnish redress for wrongs done by one person upon another in any of the States of the Union in violation of their laws, unless he also violated some law of the United States, nor to punish one person for an ordinary assault and battery committed on another in a State." *Congressional Globe,* 575–579 (42d Cong., 1st sess., 1871).

16. The amendment itself was submitted by Congressman Shellabarger, the author of the original bill (ibid., 477–478; remarks of Rep. Shellabarger). Shellabarger's amendment was based on language drafted and proposed by two moderate Republican representatives, Burton Cook and Charles W. Wil-

lard (ibid., 477, app. 188; remarks of Rep. Willard). See also ibid., 485 (remarks of Rep. Cook). See generally Marilyn R. Walter, "The Ku Klux Klan Act and the State Action Requirement of the Fourteenth Amendment," 58 *Temple Law Quarterly*, 24–27 (1985).

17. *Congressional Globe*, 478 (42d Cong., 1st sess., 1871).

18. Ch. 114, 18 Stat. 335 (Mar. 1, 1875).

19. *Congressional Globe*, 21 (42d Cong., 1st sess., 1871) (remarks of Sen. Sumner); Ulysses S. Grant, Second Inaugural Address (Mar. 4, 1873), in *The Presidents Speak: The Inaugural Addresses of the American Presidents from Washington to Nixon*, 132–134 (David Newton Lott, ed., 1969). See generally Foner, *Reconstruction*, 512–563; Stampp, *The Era of Reconstruction*, 205–210.

20. David Donald, *Charles Sumner and the Rights of Man*, 586 (1970); *Congressional Globe*, 4786 (43rd Cong., 1st sess., 1874) (remarks of Rep. Ransier).

21. *Congressional Globe*, 4175–4176 (43rd Cong., 1st sess., 1874). For Democratic opposition to the Civil Rights Act of 1875, see, e.g., *Congressional Globe*, 342–344 (43rd Cong., 1st sess. app., 1874) (remarks of Rep. Read); *Congressional Globe*, 948 (43rd Cong., 2d sess., 1875) (remarks of Rep. Finck). See also *Congressional Globe*, 1011 (43rd Cong., 2nd sess., 1875); *Congressional Globe*, 1870 (43rd Cong., 2nd sess., 1875).

22. John Hope Franklin, "The Enforcement of the Civil Rights Act of 1875," 6, 225–235 (1974); Foner, *Reconstruction*, 555–556.

23. 109 U.S. 3 (1883).

24. Ex Parte Yarbrough, 110 U.S. 651 (1884). See also Motes v. United States, 178 U.S. 458 (1900); United States v. Crosby, 25 F. Cas. 701, 1 Hughes 448 (District of South Carolina, 1871).

25. 313 U.S. 299 (1941).

26. Robert K. Carr, *Federal Protection of Civil Rights*, 1–3, 24–32, 85 (1947); J. Woodford Howard, Jr., *Mr. Justice Murphy: A Political Biography*, 204 (1968).

27. See *Classic*, 313 U.S. at 307–308; Carr, *Federal Protection of Civil Rights*, 85–88.

28. *Classic*, 313 U.S. 317–318.

29. Article I, section 4, of the Constitution provides: "The Times, Places and Manner of holding Elections for Senators and Representatives, shall be prescribed in each State by the Legislature thereof; but the Congress may at any time by Law make or alter such Regulations, except as to the Places of choosing Senators."

30. *Classic*, 313 U.S. 339 (Douglas, J., dissenting).

31. Alpheus Thomas Mason, *Harlan Fiske Stone: Pillar of the Law*, 589 (1968).

# Bibliographical Essay

The study of bias-motivated violence falls at the intersection of criminal law, criminology, free expression doctrine, and civil rights law. The purpose of this Bibliographical Essay is not to provide an exhaustive compilation of the literature in these fields, but rather to summarize many of the most helpful sources that pertain to the various topics discussed in this book. These are organized according to chapter. A number of sources deal with a wide range of issues concerning bias crimes. Jack Levin and Jack McDevitt, *Hate Crimes: The Rising Tide of Bigotry and Bloodshed* (1993), is a first-rate treatment of the sociological and criminological aspects of the study of bias crimes. Similarly, the essays in Robert J. Kelly, ed., *Bias Crime: American Law Enforcement and Legal Responses* (1991), are very helpful. For an overall collection of bias crime laws, see Lu-in Wang, *Hate Crimes Law* (1997).

James B. Jacobs and Kimberly Potter, *Hate Crimes: Criminal Law and Identity Politics* (1998), addresses many if not most of the issues dealt with in this book. In many ways, Jacobs and Potter's book provides a helpful counterpoint. The authors' analysis is careful and thoughtful, although we disagree on most important questions, including the case for enhanced punishment of racially motivated violence. The reader would do well to read both works and reach her own conclusions.

Finally, both the Southern Poverty Law Center and the Anti-Defamation League publish periodicals tracking the incidence of bias crimes. These continue to be among the very best sources for bias crime data.

## Chapter 1

A great deal of discussion surrounds which groups should be included in bias crime legislation. Much of this discussion focuses on whether women and gays and lesbians should be included. Sources addressing whether crimes against

253

women should be bias crimes include Steven B. Weisburd and Brian Levin, "On the Basis of Sex: Recognizing Gender-Based Bias Crime," 5 *Stanford Law & Policy Review*, 21 (1994); Elizabeth A. Pendro, "Recognizing Violence against Women: Gender and Hate Crime Statistics Act," 17 *Harvard Women's Law Journal*, 157 (1994); Marguerite Angelau, "Hate Crimes Statutes: A Promising Tool for Fighting Violence against Women," 2 *American University Journal of Gender & Law*, 63 (1994); and Eric Rothschild, "Recognizing Another Face of Hate Crimes: Rape as a Gender-Bias Crime," 4 *Maryland Journal of Contemporary Legal Issues*, 231 (1993). For sources addressing whether gays and lesbians should also be included, see Anthony S. Weiner, "Hate Crimes, Homosexuals, and the Constitution," 29 *Harvard Civil Rights–Civil Liberties Law Review*, 353 (1994); Gregory M. Herek and Kevin T. Berrill, eds., *Hate Crimes: Confronting Violence against Lesbians and Gay Men* (1992); and Gary D. Comstock, *Violence against Lesbians and Gay Men* (1991).

Sources detailing the various legislative responses to bias-motivated violence include Lisa S. L. Ho, "Substantive Penal Crime Legislation: Toward Defining Constitutional Guidelines Following the R.A.V. v. City of St. Paul and Wisconsin v. Mitchell Decisions," 34 *Santa Clara Law Review*, 711 (1994); Craig P. Gaumer, "Punishment for Prejudice: A Commentary on the Constitutionality and Utility of State Statutory Responses to the Problem of Hate Crimes," 39 *South Dakota Law Review*, 1 (1994); Joseph M. Fernandez, "Bringing Hate Crimes into Focus— The Hate Crimes Statistics Act of 1990, Pub. L. No. 101–275," 26 *Harvard Civil Rights–Civil Liberties Law Review*, 261 (1991); Sally J. Greenberg, "The Massachusetts Hate Crime Reporting Act of 1990: Great Expectations yet Unfulfilled?" 31 *New England Law Review*, 125 (1996); and Charles L. Neir III, "Racial Hatred: A Comparative Analysis of the Hate Crime Laws of the United States and Germany," 13 *Dickinson Journal of International Law*, 241 (1995).

## Chapter 2

Questions of intent or mental state play a key role in criminal law theory. For background on these issues, consult H. L. A. Hart, *Punishment and Responsibility: Essays in the Philosophy of Law* (1968); Joshua Dressler, *Understanding Criminal Law* (1987); Herbert L. Packer, *The Limits of the Criminal Sanction* (1968); and George Fletcher, *Rethinking Criminal Law* (1978).

Sources that consider the impact of bias crimes on the direct victim, the target community, and the general community include Lu-in Wang, "The Transforming Power of Hate: Social Cognition Theory and the Harms of Bias-Related Crimes," 71 *Southern California Law Review* (1997); Joan Weiss, "Ethnoviolence:

Impact upon the Response of Victims and the Community," in *Bias Crime: American Law Enforcement and Legal Response* (1993); Joan Weiss et al., "Ethnoviolence at Work," 18 *Journal of Intergroup Relations,* 28 (Winter 1991–92); Charles R. Lawrence III, "If He Hollers Let Him Go: Regulating Racist Speech on Campus," 1990 *Duke Law Journal,* 461 (1990); Richard Delgado, "Words That Wound: A Tort Action for Racial Insults, Epithets, and Name Calling," 17 *Harvard Civil Rights–Civil Liberties Law Review,* 136 (1982); A. P. Simester and A. T. H. Smith, eds., *Harm and Culpability* (1996).

For a discussion of the psychology of racism, the classic source continues to be Gordon Allport, *The Nature of Prejudice* (1954). Other helpful sources include Erving Goffman, *Stigma: Notes on the Management of Spoiled Identity* (1963); Robert M. Paige, *Stigma* (1984); Harold W. Stevenson and Edward C. Stewart, "A Developmental Study of Racial Awareness in Young Children," 29 *Child Development,* 399 (1958); Kenneth Clark, *Dark Ghetto: Dilemmas of Social Power* (1965); Irwin Katz, *Stigma: A Social Psychological Analysis* (1981); Harry H. L. Kitano, *Race Relations* (1974); and P. Watson, ed., *Psychology and Race* (1973).

## Chapters 3 and 4

The justification of criminal punishment has been addressed by many scholars from both a legal and a philosophical perspective. As Chapters 3 and 4 draw on similar foundational material, the sources listed here provide background for both chapters.

For a better understanding of the different philosophical rationales for society's right to punish, see H. L. A. Hart, *The Metaphysical Elements of Justice* (1968); Joshua Dressler, *Understanding Criminal Law* (1987); Jeffrie Murphy, *Retribution Reconsidered* (1992); Immanuel Kant, *The Metaphysical Elements of Justice* (John Lodd, trans., 1965); George Fletcher, *Rethinking Criminal Law* (1978); Herbert Morris, *On Guilt and Innocence* (1976); H. Acton, *Philosophy of Punishment* (R. Baird and S. Rosenbaum, eds., 1988); Alfred C. Ewing, *The Morality of Punishment* (1929); Alan W. Norrie, *Law Ideology and Punishment* (1991).

On the specific issue of severity of punishment being linked with the intent of the perpetrator, see Michael Davis, "How to Make the Punishment Fit the Crime," XVII *Nomos:* Criminal Justice (1985); Andrew von Hirsch and Nils Jareborg, "Gauging Criminal Harm: A Living Standard Analysis," 11 *Oxford Journal of Legal Studies,* 1 (1991); Anthony M. Dillof, "Punishing Bias: An Examination of the Theoretical Foundations of Bias Crime Statutes," 91 *Northwestern University Law Review,* 1016 (1997); and Mark Tunich, *Punishment: Theory and Practice* (1992).

## Chapter 5

Chapter 5 discusses the concept of freedom of speech and its legal limitations as it applies to bias crimes. The subject of hate speech has drawn far more scholarly attention than the subject of bias crimes. I will attempt here only to summarize some of the vast literature of hate speech.

For an overview and introduction to current free expression jurisprudence and its development, see Thomas I. Emerson, *The System of Freedom of Expression* (1970); Frederick Schauer, "Categories and the First Amendment: A Play in Three Acts," 34 *Vanderbilt Law Review,* 265 (1981); Kenneth L. Karst, "Equality as a Central Principle in the First Amendment," 43 *University of Chicago Law Review,* 20 (1975); Geoffrey R. Stone, "Restriction of Speech because of Its Content: The Peculiar Case of Subject Matter Restriction," 46 *University of Chicago Law Review,* 81 (1978).

For further background on the Skokie controversy, see Donald A. Downs, *Nazis in Skokie: Freedom, Community, and the First Amendment* (1985); James L. Gibson and Richard D. Bingham, *Civil Liberties and Nazis: The Skokie Free Speech Controversy* (1985); and David Hamlin, *The Nazi Skokie Conflict: A Civil Liberties Battle* (1981).

For a more specific understanding of how the First Amendment implicates bias crimes, see Kent Greenawalt, "Insults and Epithets: Are They Protected Speech?" 42 *Rutgers Law Review,* 42 (1990); David Kretzmer, "Freedom of Speech and Racism," 8 *Cardozo Law Review,* 445 (1987); Rodney A. Smolla, "Rethinking First Amendment Assumptions about Racist and Sexist Speech," 47 *Washington and Lee Law Review,* 171 (1990); Robert C. Post, "Racist Speech, Democracy, and the First Amendment," 32 *William & Mary Law Review,* 267 (1991); Samuel Walker, *Hate Speech: The History of an American Controversy* (1994); David Goldberger, "Hate Crime Laws and Their Impact on the First Amendment," *Annual Survey of American Law* (1992–1993); James Weinstein, "First Amendment Challenges to Hate Crimes Legislation: Where Is the Speech?" 11 *Criminal Justice Ethics* (Summer–Fall 1992).

Several law review symposia have dealt with the issue of hate speech, including "Symposium, Campus Hate Speech and the Constitution in the Aftermath of Doe v. University of Michigan," 37 *Wayne Law Review,* 1309 (1991); "Symposium, Critical Race Theory: Essays on Hate Speech," 82 *California Law Review,* 847 (1994); "Symposium, Free Speech and Religious, Racial and Sexual Harassment," 32 *William & Mary Law Review,* 207 (1991); "Symposium, Frontiers of Legal Thought: The New First Amendment," 1990 *Duke Law Journal,* 375; "Symposium, Hate Speech after R.A.V.: More Conflict between Free Speech and Equality?" 18 *William Mitchell Law Review,* 889 (1992); "Symposium, Race and

Remedy in a Multicultural Society," 47 *Stanford Law Review*, 819 (1995); "Symposium, the State of Civil Liberties: Where Do We Go from Here?" 27 *Harvard Civil Rights–Civil Liberties Law Review*, 309 (1992).

Among the articles discussing hate speech are Akhil Reed Amar, "The Case of the Missing Amendments: R.A.V. v. City of St. Paul," 106 *Harvard Law Review*, 124 (1992); Alan E. Brownstein, "Hate Speech and Harassment: The Constitutionality of Campus Codes That Prohibit Racial Insults," 3 *William & Mary Bill of Rights Journal*, 179 (1994); Nicole B. Casarez, "Content v. Context: Hate Speech and the First Amendment," 11 *Communications Law*, 13 (Winter 1994); Michael Kent Curtis, "Critics of 'Free Speech' and the Uses of the Past," 12 *Constitutional Commentary*, 29 (1995); Richard Delgado, "Campus Antiracism Rules: Constitutional Narratives in Collision," 85 *Northwestern University Law Review*, 343 (1991); Richard Delgado, "First Amendment Formalism Is Giving Way to First Amendment Legal Realism," 29 *Harvard Civil Rights–Civil Liberties Law Review*, 169 (1994); Richard Delgado and David Yun, "The Neoconservative Case against Hate-Speech Regulation—Lively, D'Souza, Gates, Carter, and the Toughlove Crowd," 47 *Vanderbilt Law Review*, 1807 (1994); Jane L. Dolkart, "Hostile Environment Harassment: Equality, Objectivity, and the Shaping of Legal Standards," 43 *Emory Law Journal*, 151 (1994); Murray Dry, "Hate Speech and the Constitution," 11 *Constitutional Commentary*, 501 (1994–1995); Richard H. Fallon, Jr., "Two Senses of Autonomy," 46 *Stanford Law Review*, 875 (1994); Mary Ellen Gale, "Reimagining the First Amendment: Racist Speech and Equal Liberty," 65 *St. John's Law Review*, 119 (1991); Mark A. Graber, "Old Wine in New Bottles: The Constitutional Status of Unconstitutional Speech," 48 *Vanderbilt Law Review*, 349 (1995); Alon Harel, "Bigotry, Pornography, and the First Amendment," 65 *Southern California Law Review*, 1887 (1992); Rhonda G. Hartman, "Hateful Expression and First Amendment Values: Toward a Theory of Constitutional Constraint on Hate Speech at Colleges and Universities after R.A.V. v. St. Paul," 19 *Journal of College and University Law*, 343 (1993); Elena Kagan, "Regulation of Hate Speech and Pornography after R.A.V.," 60 *University of Chicago Law Review*, 873 (1993); Donald E. Lively, "Racist Speech Management: The High Risks of Low Achievement," 1 *Virginia Journal of Social Policy and Law*, 1 (1993); Calvin R. Massey, "Hate Speech, Cultural Diversity, and the Foundational Paradigms of Free Expression," 40 *U.C.L.A. Law Review*, 103 (1992); Mari J. Matsuda, "Public Response to Racist Speech: Considering the Victim's Story," 87 *Michigan Law Review*, 2320 (1989); Martha Minow, "Surviving Victim Talk," 40 *U.C.L.A. Law Review*, 1411 (1993); John T. Nockleby, "Hate Speech in Context: The Case of Verbal Threats," 42 *Buffalo Law Review*, 653 (1994); C. Catherine Scallan, "Cross-Burning Is Not a Threat: Constitutional Protection for Hate Speech," 14 *Missis-*

*sippi College Law Review,* 631 (1994); Steven H. Shiffrin, "Racist Speech, Outsider Jurisprudence, and the Meaning of America," 80 *Cornell Law Review,* 43 (1994); Thomas W. Simon, "Fighting Racism: Hate Speech Detours," 26 *Indiana Law Review,* 411 (1993); Kathleen M. Sullivan, "Free Speech and Unfree Markets," 42 *U.C.L.A. Law Review,* 949 (1995); Cass R. Sunstein, "Words, Conduct, Caste," 60 *University of Chicago Law Review,* 795 (1993).

## Chapter 6

The history of racial violence in the United States is both tragic and well documented. Among the best sources are Michael R. Belknap, *Federal Law and Southern Order: Racial Violence and Constitutional Conflict in the Post-Brown South* (1987); Taylor Branch, *Parting the Waters: America in the King Years, 1954–63* (1988); W. E. B. Du Bois, *Black Reconstruction in America, 1960–1880* (1935); Paul Finkelman, ed., *Slavery, Race and the American Legal System, 1700–1872,* 16 vols. (1988); Paul Finkelman, ed., *Race, Law and American History, 1700–1990,* 11 vols. (1992); A. Leon Higginbotham, Jr., *Shades of Freedom: Racial Politics and Presumptions of the American Legal Process* (1996); John Hope Franklin, *From Slavery to Freedom: A History of Negro Americans* (3d ed., 1969); Aldon D. Morris, *The Origins of the Civil Rights Movement* (1984); Juan Williams, *Eyes on the Prize: America's Civil Rights Years, 1954–65* (1988); David H. Bennett, *The Party of Fear: From Nativist Movements to the New Right in American History* (1988); Stewart E. Tolnay and E. M. Beck, *A Festival of Violence* (1992); Seymour Martin Lipset and Earl Rabb, *The Politics of Unreason* (1978, 2d ed.); David Chalmers, *Hooded Americanism* (1965).

For a discussion of the issue of federalism and its impact during the adoption of the Civil War amendments, see Rory K. Little, "Myths and Principles of Federalism," 46 *Hastings Law Journal,* 1029 (1995); Bruce Ackerman, *We the People* (1991); Harold M. Hyman and William M. Wiecek, *Equal Justice under the Law: Constitutional Development, 1835–1875* (1982); Herman Belz, *A New Birth of Freedom: The Republican Party and the Freedman's Rights* (1976); James M. McPherson, *Battle Cry of Freedom: The Civil War Era* (1988); Eric Foner, *Reconstruction: America's Unfinished Revolution* (1988); Charles Fairman, *History of the Supreme Court of the United States: Reconstruction and Reunion, 1864–88* (1987).

For more directed readings on federalism and its impact on criminal law specifically, see Sara Sun Beale, "Too Many and yet Too Few: New Principles to Define the Proper Limits for Federal Criminal Jurisdiction," 46 *Hastings Law Journal,* 979 (1995); Kathleen F. Brickey, "Criminal Mischief: The Federalization of American Criminal Law," 46 *Hastings Law Journal,* 1135 (1995); and Lawrence Friedman, *Crime and Punishment in American History* (1994).

## Chapter 7

This chapter, like Chapters 3 and 4, focuses on the underlying rationale for criminal punishment. In addition to those sources listed under Chapters 3 and 4, some additional readings that bear more directly on the expressive theory of punishment include Henry M. Hart, Jr., "The Aims of the Criminal Law," 23 *Journal of Law and Contemporary Problems*, 404 (1958); Emile Durkheim, *The Division of Labor in Society* (W. D. Hall, trans., 1984); H. L. A. Hart, *Punishment and Responsibility* (1968); Ronald J. Rychlak, "Society's Moral Right to Punish: A Further Exploration of the Denunciation Theory of Punishment," 65 *Tulane Law Review*, 299 (1990); Joel Feinberg, *Doing and Deserving* (1970); and David Garland, *Punishment and Modern Society* (1990).

# Acknowledgments

This project, five years in the making, benefited from numerous contributions, direct and indirect, from colleagues and other friends. Any list of acknowledgments in a project of this sort runs the risk of omissions. It is a risk worth running, however, in order to recognize those who have lent help and support.

Much of the research and writing of this book took place during a sabbatical from Boston University School of Law and during summer breaks, thanks to generous research support from the School of Law. During the summers of 1996 and 1997, I was the beneficiary of an Inns of Court Fellowship, co-sponsored by the Institute for Advanced Legal Studies, University of London, and the Honourable Society of Lincoln's Inn.

Many colleagues at Boston University and elsewhere provided thoughtful and helpful comments on various parts of the manuscript. In this regard, I particularly wish to express my appreciation to Stan Fisher, Pnina Lahav, David Lyons, Steve Marks, Tracey Maclin, Mark Pettit, David Seipp, Ken Simons, and Larry Yackle. Joshua Dressler of the McGeorge School of Law, University of the Pacific, Roger Friedland of the University of California at Santa Barbara, and Elliot Dorff of the University of Judaism have been generous with their time and thoughts over the years and have played an important role in numerous aspects of this project. Alice Zimelman was a careful and thoughtful reader of the manuscript and provided many helpful comments. Jeff Kehoe of Harvard University Press has been a constant source of insight and support, and displayed the precisely proper balance of patience and impatience.

I will always be especially grateful to Aviam Soifer and Ronald A. Cass. Avi considered a number of my articles and ideas, some in print, some in process, some still in thought, and saw a book here before I did. His work and

261

insights were brought to bear on parts of Chapters 1 and 6, all of which are the better for it. Ron contributed as dean (in providing a timely sabbatical leave), as colleague (as careful reader and critic of several chapters), and as friend (as a constant source of encouragement and inspiration).

I also wish to acknowledge the contributions, both to this work and to the field of bias-motivated violence generally, of Richard W. Cole, Chief, Civil Rights Division of the Office of the Attorney General of Massachusetts, Sally Greenberg and Lenny Zakim of the Anti-Defamation League, and Joan C. Weiss of the Justice Research and Statistics Association. Each has helped me in this project, and each has demonstrated a deep commitment to the eradication of bias crimes in our society.

Many people played a role in making the Inns of Court Fellowship a fine opportunity to reflect on this project. The Institute of Advanced Legal Studies and its director, Barry Rider, provided me with a true scholarly home away from home during the summers of 1996 and 1997. Two individuals from Lincoln's Inn stand out from my time in the United Kingdom. Christopher McCall, Q.C., provided the bridge between scholarship and the Bar. Captain Malcolm Carver, the former Under Treasurer of Lincoln's Inn, put the inn at my disposal in order to further my research. Each displayed a generosity of spirit that can never fully be repaid, but perhaps this acknowledgment is some small step in that direction.

Many of the ideas presented in this book were thrashed out with great benefit with my most demanding yet generous critics, my students. Particular thanks are due to my students from the years since this project was conceived, my Civil Rights Crimes seminars of fall 1993 and fall 1994, and my Civil Rights Enforcement class of spring 1996. I also received great help from comments received during presentations of parts of this book at the Boston University School of Law Workshop Series, Yale University Institute for Social and Policy Studies, the Institute of Advanced Legal Studies in London, Kings College School of Law, London, University College London Faculty of Law, and the William and Mary School of Law.

I have been most fortunate over the years to have worked with a series of splendid research assistants—Jeffrey Blum, Elisabeth Hendricks, Mary Marbach, Kelly McEnaney, Helen Pfister, Gregg Rubenstein, Candace Schlichting, and Joshua Targoff. Their research and editorial work, along with their good humor and moral support, have aided me greatly. I have also benefited from the research efforts of Marlene Alderman and Stephanie

Weigmann of the Pappas Law Library at Boston University School of Law and the editorial assistance of Ken Westhassel.

Some of the discussion in this book has appeared previously in an earlier form: Chapters 2–4 in "The Punishment of Hate: Toward a Normative Theory of Bias-Motivated Crimes," 93 *Michigan Law Review*, 320 (1994); Chapter 5 in "Resolving the Hate Crimes/Hate Speech Paradox: Punishing Bias Crimes and Protecting Racist Speech," 68 *Notre Dame Law Review*, 673–723 (1993), © by Notre Dame Law Review, University of Notre Dame; and one section of Chapter 6 in "Civil Rights and Criminal Wrongs: The *Mens Rea* of Federal Civil Rights Crimes," 67 *Tulane Law Review*, 2113–2229 (1993), © Tulane Law Review Association. I thank the editors of these journals for permission to use the material.

Last and most important, there are five people without whose support and encouragement, and without whose love, this book would never have been completed. Two of them, my first and most devoted teachers, are acknowledged on the dedication page, as well they should be. The other three are the core of my life: my wife, Kathy, my daughter, Miriam, and my son, Noah. They let me work when I needed to work, and, perhaps more important, they distracted me when I needed to be distracted. This book, and any that may follow, are for Kathy. The story on p. xi is especially for Miriam and Noah.

# Index